2

FOCUS
ON
GRAMMAR
AN INTEGRATED SKILLS APPROACH

THIRD EDITION

LIDA BAKER

PEARSON
Longman

FOCUS ON GRAMMAR 2: An Integrated Skills Approach
Teacher's Manual

Pearson Education, 10 Bank Street, White Plains, NY 10606

Staff credits: The people who made up the *Focus on Grammar 2 Teacher's Manual* team,
    representing editorial, production, design, and manufacturing, are: Rhea Banker,
    Christine Edmonds, Nancy Flaggman, Ann France, Stacey Hunter, Laura Le Dréan, and
    Laurie Neaman.
Cover images: (center) Alan Kearney/Getty Images, (middle) Nick Koudis/Getty
    Images, (background) Comstock Images/Getty Images
Text composition: ElectraGraphics, Inc.
Text font: 11/13 Sabon, 10/13 Myriad Roman
Photo credit: p. 151 Henri Cartier-Bresson/Magnum Photos

ISBN: 0-13-189973-2

LONGMAN ON THE **WEB**

Longman.com offers online resources for
teachers and students. Access our Companion
Websites, our online catalog, and our local
offices around the world.

Visit us at **longman.com.**

Printed in the United States of America

5 6 7 8 9 10—BAH—12 11 10 09

Contents

Introduction

The *Focus on Grammar* series

Written by ESL/EFL professionals, *Focus on Grammar: An Integrated Skills Approach* helps students to understand and practice English grammar. The primary aim of the course is for students to gain confidence in their ability to speak and write English accurately and fluently.

The **third edition** retains this popular series' focus on English grammar through lively listening, speaking, reading, and writing activities. The new *Focus on Grammar* also maintains the same five-level progression as the second edition:

- Level 1 (Beginning, formerly Introductory)
- Level 2 (High-Beginning, formerly Basic)
- Level 3 (Intermediate)
- Level 4 (High-Intermediate)
- Level 5 (Advanced)

What is the *Focus on Grammar* methodology?

Both controlled and communicative practice

While students expect and need to learn the formal rules of a language, it is crucial that they also practice new structures in a variety of contexts in order to internalize and master them. To this end, *Focus on Grammar* provides an abundance of both controlled and communicative exercises so that students can bridge the gap between knowing grammatical structures and using them. The many communicative activities in each Student Book unit provide opportunities for critical thinking while enabling students to personalize what they have learned.

A unique four-step approach

The series follows a four-step approach:

Step 1: Grammar in Context shows the new structures in natural contexts, such as articles and conversations.

Step 2: Grammar Presentation presents the structures in clear and accessible grammar charts, notes, and examples.

Step 3: Focused Practice of both form and meaning of the new structures is provided in numerous and varied controlled exercises.

Step 4: Communication Practice allows students to use the new structures freely and creatively in motivating, open-ended activities.

Thorough recycling

Underpinning the scope and sequence of the *Focus on Grammar* series is the belief that students need to use target structures many times, in different contexts, and at increasing levels of difficulty. For this reason, new grammar is constantly recycled throughout the book so that students have maximum exposure to the target forms and become comfortable using them in speech and in writing.

A complete classroom text and reference guide

A major goal in the development of *Focus on Grammar* has been to provide students with books that serve not only as vehicles for classroom instruction but also as resources for reference and self-study. In each Student Book, the combination of grammar charts, grammar notes, a glossary of grammar terms, and extensive appendices provides a complete and invaluable reference guide for students.

Ongoing assessment

Review Tests at the end of each part of the Student Book allow for self-assessment. In addition, the tests in the new *Focus on Grammar* Assessment Package provide teachers with a valid, reliable, and practical means of determining students' appropriate levels of placement in the course and of assessing students' achievement throughout the course. At Levels 4 (High-Intermediate) and 5 (Advanced), Proficiency Tests give teachers an overview of their students' general grammar knowledge.

 ## What are the components of each level of *Focus on Grammar*?

Student Book

The Student Book is divided into eight or more parts, depending on the level. Each part contains grammatically related units, with each unit focusing on specific grammatical structures; where appropriate, units present contrasting forms. The exercises in each unit are thematically related to one another, and all units have the same clear, easy-to-follow format.

Teacher's Manual

The Teacher's Manual contains a variety of suggestions and information to enrich the material in the Student Book. It includes general teaching suggestions for each section of a typical unit, answers to frequently asked questions, unit-by-unit teaching tips with ideas for further communicative practice, and a supplementary activity section. Answers to the Student Book exercises and audioscripts of the listening activities are found at the back of the Teacher's Manual. Also included in the Teacher's Manual is a CD-ROM that includes PowerPoint® presentations that offer alternative ways of presenting selected grammar structures.

Workbook

The Workbook accompanying each level of *Focus on Grammar* provides additional exercises for self-study of the target grammar for each unit. Tests included in each Workbook provide students with additional opportunities for self-assessment.

Audio Programs

The Student Book Class Audio Program includes the listening activities, the Grammar in Context passages, and various other exercises. The symbol ⌒ identifies audio for the listening exercises. The symbol ⌒ next to the Grammar in Context passages and other exercises indicates that the listening is optional. Audioscripts for the listening exercises are located in the back of the Teacher's Manual.

Some Student Books are packaged with a Student Audio CD. This CD includes the listening exercise from each unit.

CD-ROM

The *Focus on Grammar* CD-ROM provides students with individualized practice and immediate feedback. Fully contextualized and interactive, the activities extend practice of the grammatical structures in the reading, writing, speaking, and listening skills areas. The CD-ROM includes grammar review, review tests, score-based remedial practice, games, and all relevant reference material from the Student Book. It can also be used in conjunction with the *Longman Interactive American Dictionary* CD-ROM.

Assessment Package (NEW)

A comprehensive Assessment Package has been developed for each level of the third edition of *Focus on Grammar*. The components of the Assessment Package are:

1. Placement, Diagnostic, and Achievement Tests

- a Placement Test to screen students and place them into the correct level
- Diagnostic Tests for each part of the Student Book
- Unit Achievement Tests for each unit of the Student Book
- Part Achievement Tests for each part of the Student Book

2. General Proficiency Tests

- two Proficiency Tests at Level 4 (High-Intermediate)
- two Proficiency Tests at Level 5 (Advanced)

These tests can be administered at any point in the course.

3. Audio CD

- Audio CDs include the listening portions of the Placement, Diagnostic, and Achievement Tests.
- The audioscripts for the tests are located in the Assessment Package.

4. Test-Generating Software

The test-bank software provides thousands of questions from which teachers can create class-appropriate tests. All items are labeled according to the grammar structure they are testing, so teachers can easily select relevant items; they can also design their own items to add to their tests.

Transparencies (NEW)

Transparencies of all the grammar charts in the Student Book are also available. These transparencies are classroom visual aids that help instructors point out and explain important patterns and structures of grammar.

Companion Website

The *Focus on Grammar* companion website (www. longman.com/focusongrammar) contains a wealth of information and activities for both teachers and students. In addition to general information about the course pedagogy, the website provides extensive practice exercises for the classroom, a language lab, or at home.

What's new in the third edition of the Student Book?

In response to users' requests, this edition has:

- a new four-color design
- easy-to-read color coding for the four steps
- new and updated reading texts for Grammar in Context
- post-reading activities (in addition to the pre-reading questions)
- more exercise items
- an editing (error analysis) exercise in each unit
- an Internet activity in each unit
- a Glossary of Grammar Terms
- expanded Appendices

References

Alexander, L. G. (1988). *Longman English Grammar.* White Plains: Longman.

Biber, D., S. Conrad, E. Finegan, S. Johansson, and G. Leech (1999). *Longman Grammar of Spoken and Written English.* White Plains: Longman.

Celce-Murcia, M., and D. Freeman (1999). *The Grammar Book.* Boston: Heinle and Heinle.

Celce-Murcia, M., and S. Hilles (1988). *Techniques and Resources in Teaching Grammar.* New York: Oxford University Press.

Firsten, R. (2002). *The ELT Grammar Book.* Burlingame, CA: Alta Book Center Publishers.

Garner, B. (2003). *Garner's Modern American Usage.* New York: Oxford University Press.

Greenbaum, S. (1996). *The Oxford English Grammar.* New York: Oxford University Press.

Leech, G. (2004). *Meaning and the English Verb.* Harlow, UK: Pearson.

Lewis, M. (1997). *Implementing the Lexical Approach.* Hove, East Sussex, UK: Language Teaching Publications.

Longman (2002). *Longman Dictionary of English Language and Culture.* Harlow, UK: Longman.

Willis, D. (2003). *Rules, Patterns and Words.* New York: Cambridge University Press.

About the *Focus on Grammar* Teacher's Manual

This Teacher's Manual offers a multitude of ideas for working with the material in *Focus on Grammar 2: An Integrated Skills Approach,* third edition. In this manual, you will find the following information:

- **General Teaching Tips** (pages 1–14) describe the principles underlying the course and give suggestions for teaching the activities in the Student Book. A Strategies for Teaching Grammar page offers a quick reference for some of the most common and useful grammar teaching techniques. A Frequently Asked Questions section answers some of the most common issues encountered by teachers.
- **Unit-by-Unit Teaching Tips** (pages 15–124) give you additional ideas for completing the activities unique to each unit.
- **Supplementary Activities** (pages 125–133) provide extra practice exercises for use during your presentation of a grammar point.
- **Scoring Rubrics for Speaking and Writing** are provided on pages 134 and 135 of the Teacher's Manual. You can use the rubrics to assess various speaking and writing tasks throughout the Student Book.
- **Audioscripts** and the **Student Book Answer Key** are included at the back of the Teacher's Manual for easy reference.

The **PowerPoint® presentations CD-ROM** bound into this Teacher's Manual includes additional teaching tools and resources:

- **PowerPoint® presentations** for selected units in the Student Book offer an innovative method for the contextualized instruction of grammar. These theme-based, user-friendly presentations contain a variety of colorful graphics and animations to engage a wide range of learning styles. In addition to providing a stimulating visual reinforcement of the Grammar Notes, these presentations also include interactive practice activities.
- A **PowerPoint® presentation Guide,** included on the CD-ROM in PDF format, offers guidelines for using the **PowerPoint® presentations.** It contains a variety of suggestions for getting the most out of the presentations in terms of both instructional benefit and learner participation.
- **Transparencies** of all Grammar Charts in the Student Book offer an additional teaching tool for presenting the target grammar points in the classroom.
- **Graphic Organizers** can be printed out and used in the classroom or assigned as homework. The graphic organizers provide support through the steps of pre-writing and writing a first draft.
- **Rubrics for assessing speaking and writing tasks** help teachers provide helpful feedback to students. Teachers are encouraged to use the scoring system provided, as well as write specific notes based on each student's performance.

General Teaching Tips

These tips are designed to guide you in teaching the recurring sections of the Teacher's Manual and Student Book. Experimenting with the various options will enliven your classroom and appeal to students' different learning styles.

In the following section, the icon ⊙ indicates an optional step you may wish to include if time permits.

Unit Overview

The Unit Overview (offered in the Teacher's Manual) highlights the most important grammar points of each unit. It also points out common grammar trouble spots for students. You may also find it helpful to review the Grammar Charts and Grammar Notes in the Student Book before teaching each unit.

Grammar in Context

Each unit of the Student Book begins with a reading selection designed to raise students' interest and expose them to the target grammar in a realistic, natural context. The selections include newspaper and magazine excerpts, websites, newsletters, advertisements, conversations, and other formats that students may encounter in their day-to-day lives. All of the texts are also available on the Audio Program.

Background Notes

Where appropriate, background notes are provided in the Teacher's Manual to explain cultural and historical terms or concepts that appear in a reading selection. You can introduce these terms and concepts to students during a warm-up discussion, or you can use the notes as a reference if questions come up as students are reading.

Following the Background Notes is a list of vocabulary words and expressions that may be unfamiliar to students. Rather than pre-teaching these terms, you may wish to wait until students have finished reading. This allows students to focus on reading for general comprehension, building their reading fluency. See the section on vocabulary below for some ideas on how to respond to students' vocabulary questions.

Before You Read (5 minutes)

This pre-reading activity creates interest, elicits students' knowledge about the topic, and encourages students to make predictions about the reading.

Suggested Procedure for Before You Read
1. Have the class cover up the text and look at the illustrations.
2. Ask students to respond to the questions. Ask these questions in a conversational way, instead of reading them from the book.

Option A
• Have students work in pairs to read the questions and discuss their answers.
• Call on pairs to share their ideas with the class.

Option B
• Ask pairs of students to think about what they want to know about the topic and/or to prepare some questions they have about the topic.
• Call on pairs to share some of their questions and write them on the board.
• Have students try to find the information as they read.

Option C
• Have students work in groups of three.
• Each student chooses a question to memorize and, with books closed, ask their partners.
• Call on various groups to share their answers with the class.

Reading (15–25 minutes)

Depending on the needs of your class, have students complete the reading in class or at home (procedures for both options are given below). Whichever option you choose, encourage students (1) to read with a purpose; (2) to read the passage through once or twice without stopping for unknown words; and (3) to identify and deal with new vocabulary.

Comprehension questions and discussion topics are offered in the Unit-by-Unit Teaching Tips to supplement the grammar-focused activities of the Student Book.

Suggested Procedure for Reading

1. Play the audio and have students follow along in their books.
2. Write the comprehension questions from the Unit-by-Unit Teaching Tips on the board.
3. Have students read the passage again silently, looking for answers to the questions.
4. ⏱ Have students discuss their answers with a partner or in small groups.
5. Call on individuals to share their answers with the class.
6. Spend a few minutes going over any unfamiliar vocabulary terms. (See suggested procedures for Vocabulary.)
7. ⏱ Put students in pairs or small groups to discuss the reading. Invite them to respond to the reading in a way that is meaningful to them: What was most interesting? What did they learn? Refer to the Discussion Topics in the Unit-by-Unit Teaching Tips to help generate ideas for discussion.

Option A (At Home/In Class)

- Write the comprehension questions on the board for students to copy, or prepare them as a handout for students to take home.
- Have students read the passage and answer the questions at home.
- ⏱ Have students write a few additional questions about the reading.
- In class, have students work in pairs or small groups to discuss their answers.
- ⏱ Have students take turns asking and answering questions they prepared at home.
- Follow steps 5–7 in the Suggested Procedure for Reading above.

Option B (In Class)

- Have students work in pairs. Divide the reading in half, and have each student in the pair read one half.
- Have students summarize the information in their half of the reading for their partner.
- Follow steps 5–6 in the previous notes for Suggested Procedure for Reading.

Vocabulary

After students have read the passage and answered the comprehension questions, spend a few minutes going over any unfamiliar vocabulary terms. In addition to using the definitions provided in the Unit-by-Unit Teaching Tips, you may wish to use illustrations in the Student Book or pictures that you supply to illustrate the meaning of new words.

Suggested Procedure for Vocabulary

1. Have students make lists of the words in the reading they need help with.
2. Allow them to use their dictionaries or to work with other students to discuss, search for and find the meanings, or ask you for assistance.
3. ⏱ Write the new vocabulary items on the board, or have students write them, and provide definitions.
4. Encourage students to keep a record of vocabulary items by using a notebook or by making vocabulary cards. The entries should include a definition and an example sentence. Suggest that they be on the lookout for other examples of these items and add any new examples they find to their notebooks or cards.

Where appropriate, encourage students to draw pictures on the card or to record any information that helps them remember the vocabulary item. It may be helpful for students to include a translation of the new term in their own language.

Here's one way to do a vocabulary card:

```
                                              [front]




                      thrill (n., v., adj.)
```

```
                                              [back]
    (n) + (adj) a strong feeling of excitement
    and pleasure; (v) to feel or make someone
    feel strong excitement or pleasure
    (n) My grandmother always gets a thrill
    when I call her.
    (v) The skaters thrilled their fans with their
    high jumps.
    (adj) I was thrilled to hear the good news.
```

Option A
• Write new vocabulary and definitions on the board, but do not write the definitions next to the corresponding words.
• Ask students to find the appropriate match.

Option B
• If classroom time is limited, allow students to consult their dictionaries as they are reading.
• Remind them that they will not necessarily need to know the meaning of every word in order to understand the meaning of the passage.

After You Read (5 minutes)
These post-reading questions help students focus on the meaning of the target grammar without explicitly presenting the grammar point.

Suggested Procedure for After You Read
1. Have students work individually to answer the questions.
2. Tell students to compare answers with a partner.
3. Call on volunteers to read their answers aloud.

Grammar Presentation

There are many ways to teach the material in the Grammar Presentation. As a general rule, the more varied and lively the classroom activities, the more engaged students will be—and the more learning will occur! Approaching grammar from different angles and trying out different classroom management options can help increase student motivation.

The Strategies for Teaching Grammar on page 11 provides some guidelines to keep in mind when presenting a new grammar point. In addition to these strategies and the procedures outlined below, you can find specific suggestions for presenting the unit's grammar in the Unit-by-Unit Teaching Tips.

Identify the Grammar (5–10 minutes)
This section in the Teacher's Manual provides support for you to help students identify the target grammatical structures embedded in the reading. This helps students learn the usage of the target grammar point and helps you make a smooth transition from Grammar in Context to the Grammar Presentation.

Suggested Procedure for Identify the Grammar
1. Choose an example of the target grammar from the reading and write it on the board. The Unit-by-Unit Teaching Tips provide examples that focus on specific features of that grammar point.
2. Point out that the target grammar is presented in boldfaced type in the reading for easy identification. Elicit more examples from students and write them on the board.
3. Find out what your students may already know about that grammar point. List the information you have elicited on the board. As students continue with the Grammar Presentation, encourage them to compare these notes with the information presented in the Grammar Charts and Grammar Notes.

After studying the target grammar in context, students should be ready to study the isolated forms, meanings, and usage. You can use the charts, notes, and examples to present and review the grammatical structures in a straightforward and comprehensive way.

Note that common grammatical terms are used throughout the Grammar Presentations because they help make the explanations clearer and because students often have learned them in their own language. If students are having trouble understanding the grammatical terms, encourage them to use the Glossary provided in the back of the Student Book.

Grammar Charts (5–10 minutes)

The Grammar Charts provide a clear reference of all the forms of the target grammar. Students also become familiar with grammatical terminology. The charts also enable you to pre-teach some of the Grammar Notes that follow. In addition to the charts in the Student Book, you may want to use the Focus on Grammar Transparencies (on the CD-ROM in the back of this Teacher's Manual) to help direct all of your students' attention to the same focus point.

Suggested Procedure for Grammar Charts

1. Using the examples you wrote on the board (see Identify the Grammar above) and/or Focus on Grammar Transparencies, draw students' attention to important features in the models by asking them questions or by pointing out the key features.
2. Confirm students' understanding by engaging them in some recognition activities. Try one or two activities from Strategies 3, 4, 5, or 6 (page 11).
3. Get students to manipulate the new structures through substitution or transformation drills. See Strategy 7 (page 11) for an example of a transformation drill.
4. Encourage students to make sentences that are personally meaningful using the new grammar.

Option A
- Have students study the Grammar Charts at home.
- In class, follow step 1 in the suggested procedure above.
- Move directly to the Grammar Notes section. Carry out steps 2, 3, and 4 in the suggested procedure above using the notes together with the charts.

Option B
- Assign individual students responsibility for presenting a topic to the class by combining the information in the charts and the relevant notes. Give them newsprint and a marker to prepare a display in class or at home.
- ⏰ Meet with students individually. Allow them to rehearse their presentations and provide any coaching needed.
- Call on students to present their topics to the class. Encourage class questions.
- Choose appropriate practice activities from Strategies 4–8 (page 11) OR move directly to the Grammar Notes section.

Grammar Notes (10–30 minutes)

These notes provide helpful information about meaning, use, and form of the grammatical structures that students have encountered in the introductory reading selection and Grammar Charts. They include the following features to help students understand and use the forms.
- Where appropriate, time lines illustrate the meaning of verb forms and their relationship to one another.
- *Be careful!* notes alert students to common errors among English language learners.
- *Usage Notes* provide guidelines for using and understanding different levels of formality and correctness.
- *Pronunciation Notes* are provided when appropriate.
- Below the notes and examples, references to related structures are provided.

The Grammar Notes section includes cross-references to the Focused Practice exercises in the Student Book and to the Supplementary Activities in this Teacher's Manual. Have students complete the appropriate exercises after you present each note. This breaks up the grammar presentation into manageable chunks and allows students to check their understanding of the note.

Suggested Procedure for Grammar Notes
1. Have students read each note at home and/or in class.
2. For each note, write examples on the board and elicit from students the important features of the form (see Strategy 1, page 11, for suggestions) or point out the key features yourself.
3. If possible, demonstrate the meaning of the grammatical form(s) by performing actions (see Strategy 6, page 11).

4. Model the examples and have students repeat after you so that they become comfortable with the appropriate stress, intonation, and rhythm.

5. Engage students with the grammar point by choosing appropriate activities, for example:
   • Elicit examples of the target structure.
   • Confirm students' understanding by having them categorize examples or perform actions that illustrate structure. See Strategies 5 and 6 (page 11) for examples.
   • Provide controlled practice with quick substitution or transformation drills.
   • Encourage students to make personally meaningful sentences using the new grammatical forms.
   • Use the Focused Practice exercises in the Student Book and/or the Supplementary Activities starting on page 125 of this Teacher's Manual.

6. You may want to repeat steps 2–5 for each Grammar Note. Where appropriate, the Unit-by-Unit Teaching Tips give suggestions for presenting two or more notes simultaneously.

Option
• Photocopy one set of Grammar Notes for each group of three or four students in your class. Cut them up so that the notes and their corresponding examples are not attached.
• Divide the class into groups of three or four students and give a set of cut-up notes to each group.
• Give students their task:
  1. Match the examples with the correct notes.
  2. Attach the notes and corresponding examples to a sheet of newsprint (a large piece of paper).
  3. Have students create more examples for each note.
• Circulate to ensure that students are on the right track, and provide help as needed.
• Have students post their results around the room, and invite groups to look at each other's work.
• Regroup as a whole class to answer questions.

Focused Practice

The exercises in this section provide practice for the structures in the Grammar Presentation. You may wish to have students complete the corresponding exercise immediately after you have presented the relevant Grammar Note. Another option is for students to complete one or more of the exercises at home, using the cross-references to the Grammar Note(s) for support.

If you decide to have students complete the exercises in class, you can keep them motivated by varying the order of the exercises and/or the way you conduct them. Following are various ways of conducting the exercises. In the Unit-by-Unit Teaching Tips, you will find definitions for potentially unfamiliar words and phrases that appear in the Focused Practice exercises.

Discover the Grammar (5–10 minutes)

This opening activity gets students to identify the target grammar structures in a realistic context. This recognition-only activity raises awareness of the structures as it builds confidence.

Suggested Procedure for Discover the Grammar
1. Go over the example with the class.
2. Have students complete the exercise individually or in pairs.
3. Elicit the correct answers from students.

Controlled Practice Exercises (5–10 minutes each)

Following the Discover the Grammar activity are exercises that provide practice in a controlled, but still contextualized, environment. The exercises proceed from simpler to more complex and include a variety of exercise types such as fill in the blanks, matching, and multiple-choice. Exercises are cross-referenced to the appropriate Grammar Notes so that students can review as necessary. Students are exposed to many different written formats, including letters, electronic bulletin boards, résumés, charts, and graphs. Many exercises are art-based, providing a rich context for meaningful practice.

Options
• Have students work in pairs to complete the exercises.
• If the exercise is in the form of a conversation, have students complete the exercise and then work in pairs to practice and perform the conversation for the class.
• When going over answers with students, have them explain why each answer is correct.
• Whenever possible, relate exercises to students' own lives. For example, if an exercise includes a time line, elicit from

students some important events that have happened in their own lives.

Editing (10 minutes)

All units include an editing exercise to build students' awareness of incorrect usage of the target grammar structures. Students identify and correct errors in a contextualized passage such as a student's composition, a journal entry, or an online message-board posting. The direction line indicates the number of errors in the passage.

Suggested Procedure for Editing

1. Have students read through the passage quickly to understand its context and meaning.
2. Tell students to read the passage line by line, circling incorrect structures and writing in the corrections.
3. Have students take turns reading the passage line by line, saying the structures correctly. Alternatively, read the passage aloud to the class and have students interrupt you with their corrections.
4. There are also usually examples of the correct usage of the structures in each editing exercise. After students have identified the errors, point out the correct usages and ask why they are not errors.

Communication Practice

These in-class exercises give students the opportunity to use the target structure in communicative activities. These activities help develop listening and speaking fluency and critical thinking skills, as well as provide opportunities for students to "own" the structures. As with the Focused Practice exercises, you may wish to vary the order of these activities to keep student motivation high.

Since there are many different exercise types in the Communication Practice section, specific ideas and guidelines are provided in the Unit-by-Unit Teaching Tips. Following are general suggestions for the three main types of exercises. (Note: See the FAQ on pages 12–14 for more information about setting up pair work and group work.)

Listening (10 minutes)

Each Communication Practice section begins with a listening and a comprehension exercise. Students hear a variety of listening formats, including conversations, television scripts,

weather forecasts, and interviews. After listening, students complete a task that focuses on the form or meaning of the target grammar structure. The listening exercises are included on the Student CD so that students may also complete these exercises outside of class.

Suggested Procedure for Listening

Before students listen
1. Explain the situation or context of the listening passage. Provide any necessary cultural information, and pre-teach any vocabulary students may need to know. Definitions are provided in the Unit-by-Unit Teaching Tips for words and phrases that may be unfamiliar to students. (Note that some of these words and phrases may appear in the listening, not in the exercise itself.)
2. Ask students to read the exercise questions first so that they know what to listen for.

Listening
1. Play the audio or read the audioscript aloud. If you choose to read:
   • Speak with a lot of expression and at a natural pace.
   • Change positions and tone of voice to indicate who the speaker is. Another method is to draw stick figures on the board and label them with the characters' names so that you can point to the appropriate character as you change roles.
2. Have students listen the first time with their pencils down.
3. Have students listen again and complete the task.
4. You may want to let students listen as many times as necessary to complete the task.

After students listen
1. Elicit answers for the exercise items and write them on the board. Answer any questions the students may have.
2. ⏱ Students listen a final time and review the passage.

Option A
• Make photocopies of the audioscript and hand it out to students.
• Play the audio recording and have students read along with it in chorus. Explain that this exercise will help them to hear and practice the rhythms, stresses, and clusters of English sounds.

Option B
Have students listen and complete the exercise at home or in a language lab.

Role Plays (10–20 minutes)

In these classroom speaking activities, students role-play a real-life encounter, such as a business meeting or an interview.

Advantages of Role Plays
- They are fun and motivating for most students.
- Role-playing characters often allows the more hesitant students to be more outgoing than if they are speaking as themselves.
- By broadening the world of the classroom to the world outside, role playing allows students to use a wider range of language than less open-ended activities.

Suggested Procedure for Role Plays
1. When possible, bring in props or costumes to add drama and fun.
2. Review the task so students understand what is required.
3. Perform a sample role play with a volunteer in front of the class.
4. Divide the class into the suggested groupings and give them a fixed time limit for completing the task.
5. Have students write a script for the role play. Then have them write key words on cards and perform the role play using the cards as prompts. OR Have students plan the action without a script and present it extemporaneously.
6. While students are working, circulate among the pairs or groups to answer students' questions and help them with the activity.
7. Have various pairs or groups perform their role plays in front of the class. If possible, tape-record or videotape the role plays for students' own listening or viewing. You may want to use the Speaking Rubric on page 134.

Information Gaps (10–20 minutes)

These games are designed to encourage communication between students. In these activities, each student has a different set of information. Students have to talk to their partners to solve a puzzle, draw a picture (describe and draw), put things in the right order (describe and arrange), or find similarities and differences between pictures.

Advantages of Information Gaps
- Like role plays, information gaps are motivating and fun.
- Information gaps are additionally motivating because there is a real need for communication in order to combine the information to solve a problem and complete the task.
- Information sharing allows students to extend and personalize what they have learned in the unit.

Suggested Procedure for Information Gaps
1. Explain how the Student A and Student B pages relate to each other (how they are different or similar).
2. Refer students to the examples and to any language provided.
3. Divide the class into pairs (Student A and Student B) and have them position themselves so that they cannot see the contents of each other's books.
4. Tell the Student Bs what page to turn to, and circulate to check that they are looking at the correct page.
5. Have students read their separate instructions. Check comprehension of the task by asking each group, "What are you going to do?"
6. Remind students not to show each other the contents of their pages.
7. As students are working, circulate to answer individual questions and to help students with the activity.

Writing (15–25 minutes in-class time)

These activities give students the opportunity to develop their writing skills and provide additional practice using the target grammatical structures. There is a variety of realistic formats, including paragraphs, essays, letters, and journal entries. The themes are related to material covered in the unit so that students already have some preparation for the writing task.

A Scoring Rubric for Writing is included on page 135 so that you can assess students' general writing skills as well as their ability to apply the target grammar point within a written context. This rubric allows you to give students a holistic score from 1 to 5 that reflects how well students have responded to the topic, organized their ideas, and incorporated the new grammar points from the unit. It is best to hand out copies to students before they begin working on the assignment, so that they understand what competencies are required.

The rubric provided in this book is for classroom use. To see an example of a rubric used to evaluate writing in a formal assessment situation, you can look at the one used by raters of the writing section on the TOEFL® iBT. This is available to download at http://ftp.ets.org/pub/toefl/Writing_Rubrics.pdf.

Suggested Procedure for Writing

Pre-writing

1. Go over the requirements of the assignment to make sure students understand what they are expected to do.
2. Write some questions on the board, and have students work in pairs or small groups to brainstorm ideas for the writing assignment. The Unit-by-Unit Teaching Tips provide suggestions for questions you might write on the board.
3. Call on volunteers to answer the questions as you write key words and phrases on the board.
4. Remind students to include the grammar studied in the unit as they complete the assignment.

Composing and correcting

1. Have students compose a draft of the writing assignment at home and then submit it to you or share it with a partner in class.
2. Give students feedback on the following features:
   - Content: Has the student responded appropriately to the task? Are the main points well supported?
   - Organization: Is the flow of ideas logical and effective?
   - Accuracy: Are there any major errors in the grammar points taught in the unit? (At this stage, you may want to focus your comments on errors related to the target grammar point. Circle the errors, but let students make the corrections. If students are providing feedback to each other, encourage them to focus on content and organization.
3. ⏱ For longer assignments, have students complete a second draft. When you check these drafts, point out any further areas needing correction, concentrating especially on errors in the target grammar point or grammar points from a previous unit.
4. Have students prepare their final draft at home.

Presentation

1. In class, have students share their final drafts. There are a variety of ways to do this:
   - Post students' work on the class bulletin board.

- Publish it in a website or a magazine that the class creates.
- Exchange papers with others in the class.
- Read papers aloud.

2. ⏱ Have your students put all their corrected written work into a folder, or portfolio, which you can review at the end of the course. This will allow your students and you to see the progress they have made.

Internet Activity (20 minutes in-class time)

This activity gives students an opportunity to do research related to the content of the unit and to discuss or present their findings in class. The activity varies from unit to unit. In some cases students are given very specific questions to research, and the reporting task is brief. In other cases, the investigation is more open-ended, and there is potential for a more extensive presentation.

Suggested Procedure for Internet Activity

Before class

Try the activity yourself, and prepare a list of appropriate key words or specific websites. Note: some suggested website addresses are listed on the *Focus on Grammar* Companion Website (www.longman.com/focusongrammar).

In class: preparation

1. Go over the directions to be sure students understand them. Have students work in small groups to brainstorm ideas for their research.
2. For some projects, you may want to have students work in small groups to divide up the research tasks.
3. Ask students to think about how they would search for their topics. Discuss useful key words and/or write some suggested websites on the board. Remind students that they can find websites on the *Focus on Grammar* Companion Website (www.longman.com/focusongrammar).
4. Elicit language that students are likely to use when discussing their research results. Remind them to review language they have studied in the unit.

At home / language lab

1. Students research their topics and take notes.
2. Ask students to review the notes they made on each website and summarize the most important information.

In class: wrap-up

1. During the next class session, put students into small groups to discuss their research findings.

2. Call upon a spokesperson for each group to report what the group discussed and, if appropriate, what conclusions they came to.

Option (40–60 minutes in-class time)

• Follow the above procedure, but instead of having small group discussions, have students deliver more formal spoken presentations. You may wish to use the Speaking Rubric on page 134.

• When going over the directions to the activity, tell students that they should take notes as they do their research and prepare a short (5-minute) presentation.

• Talk with students about elements of successful spoken presentations, including the importance of making eye contact and using body language. Encourage them to practice at home and to bring in visuals if possible.

• Coach students as they present and provide feedback on their presentations. You may wish to have students complete feedback forms for other students' presentations.

Further Practice

One or more Further Practice activities (in the Teacher's Manual only) can be found at the end of every unit in the Unit-by-Unit Teaching Tips. These exercises offer additional communicative practice with the target structure of the unit. Most can be done in class with no before-class preparation.

GRAMMAR OUT OF THE BOX ......

This activity (in the Teacher's Manual only) offers ideas for how to bring "real life" into your grammar classroom. Using video, pictures, news articles, or other realia, these activities help students make the connection between the structures they learn in the classroom and their application in the real world.

From Grammar to Writing

The From Grammar to Writing section at the end of each Part of the Student Book includes a grammar point and relates this grammar point to the writing focus. Students first practice the teaching point in a controlled exercise such as fill in the blanks, identification, or editing. Following these exercises, students practice pre-writing strategies such as making charts, time lines, schedules, story maps, Venn diagrams, notes, and outlines. Finally, students apply the teaching point in a writing task. Text types include both formal and informal writing, such as personal letters, business letters, essays, summaries, and reports. The section concludes with peer review and editing.

Suggested Procedure for From Grammar to Writing

Pre-writing

1. Have students work individually to complete the controlled practice exercises. Then have them exchange books and compare answers.

2. Go over the answers as a class and answer any questions that students have at this point.

3. Explain the pre-writing task. Where appropriate, provide a model for students on the board or on an overhead.

4. Have students work in pairs or small groups to complete the pre-writing task. Circulate while they are working to answer any questions and to help them with the activity.

Composing and correcting

1. Go over the requirements of the assignment to make sure students understand what they are expected to do.

2. Have students complete the writing assignment at home.

3. In class, complete the peer review portion of the task. Circulate while students are working together to make sure they are on task and to provide appropriate feedback. (See Suggested Procedure for Writing on page 8 for examples of what kind of feedback to provide.)

4. ⏱ Have students revise their writing and turn in the second draft to you. You may wish to use the Scoring Rubric for Writing on page 135 to correct these drafts and to include the drafts as part of the students' writing portfolios.

Option

- Have students complete the controlled practice exercise(s) at home.
- In class, have students work in pairs to compare answers.
- Follow the suggested procedure, starting from step 4 in the pre-writing phase.

Review Test

The last section of each Part of the Student Book is a review feature that can be used as a self-test. These exercises test the form and use of the grammar content presented and practiced in that Part. They give students a chance to check their knowledge and to review any problematic areas before moving on to the next part. An answer key is provided at the back of the Student Book, with cross-references to units for easy review.

Suggested Procedure for Review Test

1. Have students complete the exercises at home and check their answers in the Answer Key.
2. During the next class, go over any remaining questions students may have.

Option

- Have students complete the exercises in class. Give them a time limit of 20–30 minutes and circulate as they work.
- Have students use the Answer Key to check and correct their answers in pairs. Or you can go over the answers as a class.

Strategies for Teaching Grammar

1. Develop awareness
- Ask questions that help students become aware of the form of the structure. For example, for the present of *Be*, affirmative statements (FOG 2, page 5), read the statement *David is popular.* Ask students what the subject is *(David)*. Ask, "Is it singular or plural?" *(singular)* Ask "What is the verb?" *(is)*
- Compare information in the Grammar Charts. For example, for the simple past (FOG 2, page 200) there are Grammar Charts for the past of *be* and for other verbs. Ask, "How many forms are there for the simple past of *be*?" *(two: was and were)* "How do you form the negative with *be* in the simple past?" *(wasn't, weren't)* "How many forms are there for the negative with other verbs?" *(one: didn't + base form)*

2. Present meaning
Show the meaning of a grammatical form through a classroom demonstration. For example, to illustrate the use of present perfect progressive, you could show a picture of a person carrying grocery bags full of food. *(He/She has been shopping.)*

3. Identify examples
Ask students to go back to the Grammar in Context section and label examples in the reading passage with the grammatical terms in the Grammar Charts.

4. Generate examples
Find examples from the reading or elsewhere that could fit into the Grammar Charts. An interesting way to do this is to photocopy and enlarge the Grammar Chart. White out the targeted structures and replace them with blank lines for each missing word. Make copies and distribute them to students in pairs or small groups. Have students fill in the blanks, using examples from the reading. Then generate more examples. Books can be open or closed, depending on the level of challenge desired.

5. Show understanding by categorizing
Check comprehension of a grammatical principle by asking students to label multiple examples appropriately. For example, students can label verbs "present" or "future" or they can label examples "correct" or "incorrect."

6. Show understanding by performing actions
Check comprehension of the meaning of a grammatical form by having students follow instructions. Ask students, for example, to think of and perform a set of actions that they could describe using the present progressive.

7. Manipulate forms
Have students manipulate the examples in the Grammar Charts to practice the form. Drills such as substitution or transformation help students to build fluency. For example, in Unit 17 (FOG 2, page 161), you might have students look at examples in Note 1 and change the affirmative statements to negative ones.

8. Personalize
Ask students to provide personal examples. For example, on page 76 in Exercise 7, students are asked to check the sentences that are true for them. To expand on this exercise and have students personalize the material even more, you might ask them to write three more true affirmative statements and three more true negative statements about themselves using the simple present.

9. Repeat, reinforce
Students need to be exposed to new grammar many times in order to internalize it completely. You can first present a new structure on the board, then point it out in the book, then have students use it in an informal oral exercise, then do a written exercise in pairs, and finally review the same structure in homework. Varying the content and focus of these activities will keep students interested, and the grammar will be reinforced almost automatically.

Frequently Asked Questions (FAQ)

1. When should I have students work in pairs or groups rather than individually or as a whole class?

Varying your classroom organization to suit particular activity types will result in more effective and more interesting classes. Many students are not accustomed to working in pairs or groups, so it is important to use these groupings only when they are most beneficial.

- **Whole-class teaching** maximizes teacher control and is especially good for:
  —presenting information, giving explanations and instructions
  —showing material in texts and pictures or on audio or videotape
  —teacher-led drills (such as substitution or transformation) or dictations
  —reviewing answers or sharing ideas after students have completed an activity
  —enabling the whole class to benefit from teacher feedback to individuals
- **Students working individually** allows quiet, concentrated attention and is most effective for:
  —processing information or completing a task at students' own pace
  —performing writing tasks

For objective exercises such as fill-in-the-blank, matching, multiple choice, and editing, vary your class organization to keep student motivation high. Students can sometimes complete these exercises individually, and sometimes they can work with a partner.

- **Students working in pairs** maximizes student speaking time, breaks up the routine and "teacher talk," and is ideal for:
  —information-gap activities
  —role plays
  —writing and/or reading dialogues
  —predicting the content of reading and listening texts
  —comparing notes on what students listen to or see
  —checking answers
  —peer assessment

Pair work can also be very effective for completing objective exercises such as fill-in-the-blank, matching, multiple choice, and editing.

- **Students working in groups** creates ideal conditions for students to learn from each other and works well for:
  —generating ideas
  —pooling knowledge
  —writing group stories
  —preparing presentations
  —discussing an issue and reaching a group decision

2. How should I set up pair work and group work?

- **Streaming:** Grouping students according to ability or participation has certain advantages.
  —**ability:** Grouping weaker and stronger students together allows more able students to help their less fluent classmates.
  —**participation:** If you see that some students participate less than others, you could make a pair or group of weak participators. By the same token, you can also put especially talkative students together.
- **Chance:** Grouping students by chance has many benefits, especially if it results in students working with varied partners. You can group students by chance according to:
  —**where they sit:** Students sitting next to or near one another work in pairs or groups. This is the easiest option, but if students always sit in the same place, you will want to find other ways of grouping them.
  —**the "wheels" system:** Half the class stands in a circle facing outwards, and the other half stands in an outer circle facing inwards. The outer circle revolves in a clockwise direction, and the inner circle revolves in a counterclockwise direction. When you tell them to stop, students work with the person facing them. This is a very effective way to have students engage in meaningful repetition, such as asking the same question of many different partners.
  —**assigned letters:** Assign each student a letter from *A* to *E*. Then ask all the As to form a group, all the Bs to form a group, and so on.
  —**birthdays:** Students stand in a line in the order of their birthdays (with January at one end and December at the other). The first five students form one group; the second five students another group, and so on.

—**native language:** If possible, put students in groups or pairs with others who don't share a native language. This helps create an "English-only" classroom.

3. How can I make activities more successful?

Before the activity:
- **Motivate students and explain the purpose.** Make it clear that something enjoyable or interesting is going to happen. Explain the rationale for the activity. Making sure students understand the purpose of the activity is to practice what they learned and encourage them to participate.
- **Provide clear directions.** Explain what students should do in every step of the activity. Have students paraphrase or demonstrate the task to be sure they understand it.
- **Demonstrate.** Show the class what is supposed to happen in an activity. This might involve asking a student to demonstrate the activity with you or having two students role-play in the front of the room.
- **Provide a time frame.** It is helpful for students to know how much time they have and exactly when they should stop. Approximate times are given for all the activities in this Teacher's Manual.

For open-ended activities, such as the Internet Activity or writing exercises, you will also want to:
- **Stimulate thinking.** When there are choices for students to make, it is often helpful to set up small-group and/or whole-class brainstorming sessions to define the focus and/or content of their task.
- **Prepare language.** Review grammar and vocabulary that students may need to complete the task. This can be done as a follow-up to a brainstorming activity where you elicit ideas and write key language on the board.

During the activity:
- **Observe students.** Walk around the room watching and listening to pairs or groups.
- **Provide assistance as needed.** (See FAQ #5 for suggestions on giving feedback and correcting errors.)

After the activity:
- **Elicit student responses.** For some activities, you may ask for volunteers or call on students to share some of their ideas with the class. For other types of activities, a few pairs or groups can be asked to role-play

their discussions to demonstrate the language they have been using.
- **Provide feedback.** In many cases, this is most conveniently done in a whole-class setting. It may be preferable, however, for you to meet with individuals, pairs, or groups. While the principal focus in a grammar class is language use, it is also important to acknowledge the value of students' ideas. See FAQ #5 below for suggestions on feedback and error correction.

4. What can I do to encourage students to use more English in the classroom?

It is perfectly natural for students to feel the need to use their first language in an English class. There are a number of actions that teachers can take to promote the use of English.
- **Set clear guidelines:** Some teachers in monolingual classes find that activities such as providing vocabulary definitions, presenting a grammar point, checking comprehension, giving instructions, and discussing classroom methodology are best done in the students' native language.
- **Use persuasion:** Walking among the students during speaking activities and saying things like "Please speak English!" or "Try to use English as much as possible." helps to ensure that students will speak English most of the time.

5. What's the best approach to giving feedback and correcting errors?

Be selective in offering correction. Students can't focus on everything at once, so concentrate first on errors relating to the target grammar point and grammar points from units previously studied, as well as any errors that interfere with communication. Whether you respond to other errors depends on your judgment of students' readiness to take in the information. If you see a teachable moment, seize it! Rather than correct every error individual students make in the course of activities, it is generally preferable to note commonly occurring mistakes and give a short presentation for the whole class at the end of the activity.
- **Recasting.** If a student makes an error—for example, "I *didn't came* to class yesterday because I was sick."—you can recast it as, "You *didn't come* to class yesterday because you were sick?" The student ideally notices the difference and restates the original

sentence: "Right. I didn't come to class yesterday because I was sick." This process can be effective because the student has the opportunity to self-correct an error that is still in short-term memory. As a variation, you can restate but stop, with rising intonation, right before the potential error: "You didn't . . . ?"

6. What can I do to accommodate different learning styles?

Focus on Grammar recognizes different styles of learning and provides a variety of activities to accommodate these different styles. Some learners prefer an analytical, or rule-learning (deductive) approach. Others, especially younger learners, respond best to an inductive approach, or exposure to the language in meaningful contexts. Indeed, the same students may adopt different styles as they learn, or they may use different styles at different times.

As teachers, we want to help the students in our classes who prefer to follow rules become more able to take risks and to plunge into communicative activities. We also want to encourage the risk-takers to focus on accuracy. *Focus on Grammar* provides the variety to ensure that students achieve their goal: to learn to use the language confidently and appropriately.

Unit-by-Unit Teaching Tips

 UNIT 1 **The Present of *Be*: Statements**

Unit Overview

Students will learn the structure and use of *be* in present-tense statements to include:
- singular and plural forms of *be* in affirmative and negative statements
- contractions
- subject pronouns
- placement of *be* in affirmative and negative sentences

Grammar in Context (pages 4–5)

Background Notes
- Posh Spice was a member of the British girl-band The Spice Girls, famous in the 1990s.
- Foot-volley is a beach sport that combines soccer and volleyball. It was invented in Brazil and is also popular in Italy.
- Ronaldo is a famous Brazilian foot-volley player.

Vocabulary

talented: very good at something that not everyone can do

popular: liked by a lot of people

favorite: liked more than others of the same kind

Comprehension Questions
- Who is David Beckham? (*He is a famous British soccer player.*)
- What is his wife's name? (*Her show-business name is Posh Spice, but her real name is Victoria Adams.*)
- Where is their home? (*Their home is in England.*)
- Is Ramon Gomes famous? (*No, he isn't famous.*)
- Where is he from? (*He's from Rio de Janeiro, Brazil.*)
- What is his favorite sport? (*His favorite sport is foot-volley.*)
- Who is his favorite player? (*His favorite player is Ronaldo.*)

Discussion Topics
- Ask students to name other well-known talented people in the following categories: sports, music, literature, acting, visual arts, science. Ask if they can think of other categories and other examples.
- Many talented people are not famous. Ask students to talk about their own special talents.

Grammar Presentation (pages 5–7)

Identify the Grammar

David Beckham is a soccer player.
David and Victoria are rich and famous.

Beckham isn't his favorite soccer player.
He's from England.
David's married to Posh Spice.

Grammar Charts
- Give students time to read the charts on pages 5 and 6.
- On the board, write affirmative sentences: *I am popular. You are popular. [Student's name] is popular. [Student's name] and [Student's name] are popular.*
- Ask students to read the sentences. Ask questions to draw students' attention to the forms in the sentences, such as "What is the subject here?" "Is it singular or plural?" "What is the verb?" "Is it singular or plural?"
- Matching drill: Say a noun or pronoun, singular or plural. Have the class respond with the appropriate form of *be* (is/am/are).
- Put a chart like the following on the board. Have students combine elements to make their own affirmative statements.

I	am	tired
you	is	a student
he, she, it	are	cities
Anita		students
we		young
you		hungry
they		
Seoul and Moscow		

- Explain contractions. Use mathematical formulas, such as *you + are = you're*. Do this for all forms. Have students repeat the forms after you.
- Have students repeat the affirmative statements using contractions. *(Anita's hungry. They're students.)*
- Give students time to read the charts on page 6.
- Repeat the previous steps with negative sentences. Add the word *not* to the chart above.
- Tell students to cover the charts in the book with their hands. Do a rapid transformation drill with the two types of negative contractions. Example:

  TEACHER: We are not from London.

  A: We aren't from London.

  B: We're not from London.

Grammar Notes

Note 1 *(Exercises 3–4)*
- Write on the board: *David Beckham is a soccer player. He is from England.*
- Have students identify the following: subject, verb, noun, pronoun. If necessary, provide another example: *Victoria Adams is from England. She is Beckham's wife.*
- Have a student read the first rule.
- Have another student read Be Careful aloud. Then write the following wrong sentences on the board. Call students up to the board to fix them. Ask students to explain the problem in each sentence.

  —Is a student. *(He/She is a student.)*

  —Tom a student. *(Tom is a student.)*

  —My sister she a student. *(My sister is a student.)*

  —We students. *(We are students.)*

Note 3 *(Exercises 3–4)*
- On the board, write *a singer, singers, big, from Japan.* Have students identify the following: singular noun, plural noun, adjective, prepositional phrase. Elicit more examples from the class.

- Read each sentence in the book and have the class repeat.
- Write *It is bigs.* on the board. Ask the class, "Do English adjectives have an *-s* ending?" *(no)* Draw attention to the incorrect *-s* ending by putting a big *X* through it.

Note 5 *(Exercise 4)*
- To review all contractions in the affirmative and negative, make a handout with a chart like this:

Affirmative	Negative
1. (I) *I'm* _____	1. (I) _____
2. (you) _____	2. (you) _____
3. (he) _____	3. (he) _____
4. (she) _____	4. (she) *She's not, she isn't*
5. (it) _____	5. (it) _____
6. (we) _____	6. (we) _____
7. (you) _____	7. (you) _____
8. (they) _____	8. (they) _____

- Put students in small groups. Have them fill in the missing forms. Remind them to fill in both negative forms wherever possible.
- Have students make sentences using all the forms in the chart.

Focused Practice (pages 7–9)

Exercise 2
fan: someone who likes a particular sport, type of music, etc., very much, or who admires a famous person

Exercise 3
comedy: a funny movie, play, or other performance
traditional: following ideas or methods that have existed for a long time rather than doing something new or different

Exercise 5
supervisor: someone who is responsible for making sure a group of people does its work correctly

Communication Practice (pages 10–11)

Exercise 7
- Before students listen, have them look at the pictures. Ask where the people are from.
- Follow the directions for speaking and listening.

Exercise 8
- Put students in pairs.
- Choose one student. Together, model the activity using the examples.
- After students do the activity in pairs, follow up by having a few students say their statements to the whole class. The class responds, "That's right" or "That's wrong."

Exercise 9
Questions to generate ideas and elicit vocabulary:
- Do you have a talented friend or family member?
- Who is this person? How old is he or she? Where does he or she live?
- What is this person's special talent?
- How do you feel about this person's talent?
- Will this person be famous someday?

Further Practice
Have the students play a guessing game. Write the names of the students on slips of paper. Distribute the slips so that each student has a "mystery partner." Have each student write five sentences about the mystery partner. Sentences should be both affirmative and negative. They should have contractions if possible. Have the students read their sentences out loud. The class guesses who the "mystery partners" are. Example sentences:
My mystery partner's from Morocco.
He's a man.
He isn't tall and he isn't short.
He's handsome. He's shy.

GRAMMAR OUT OF THE BOX......

Movie talk. Consider showing parts of the film *Bend It Like Beckham*. Although students will not be able to understand most of the dialogue, they can appreciate the soccer scenes. The scenes in which the young Indian girl argues with her parents are also interesting; students will understand the conflict even without knowing the words. After viewing, ask students questions like the following:
- Who is right—the girl or her parents?
- Are your parents like the girl's parents?
- Is it OK for girls to play soccer?

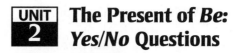
UNIT 2 **The Present of *Be*: *Yes/No* Questions**

Unit Overview

Students will learn the structure and use of the *be* verb in:
- *yes/no* questions, singular and plural
- short and long answers

Grammar in Context (pages 12–13)

Background Notes
- Claudia is a woman's name in Spanish.
- Al is a man's name in English.
- Latin America includes the countries of South and Central America.

Vocabulary
Whew!: an interjection spoken when a person feels tired, hot, or relieved

Comprehension Questions
- Is Claudia late? *(No, she isn't.)*
- Is Claudia a new student? *(Yes, she is.)*
- Is Al a new student? *(No, he is not.)*
- Where is Claudia from? *(Mexico)*
- Where is Al from? *(Michigan)*

Discussion Topics
Use students' names to ask who is here, absent, or late. Ask:
- Is Carlos here? Is he absent? Is he late?
- Is Sang Hee late for class today?

Grammar Presentation (pages 13–14)

Identify the Grammar

YES/NO QUESTIONS
Am I late for class?
Are you new here?

SHORT ANSWERS
No, you're not.
Yes, I am.

Grammar Charts
- Write the following on the board. Don't write the final punctuation.
I am late for class
Am I late for class

- Ask the class, "Which one is a question? How do you know?" *(word order)*
- Write the following on the board, using names of students from the class:
  Is _____ here?
  Yes, she is here. / Yes, she is.

  Is _____ here?
  No, he's not here. / No, he's not.
  No, he isn't here. / No, he isn't.
- Call a student to the board. Have the student point to each answer and say "long answer" or "short answer."
- Repeat using plural forms:
  Are _____ and _____ here?
  Yes, they're here.

  Are _____ and _____ here?
  No, they're not. / No, they aren't.
- Read all the singular and plural questions in the Student Book. Emphasize the rising intonation of the questions. Show the rising contour with your hand. Have students repeat.
- Do a transformation drill. Include all the singular and plural forms.

  TEACHER: I am hungry.

  CLASS: Am I hungry?

  TEACHER: You are hungry.

  CLASS: Are you hungry?
- Drill the short answer using a question-and-answer format. Ask questions using all pronouns, singular and plural. Students should answer truthfully. Begin with questions that take affirmative answers:

  TEACHER: Am I in room 202?

  STUDENT: Yes, you are.

  TEACHER: Are you in room 202?

  STUDENT: Yes, I am.
- Repeat the previous step with questions that take a negative answer.

  TEACHER: Is today Thursday?

  A: No, it's not.

  B: No, it isn't.

  TEACHER: Are we learning to speak French?

Grammar Notes

Note 1 *(Exercises 2–4)*
- To reinforce the word order of *yes/no* questions, write the sentences from the book on an overhead transparency. (Note: If you do not have an overhead projector, you can use pieces of cardboard or strips of paper.) Use all capital letters. Then cut up each sentence into words and phrases.

- Mix up the pieces of one sentence (question mark and period included) and project them for the whole class to see.
- Call students up and instruct them to put the pieces in the correct order to make either a question or a statement.
- Do this with just one sentence the first time. After that, mix several sentences together and instruct students to combine them in any way that makes sense.

Note 2 *(Exercises 3–4)*
- Read the note with the class. Read the examples as a dialogue between you and two students. To reinforce the incorrect form *Yes, I'm,* write it on the board and say "incorrect." Then draw a big *X* through it.
- Practice questions and short answers as follows: Choose a question and have students ask each other in turn. Instruct them to answer truthfully. Here is an example:

  TEACHER: Paru, are you married?

  PARU: No, I'm not.

  TEACHER: Ask Zena the same question.

  PARU: Zena, are you married?

  ZENA: Yes, I am.
- After three or four students have answered the same question, substitute a different question as follows:

  ZENA: David, are you married?

  DAVID: No, I'm not.

  TEACHER: Sleepy.

  DAVID: Ali, are you sleepy?

  ALI: No, I'm not.

Note 3
Follow the same procedure as for Note 2. Change the question frequently to help students stay alert.

Note 4 *(Exercise 4)*
- On the board write *I don't know; Yes, I think so; No, I don't think so.*
- Demonstrate the meanings with gestures. Say, "I don't know" and shrug your shoulders. Say, "Yes, I think so," pointing to your brain and nodding your head. Say, "No, I don't think so," pointing to your brain and shaking your head from side to side.
- Ask a few questions like the ones in the Student Book. Have students answer truthfully using one of the three expressions.

Focused Practice (pages 15–19)

Exercise 3
pronounce: to make the sound of a letter or word in the correct way

Exercise 4
psychologist: someone who is trained in the scientific study of the mind and how it works

on time: at the correct time

plan: to think about something you want to do and how you will do it

Communication Practice (pages 19–21)

Exercise 7
- Clarify the meaning of *occupations*. Give students cues such as jobs and work.
- Say, and have students repeat, all the occupations on page 20. Check for comprehension.
- Model the Part B conversation with a student. Explain the vocabulary in the box. Use gestures and pantomime to make meanings clear.
- To extend this activity, elicit more occupations from the class. Have students explain occupations in words or use gestures for classmates.

Exercise 8
- For Part A, follow the directions in the text.
- For Part B, pronounce the items in the box and have the class repeat. Clarify meanings. Model the example conversation.

Further Practice
Have the class play 20 questions. The game can be played with the whole class, or you can divide students into groups of at least four people. One student is "it." This student thinks of a mystery person. The other students ask *yes/no* questions in order to guess who the mystery person is. If listeners guess in 20 questions or fewer, they win, and a new person becomes "it." The student who is "it" should answer with short answers. If students have trouble getting started, a good opening question is always, "Is it a man or a woman?"

 **OUT OF THE BOX** ......

Job talk. Have a discussion about unusual jobs. Do an Internet search for *unusual jobs*.

Give students a list of jobs and a list of questions to discuss. Use the vocabulary from this unit. For example:
- Is this job interesting/dangerous/fun/etc.?
- Is this a good job for you? Why?

Sample jobs:
A - Assistant to a Magician
B - Blueberry Counter
C - Carnival Ride Operator
D - Dynamite Packer
E - Eye Bank Procurer
F - Fantasy Theme Park Character
G - Gold Miner
H - High Priority Document Escort
I - Instructor for Prison Education Program
J - Janitor for Zoo Cages
K - Karaoke DJ
L - Scout for Filming Locations
M - Mountain Cave Tour Guide
N - Nanny for Company Guard Dog
O - Obituary Writer
P - Pet Photographer's Apprentice
Q - Quality Control Manager for Fast Food Chain
R - Recreational Therapist for Psychiatric Hospital
S - Shopper
T - Trapper of Black Bears
U - Undercover Investigator
V - Voice for Recorded Announcements
W - Whisker for Carpet Company
X - Xmas Gift Wrapper
Y - Yoga Instructor
Z - Zip Code Finder

UNIT 3 The Past of *Be*

Unit Overview

Students will learn the structure and use of the *be* verb in past time, including:
- singular and plural forms of *be* in affirmative and negative statements
- *yes/no* questions
- past time markers

Grammar in Context (page 22)

Background Notes
Ottawa is the capital of Canada.

Comprehension Questions

- Was Emily at the party? *(yes)*
- Why is Emily calling? *(to say thank you)*
- Was Dave at the party? *(no)*
- Where was Dave? *(in Ottawa, at the airport)*

Discussion Topics

- Ask students if they have an answering machine. If they are in an English-speaking country, help them compose a simple outgoing message like the following: "This is Kazuo. I'm not home right now. Please leave me a message."
- Ask students, "Did you go to a party last night/Friday/weekend? Was it fun? Who was there? Was the food good?"

Grammar Presentation (pages 23–24)

Identify the Grammar

The party was great.
We were happy to meet Gina.
I'm sorry I wasn't at the party.

Grammar Charts

- Model the affirmative statement form with singular and plural subjects. As you say each sentence, write it on the board. Example:
  Yesterday evening I was at home.
  You were at home.
  He was at home.
- Point to the sentences and ask, "What is the subject? What is the verb? Is it singular or plural?"
- Do a substitution drill. Provide a base sentence. Cue the class with different subjects and have students repeat the sentence with the proper verb. Example:

  TEACHER: Yesterday Jack was late. You.

  CLASS: Yesterday you were late.

  TEACHER: They.

- Repeat the previous steps with non-contracted negative forms. Example:
  I was not here last night.
  You were not here last night.
- Repeat the previous steps, this time with contracted forms:
  I wasn't here last night.
  You weren't here last night.
- Model and drill the word order of questions and short answers. See page 18 of this Teacher's Manual, Note 2.

Grammar Notes

Notes 1–3 *(Exercises 2–7)*

- Have students generate their own true sentences for each verb form. First, write three columns on the board:

I	at a party	yesterday
you	absent	last night
he, she, it	late	
we	at home	
you	at the library	
they	in class	
[Student's name]	at the airport	
[Student's name and Student's name]	tired	

- Next, on their own piece of paper, have students draw a large square and divide the square into four smaller squares, like this:

was	were
wasn't	weren't

- Have students form pairs or small groups. Tell them to write three true sentences for each verb form, using the vocabulary on the board and the verb forms on their papers. Have groups share their sentences with other groups, or ask volunteers to read selected sentences to the class.

Notes 4–5 *(Exercises 2, 4, 6–7)*

- Put students in pairs and have them interview each other using *yes/no* questions, short answers, and past time markers. Have students use the prompts below to form questions. Remind students to use rising intonation at the end of questions. Instruct them to answer truthfully.

Were you in this country last year?

Student A's questions	Student B's questions
this country / last year	here / two months ago
in class / yesterday	with [Student's name]
at home / last night	/ last night
absent / the day	tired / yesterday
before yesterday	sick / last week

Focused Practice (pages 24–28)

Exercise 3
sunny, cloudy: Refer students to the Student Book, page 29 for illustrations.

Communication Practice (pages 29–30)

Exercise 9
• Before listening, have students look at the items and try to guess which words fit in the blanks.
• After listening, have students work in pairs and compare answers.

Exercise 10
• Say the weather words in the box and have students repeat. Clarify meanings if necessary. Use gestures or pantomime.
• Model the activity. Read the example with a student. Show students where to write the information they get from their partners.
• Put students in pairs and direct each partner to the page with his/her information.
• Follow-up: Ask the class to describe the local weather today and yesterday.

Exercise 11
• Follow the instructions for Part A.
• Ask the following questions to generate ideas and elicit vocabulary for Part B:
  —Which friend will you write an e-mail message to?
  —What can you say about your life now?
  —What can you say about last weekend?
  —What can you say about the weather?

Further Practice
Make a handout like the chart that follows. In class, give students the following instructions:
• Stand up and walk around. Talk to your classmates.
• Ask questions with "Were you . . ." Use the information in the chart.
• Find someone who says yes. Write the person's name in the space. Then talk to a different person.

Find someone who ...	
was absent yesterday	
was in Europe, South America, or Asia last year	
wasn't here on the first day of class	
was born after 1985	
wasn't at home last weekend	
wasn't in school last year	

Follow-up: In a small class, call out the name of each student and elicit two to three sentences about him or her. Example:

TEACHER: Zahra.

CLASS: She was absent yesterday. She was born after 1985.

In a large class, call out each question and elicit sentences about the students. Example:

TEACHER: Who was absent yesterday?

CLASS: Zahra was absent yesterday. Theo was absent yesterday. Bijan was absent yesterday.

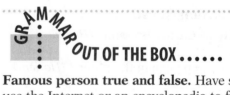

GRAMMAR OUT OF THE BOX ......

Famous person true and false. Have students use the Internet or an encyclopedia to find information about a famous person who interests them. They should try to obtain a photo of the person as well. Instruct students to write a true/false quiz about their famous person. On the top of a piece of paper they should write the person's name and paste the person's photo. Then they should write six to seven statements about the person in the following format:
1. Elvis Presley was born in Memphis, Tennessee. _____
2. His mother and father weren't married. _____
Some of the statements should be false.

Have students post their quizzes around the room. Students should circulate and take each other's quizzes. They should write *T* for true and *F* for false on the line following each statement, along with their initials. For example:
1. Elvis Presley was born in Memphis, Tennessee. T-LB
At the end, students should share the correct answers to their quizzes by writing them on the quiz paper in a different-colored ink.

UNIT 4 — Count Nouns; Proper Nouns

Unit Overview

Students will learn the following:
- singular and plural count nouns
  (*a photographer, photographers*)
- irregular plural nouns (*children*)
- proper nouns (*New York City*)
- nouns that are always plural (*pants*)

Grammar in Context (pages 38–39)

Background Notes

- Before World War II, Harlem was a center of great artistic expression, especially among black Americans. The area was famous for its jazz and dance clubs.
- Henri Cartier-Bresson died on August 8, 2004. He was a master of candid photography. Many consider him to be the father of photojournalism.

Comprehension Questions

- Who is Henri Cartier-Bresson? (*He was a photographer.*)
- Where are the people in the photo? (*Harlem*)
- What year is it? (*1947*)

Discussion Topics

- Ask students why they think the photo is famous. Ask if they like it.
- Find out if there are students in the class who enjoy taking pictures.

Grammar Presentation (pages 39–40)

Identify the Grammar

Henri Cartier-Bresson is a photographer.
He was born in France.
His photos are famous.

Grammar Charts

To demonstrate the five categories of nouns in the charts, use objects, photos, items in the classroom, or the students themselves. Make sure to have at least two of some items in order to demonstrate the plurals.

Grammar Notes

Notes 1–3   (*Exercises 2–3*)

- On the board, sketch a graphic organizer like the following:

singular
a   an

- Demonstrate singular nouns with the article *a*. Hold up objects or photos or point to objects in the room. Name the items using *a*. (Examples: *a book, a pencil, a phone,* etc.) Write the items under the article *a* on the board.
- Repeat with objects or photos that take the article *an*. (Examples: *an orange, an apple, an eye, an earring*) Again, write the examples on the board, this time under *an*.
- Ask the class for additional examples of singular nouns with *a/an*. Write them on the board.
- Now write two columns on the board, or use an overhead projector slide:

hour   hot
honor   hand
*   house*

Point to each word and say it with *a/an*. Put an *X* through the first letter of *hour* and *honor* so students understand that this sound is not pronounced. Have students repeat the phrases after you: "an hour, an honor, a hot day, a hand, a house."

- Follow the same procedure for the two pronunciations of the letter *u* (Note 3), as in the following pairs:

umbrella   university
undershirt   uniform

Note 4   (*Exercises 3–4*)

- Sketch another organizer on the board:

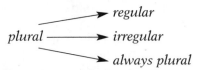

plural
regular
irregular
always plural

- Demonstrate examples of regular, irregular, and always plural nouns and write them on the board. Elicit further examples from the students.
- Drill the irregular plurals. Have students listen and repeat: "One man, two men. One woman, two women. One child, two children."

- Say the singular noun and have the class fill in the plural. Then do the reverse.

TEACHER: One man, two . . .

CLASS: Men.

TEACHER: One tooth, two . . .

CLASS: Teeth.

TEACHER: Two feet, one . . .

CLASS: Foot.

Note 5 *(Exercises 3, 5)*
- On the board, write *proper nouns*. Write several names of places and people as examples.
- Ask the class for further examples. Call students up to the board to write them.
- Point to the capital letters and underline them.

→ For additional practice, see the Supplementary Activities on page 125.

Focused Practice (pages 41–44)

Exercise 1
accountant: someone whose job is to take care of accounts (money)

Exercise 3
pianist: someone who plays the piano

Communication Practice (pages 45–47)

Exercise 8
A variation on this activity is for students to switch partners several times. At the end of class, have students hang their pictures on a bulletin board.

Exercise 9
- Part A: Model the example with a student. Then put students in pairs to do the activity.
- Part B: Students can work in pairs or in small groups.
- As a variation, put the chart on an overhead transparency and do the activity with the whole class. As students name the objects in the room, call them up to write on the transparency.

Exercise 10
Questions to generate ideas and elicit vocabulary:
- Who is a famous photographer?
- What is a famous city?
- What are some famous countries?

Further Practice
1. Play a kind of chain game. Have students sit in a circle. Students will speak in turn. Take the first turn and say, "I'm going shopping. I need to buy a/n _____." The student on your right will then say your sentence and add an item of his or her own: "I'm going shopping. I need to buy a/n _____ and a/n _____." Each speaker repeats what has been said and adds one item until you make it all the way around the circle.
2. Play a game similar to the card game concentration. You will need a deck of cards consisting of pairs of items, one singular and one plural. It's best to use pictures, but if none are available, you can also write the words on cards, e.g., *cat, cats.* Don't write the articles. Be sure to have cards representing words that take both *a* and *an.* Also include irregular plurals. Include 15–20 pairs in a deck and have a deck for every 2–3 students. If your class is large and you don't have time to prepare so many sets, have the students themselves do it. To play the game, spread out all the cards face-down. Students take turns turning over pairs of cards and saying what is on them. If the two cards match, the student keeps them. If they don't match, the student turns them back face-down. The winner is the student who collects the most pairs of cards.

GRAMMAR OUT OF THE BOX . . . . . .

Fun and games. Have students bring in photos, postcards, or posters that they like. Many things can be done with these visual items:
- Show and tell: Students show their item to the class or to their group and talk about the people, places, or things they have seen.
- A classroom art gallery: Students write captions for their items. The items and captions should be displayed in the classroom. Students can "visit" the gallery and discuss the items.
- Play the children's game "I spy." Divide students into groups of five or six. Give each group a bunch of photos. These should be spread on a large table or taped to the wall. In each group, one student looks at the photos and silently selects an object in one of them. Then the student says, "I spy" and names the object, using the proper article:

"I spy a black hat." The other students in the group compete to be the first person to point to the object the speaker named.

5 Descriptive Adjectives

Unit Overview

Students will learn the formation of descriptive adjectives and the positions of adjectives in sentences with and without *be*.

Grammar in Context (page 48)

Vocabulary

unusual: strange

underground: under the earth's surface

cave: a large natural hole in the side of a mountain or under the ground

hike: to walk in the mountains

landscape: view across an area of land, including hills, forests, fields, etc.

mild: not too severe or serious

Comprehension Questions

• Where is Cappadocia? *(in the center of Turkey)*
• Why is it unusual? *(It has underground cities and cave homes.)*
• How does the landscape look? *(like a different world)*
• Which movie was filmed there? *(Star Wars)*
• In the past, where did people live? *(in caves)*
• How is the climate? *(The climate is mild; the days are sunny and warm, and the nights are cool.)*

Discussion Topics

• Ask if students would like to visit Cappadocia.
• Ask if students have visited places that have unusual landscapes.

Grammar Presentation (page 49)

Identify the Grammar

It is an unusual place.
There are interesting things to see.
The landscape looks like a different world.
The climate is mild.

Grammar Charts

• Write the example sentences from Identify the Grammar on the board. Read them aloud. Point to the word *place* and say, "noun." Ask, "What kind of place is it?" *(an unusual place)* Say, "Unusual is an adjective."
• Repeat with the other examples.
• Erase the sentences except for the nouns. Ask the following questions:
  —What kind of place? *(an unusual place)*
  —What kind of things? *(interesting things)*
  —What kind of world? *(a different world)*
  —How is the climate? *(mild)*
• To reinforce the word order, write the following on the board:
  The [noun] is [adjective].
  It's a/an [adjective] [noun].
• Provide several sentences using the first pattern and have students transform them to the second pattern. Example:
  TEACHER: The day is warm.
  CLASS: It's a warm day.

Grammar Notes

Go over the notes with the whole class. Call on one student to read a rule and another student to read the examples.

Note 3 *(Exercise 2)*
It may be useful to contrast English with other languages. For example, write on the board:
Spanish: Las muchachas bonitas.
English: The pretty girls.
Circle the *-s* on the adjective in Spanish (or another language). Point to the English adjective and say, "no *-s*."

Note 4 *(Exercise 2)*
Write the examples on the board, but replace the articles with a blank. Elicit the correct article from the class. Ask them to state the rule:
"Use *a* if the adjective starts with a _____" *(consonant sound)*
"Use *an* if the adjective starts with a _____" *(vowel sound)*

Note 5 *(Exercise 2)*
Try to elicit more adjectives from the class by providing different contexts. Examples of adjectives include *bored, exciting, confusing, worried, early, used.*
• How do you feel when you have to wait for a long, long time? *(bored)*
• Is English grammar confusing? *(yes)*

- What kind of city is this? *(exciting)*
- Do you have a car? Is it new? *(No, it's used.)*

→ For additional practice, see the Supplementary Activities on page 125.

Focused Practice (pages 50–51)

Exercise 1
in the heart of: in the center of

modern: new

rates: prices

Exercise 2
carpet: rug

reasonable: not expensive

Exercise 3
bowls: wide, round containers that are used for holding food or liquids

Communication Practice (pages 51–52)

Exercise 4
Before students listen, show the location of Mesa Verde on a map, if possible. Tell students Mesa Verde means "green table" in Spanish. Ask students to describe the picture.

Exercise 5
- Part A: Read the lists out loud and have students repeat the words. Have students work in groups. Circulate and help with vocabulary.
- Part B: Circulate and help as students are writing.
- Part C: Circulate as students are working. Note sentences with errors. Write a few on the board and ask students to find and correct the errors.

Exercise 6
Variation: Have students sit or stand in a circle and share their sentences. No one is allowed to repeat a sentence that has already been said.

Further Practice
Have students prepare a short talk about a vacation. Write some questions on the board to guide students. For example,

Where did you go?
When did you go?
With whom did you go?
What does this place look like?

What did you see and do?
How was the vacation?

Read and give students a copy of the following example:

"In December 2003 I went to London with my parents. It is an exciting, beautiful city. The shopping is great in London, but it's very expensive. We saw many museums, the Queen's palace, big parks, and the famous Thames River. Our hotel was small and comfortable. The food was excellent. The weather was cold, but it was sunny. We had a wonderful vacation."

GRAMMAR OUT OF THE BOX ......

Check the library. Explore your local library to find a videotape or television program about the places listed in Exercise 7. The reference librarian can help you find appropriate materials.

UNIT 6   Prepositions of Place

Unit Overview

Students will learn prepositions of place in three contexts:
- locations: *My bag is under my seat.*
- addresses: *We're at 79 Main Street.*
- idiomatic expressions: *No one is home / at home.*

Grammar in Context (pages 53–54)

Background Notes
- In the United States, people who examine eyes and prescribe glasses go to a special school and are called "Doctor" after they graduate. People who make the glasses are not doctors.
- The *ground floor* is the entry level of a building. In the United States, it is also called the *first floor.*
- The idiom *a piece of cake,* meaning something easy, goes back to a nineteenth-century dance called the "cakewalk."

Vocabulary
appointment: a meeting that has been arranged for a particular time and place

chart: a large poster with letters on it, used for testing patients' vision

I guess: I think (used for expressing an opinion)

Comprehension Questions
- What kind of doctor is Dr. Green? *(eye doctor)*
- Where is his office? *(7 East 89th St., between Madison and Fifth Avenues, on the ground floor near the art museum)*
- When is the patient's appointment? *(Monday at 11)*
- Does the patient need glasses? *(yes)*

Discussion Topics
Ask who wears glasses or contact lenses. Then ask selected students, "Where is your eye doctor?"

Grammar Presentation (pages 54–55)

Identify the Grammar
We're at 7 East 89th Street. That's between Madison and Fifth Avenues. We're on the ground floor near the art museum.

Grammar Charts
- Read the examples of the target grammar from the reading out loud. Underline the word *at* and say, "At is a preposition. Prepositions tell where something is."
- Call a student up to the board to underline the other prepositions in the examples *(between, on, near).*
- You will need a collection of objects in order to demonstrate the prepositions. Cuisinaire rods and multicolored children's blocks work well. Objects found in the classroom, such as keys or pencils, can also be used.
- Write the following prepositions on the board: *next to, between, under, behind, near, in, in front of, in back of*
- Use the objects to make sentences on the board. Examples:
  My keys are next to my glasses.
  The pencil is on the floor. It's under the table.
- Ask a student to read the sentences you wrote on the board. The student should position the objects according to the information in the sentences. Do this with several students.
- Next, position a pair of objects and have the whole class, then individual students, make sentences. Provide the preposition if students need help.

- Have students pair up. Have them make sentences using the prepositions on the board with objects from their bags, pockets, or purses.

→ For additional practice, see the Supplementary Activities on page 125.

Grammar Notes

Note 1 *(Exercises 2–4)*
- Read the explanation out loud. Call on students to read the examples.
- Use objects to demonstrate the difference between *near* and *next to.*

Note 2 *(Exercises 2–4)*
- Before class, prepare a handout or an OHP slide with a map of your neighborhood. Draw an *X* to show where your school is, and include several streets and other buildings. Write the address at the top.
- Model sentences, using the map, like the ones in the note. Say the sentences and have the class repeat. Also model sentences with the words *street* or *avenue* omitted as explained in the Usage Note. Example: "My house is on the corner of Center Street and Broad Avenue. It's on the corner of Center and Broad."
- Say an address to emphasize the contrast among *in, on,* and *at.* Examples:
  —I live on Center Street.
  —I live at 2110 Center Street. My apartment is on the second floor.
  —I live in Detroit.
  —I live in Michigan.
  —I live in the United States.
- Call one student up to the board to write his or her address. Have the class make sentences like those above.
- Put students in pairs or small groups. Have them sketch a quick map of their neighborhood and write their addresses at the top. Use this opportunity to make sure students know what their addresses are and how to write them. Then have them make sentences like those in the note.

Note 3 *(Exercise 4)*
- Draw a horizontal line on the board representing your daily schedule. Underneath the line, fill in some times. Example:

7	8	9	10	11	12	1	2	3	4	5	6
Morning					*Afternoon*					*Evening*	

- Make sentences using the expressions in the note.

- Call one student to the board. Have him or her make sentences like yours.
- Put students in pairs. Have them repeat steps 1 and 2.

Focused Practice (pages 56–58)

Exercise 2

stationery: special paper used for writing letters

bakery: a place where cakes, cookies, and pastries are made and sold

drugstore: a store where you can buy medicines, beauty products, and other supplies

Communication Practice (page 58)

Exercise 6

Before students listen, pronounce the names of the continents and point to them on the map.

Exercise 7

Read the directions and do the activity as a class. Write the alphabet on the board. Encourage students to write a word puzzle like the one on page 56, using the alphabet to give clues. Students can exchange their puzzles with a partner and try to solve them, or they can read their puzzles out loud to their partners for them to solve.

Further Practice

Play a game of thief with the students. This game offers students practice forming *yes/no* questions and using prepositions of place. Explain that one of the students in the class is a thief. Have students ask *yes/no* questions with prepositions of place to determine who the thief is. For example, students might ask, "Is the thief behind me?" or "Is the thief next to Juan?" If the thief figures it out before the other students do, give him or her two points. Give other students who figure it out one point.

 **OUT OF THE BOX** ......

Map activity. In this activity, students ask each other for the location of buildings on a map. There are two versions of the map, A and B (See page 28 of this Teacher's Manual.) One student receives map A, and the other gets map B. Students should not look at their partners' maps. At the bottom of each map is a list of places. Students ask their partners to tell them

the location of each place on the list. Then they write the name of the place on their map. For example:

B: Where is the gas station?

A: It's on the corner of Lincoln and 2nd Avenue. Where's the bookstore?

B: It's on Adams Street next to the fire station.

At the end of the activity, students put their maps side by side. They should look the same. (Note that students are not expected to use the definite article *the* correctly at this time.)

UNIT 7 *Wh-* Questions

Unit Overview

Students will learn to ask for and give information using:
- questions with *who, what, where,* and *why: Who is René Magritte?*
- short and long answers: *An artist / He is an artist.*

Grammar in Context (pages 59–60)

Background Notes

- The number *101* denotes an introductory university course.
- René Magritte (1898–1967) was a surrealist painter born in Belgium.
- *The Son of Man* was painted in 1964. It shows a man in a gray suit with a red tie posing in front of the ocean. The apple obscuring his face is green. Magritte said about the painting, "Everything we see hides another thing, we always want to see what is hidden by what we see. There is an interest in that which is hidden. . . ."

Vocabulary

unusual: different from what is ordinary or usual

Comprehension Questions

- How many paintings are on the test? *(12)*
- What should students do first? *(look at the questions)*
- What should they do next? *(look at each painting)*
- What should they do last? *(answer the questions)*
- How long is the test? *(one hour)*

Map B

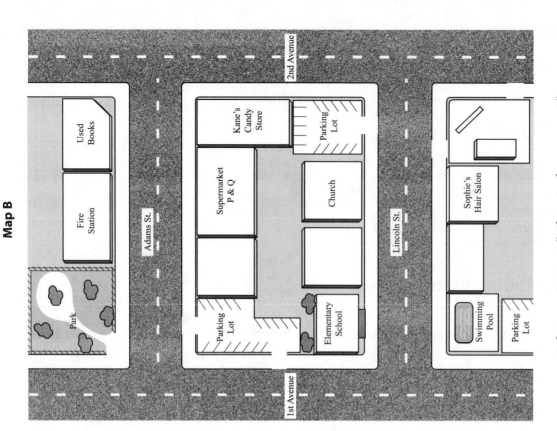

Ask your partner, *"Where is the _____?"*

- pet store
- language school
- gas station
- drugstore

Map A

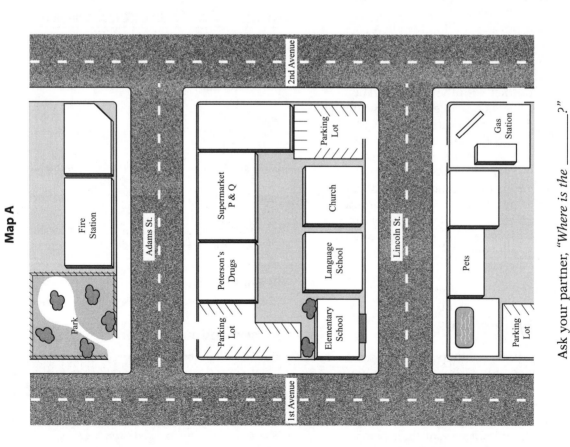

Ask your partner, *"Where is the _____?"*

- bookstore
- swimming pool
- hair salon
- candy store

Discussion Topics

- Ask students for their opinion about the Magritte painting. Is *The Son of Man* a good name for it? Can they imagine the colors of the painting? Do they like the painting?
- Do students have a favorite painter or a favorite painting?

Grammar Presentation (pages 60–61)

Identify the Grammar

<u>Who</u> is the artist?
<u>Where</u> is the artist from?
<u>What</u> is the name of the painting?
<u>Why</u> is this painting unusual?

Grammar Charts

- Make it clear that the sentences in Identify the Grammar refer to the Magritte painting on page 59. Write them on the board, then read them out loud. Underline the *wh-* words.
- Model short and long answers for the first question and write them on the board next to the questions:
Short: From Belgium.
Long: He's from Belgium.
- Elicit short and long answers to the other questions and write them on the board.
- Repeat using a reproduction of another painting. Do it once with the questions and answers on the board. Then erase the board and repeat with a different painting.

Grammar Notes

Note 1   *(Exercises 2–3)*
- On the board, write:
Where _____ Belgium?
Where _____ the paintings?
- Call a student up to the board to fill in *is* and *are*. Elicit the rule. Point and say,
"If the subject is singular, use _____." *(is)*
"If the subject is plural, use _____." *(are)*
- Drill: Teacher provides singular and plural proper nouns, and students form questions with *Where is/are*. Example:

TEACHER: New York.

CLASS: Where is New York?

TEACHER: David and Shin.

CLASS: Where are David and Shin?

Note 2   *(Exercises 2–3)*
- Say the answer and elicit the question with *Who*:

TEACHER: He's a Belgian artist.

CLASS: Who is Magritte?

- Drill with names of other famous people (not just artists), such as George Bush and Michael Jordan. Teacher provides the answer, students respond with the question.
- Repeat, but have students compose the answer sentences and respond to each other.

Notes 3–5   *(Exercises 2–3)*
Repeat the same procedure as for Note 2.

Note 6   *(Exercises 2–3)*
- Write math notation on the board to illustrate the formation of contractions:
Who + is = Who's
What + is = What's
Where + is = Where's
Why + is = Why's
- Point out that *wh-* words are not contracted with plural verbs.
- Drill the pronunciation of the contractions. Provide short answers. Students form contracted questions. Example:

TEACHER: Who. Georgia O'Keeffe.

CLASS: Who's Georgia O'Keeffe?

TEACHER: When. Lunch.

CLASS: When's lunch?

TEACHER: Why. He's late.

CLASS: Why's he late?

Note 7   *(Exercises 2–3)*
Do a transformation drill. Ask questions with *who, what, where,* and *why.* Use contracted forms. One student responds with a short answer. A second student responds with a long answer. Example:

TEACHER: Where's Rada today?

A: Absent.

B: She's absent.

TEACHER: What's a noun?

B: A person, place, or thing.

C: A noun is a person, place, or thing.

→ For additional practice, see the Supplementary Activities on page 126.

Focused Practice (pages 61–63)

Exercise 2

sculpture: work of art made from stone, wood, metal, or other materials

eternal: continuing forever

Exercise 3

style: a way of doing or making something that is typical of a particular period of time, place, or group of people

persistence: determination to do something even though it is difficult or other people oppose it

Communication Practice (page 63)

Exercise 5

Before students listen, have them read the questions and try to predict what the listening is about.

Exercise 6

• Part A: Clarify the directions. This activity resembles the television program *Jeopardy*. Contestants read the answer, and the response must be a question. Choose a student to read the example with you.

• Part B: Prepare two or three items to "feed" students in case they are unable to think of any artists on their own. Example: "He was a Dutch painter. One famous painting was *Sunflowers*. He had one ear." *(van Gogh)*

Further Practice

Play a game of "Jeopardy." On index cards, write answers to questions beginning with *who, what, where,* or *why*. Include information from a variety of fields—art, sports, people in the news, fashion, school, etc. Write the matching questions on the back of the cards. Example: *Answer: This person won the Tour de France bicycle race six times. He has two Olympic gold medals.*

Question: Who is Lance Armstrong?

In class, play the game as it is played on television. You will need a program host and three contestants. You can be the judge in case there are disputes. Have the contestants sit side by side, facing the class. The host can stand off to the side. Give the stack of cards to the host. To start play, the host takes a card and reads an answer. A contestant who wants to answer hits the table or rings a bell. The first person to do so gets to ask the question. If he or she is correct, the contestant gets 3 points. If the contestant is wrong, another contestant can try to ask the

question. If this contestant responds correctly, he or she gets 2 points. If the second contestant is also wrong and the third contestant responds correctly, he or she gets 1 point. The round is finished after 10 questions. At that point, you can call up different students and play the game again. A variation of the game is to have the students write the questions and answers.

GRAMMAR OUT OF THE BOX ......

Talk about art. Find posters, postcards, slides, or magazine pictures of pieces of art. Find or write a short description of each, giving the name of the artist and some facts about the piece. Paste each description on an index card. In class, put students in pairs. Hand out one index card to each pair. Instruct them to read the information on the card and become familiar with it because their classmates are going to ask them questions about it. Call one pair at a time to the front of the class. Have them display the art piece so the class can see it and answer their classmates' questions about the piece of art. Encourage the class to ask questions such as the following:

• Who's the artist?
• Where's he or she from?
• What's the name of the painting?
• Who is the person in the painting?
• Where is the painting?
• What style is it?

UNIT 8

The Simple Present: Affirmative and Negative Statements

Unit Overview

Students will learn:
• the form and meaning of the simple present tense in affirmative and negative statements
• use of the simple present with non-action verbs
• three pronunciations of third-person singular *-s*
• irregular conjugations of *be, have, go,* and *do*

Grammar in Context (pages 70–71)

Vocabulary

label: a piece of material that is attached to an item of clothing and is imprinted with the brand name *trend:* a fashion or current style

junior high: in the United States, years 7–8 of school (sometimes 6–8 or 7–9)

"look": appearance

Comprehension Questions

- How old is Yumi? *(17.)*
- Where does she live? *(Japan.)*
- What does she wear? *("Kawaii" boots, jeans, and sunglasses)*
- What does "kawaii" mean? *(cute)*
- What is a trendsetter? *(the first to start a trend)*
- Who are the trendsetters now? *(high school girls)*
- Are trendsetters always girls? *(No.)*

Discussion Topics

- Ask students if they think the girls in the picture look "kawaii." Do students like the style of the girls' clothes and hair?
- Ask students what trends they like in hair, clothes, music, cars, and art.
- Ask students if they are trendsetters or trend followers.

Grammar Presentation (pages 71–72)

Identify the Grammar

Affirmative	Negative
Yumi <u>wears</u> "kawaii" boots. Yumi and her friends <u>buy</u> the same things.	She <u>doesn't buy</u> "non-kawaii" things. Their clothes <u>don't</u> always <u>cost</u> a lot.

Grammar Charts

- Before the start of the lesson, prepare a large cutout of the letter *s,* or draw a large *s* on a piece of paper that you can hold up for the class to see.
- To begin the lesson, write the example sentences from the reading on the board and read them out loud. Point to the sentences in turn and ask questions to focus students' attention on the form:
  —What is the verb in this sentence?
  —Is it singular or plural?
  —Is the verb always the same in affirmative sentences? *(No. Third-person singular takes an -s ending.)*
  —How do we make negative sentences? *(do/does + not + verb)*
  —What is the *-n't* in *don't* and *doesn't*? *(not)*

- Model the affirmative forms: *I work, you work, he works,* etc. When you get to the third person, hold up the cutout of the letter *s.*
- Drill the affirmative forms. Say the pronouns. Students should respond with the verbs. Hold up the *s* cutout at the appropriate times. Mix up the order of the pronouns until students get the *s* every time. Then substitute other verbs. For example:

A: She works.

TEACHER: Learn.

B: She learns.

TEACHER: We.

C: We learn.

- Repeat the previous two steps with negative verbs. Use the contracted forms only.
- Mix the affirmative and negative forms and all persons in a quick-moving substitution drill. For example:

TEACHER: I like dogs. Maria.

CLASS: Maria likes dogs.

TEACHER: Negative.

CLASS: Maria doesn't like dogs.

TEACHER: We.

CLASS: We don't like dogs.

TEACHER: Affirmative.

CLASS: We like dogs.

Grammar Notes

Note 1 *(Exercises 3–4)*

- Review frequency adverbs and time expressions. Write the following on the board: *sometimes, often, always, never every day, once a week, on Saturday, in the morning*
- Use the time expressions to tell about your own life. Examples: *I always sleep late on Saturday morning. I read the newspaper every day.*
- Elicit similar sentences from the students. Choose time expressions and ask students to make sentences by asking questions like, "What do you do on Saturday morning, Yuki?"
- Elicit the meaning from the students. Note that you may need to tell students that English tenses have meanings beyond just time. Follow up by reading Note 1 from the Student Book.

Note 2 *(Exercises 3–4)*

- Write four facts on the board. All but one should be true. Call on students to read the sentences out loud. Then point to each sentence and ask, "Is it true?" When students identify the false statement, have them correct it to make it true. Here are examples of sentences you can use:

Dogs love cats.
The sun is hot.
Carlos isn't here today.
Nicole Kidman lives in New Zealand.

- Use the sentences to explain that the simple present is used to tell facts. Elicit several other facts from the class. Then read Note 2 together.

Note 3   *(Exercises 3–4)*

- Write a mix of action and non-action verbs on the board: *eat, like, run, want, write, have, smile.*
- Pantomime each action verb and say "action verb." Stand still for each non-action verb and say "non-action verb."
- Have students stand up. Recite a mix of action and non-action verbs. Students should pantomime the action verbs and stand still for the non-action ones.
- Read the note with the class.

Note 4   *(Exercises 3–4)*

- Hold up your cutout of the letter *s* and say a few third-person verbs, such as *eats, likes, watches, kisses.*
- Use the overhead projector or a handout like the one below to introduce the spelling rules. Read the lists out loud. Underline the last sound of each word and add *-s* or *-es.*

-s	-es
stop	kiss
kick	teach
eat	wash
need	box
learn	buzz
sing	
live	
laugh	
fall	
remember	
play	

- State the rules:
  "If a word ends in *s, z, sh, ch,* or *x,* add _____." (*-es*)
  "For other third-person singular verbs, add _____." (*-s*)
- Optional game: Make up a list of verbs that take both *-s* and *-es* in the third person. Put students into pairs. Give them the list and

instruct them to add *-s* or *-es.* The first team to finish with no mistakes is the winner.

Note 5

- Teach students the difference between voiceless /s/ and voiced /z/. (Note that many languages do not have a /z/, and students will have difficulty making this sound.) Model by putting your hand on your throat and saying "sssss." Have students copy you. Ask, "Did you feel anything?" Repeat with /z/. Students should feel their vocal cords vibrating. If a student is unable to do this, put the student's hand on your own throat and let him or her feel the vibration.
- Write three columns of words on the board, an overhead slide, or a handout as follows:

/s/	/z/	/ɪz/
stop	need	kiss
kick	learn	teach
eat	sing	wash
laugh	fall	box
	remember	
	play	
	go	
	do	

- Have students put their hands on their throats. Put your hand on your throat and say each verb with its ending together with the class.
- Go back and underline the last sound of each word. Put your hand on your throat to show whether the sound is voiced or voiceless. You need to convey to students that a voiceless sound is followed by /s/, another voiceless sound. Likewise, voiced sounds are followed by the voiced /z/.
- Elicit the rules:
  —After voiceless sounds, third-person *s* is pronounced _____. (*/s/*)
  —After voiced sounds, third-person *s* is pronounced _____. (*/z/*)
  —After /s/, /ch/, /sh/, and /x/, third-person *s* is pronounced _____. (*ɪz*)
- Elicit 10–12 verbs from students and write them on the board. (It helps to provide a context. For example, ask students to tell you about things they do every day.) Have students copy the verbs, underline the last sound, and practice pronouncing the third-person form.

Note 6   *(Exercises 2–4)*

- Do a quick transformation drill to review the contracted forms. Say affirmative sentences and have students say the negative. Example:

TEACHER: I eat eggs for breakfast.

CLASS: I don't eat eggs for breakfast.

- Write the contractions on the board. Draw an arrow, then write the uncontracted forms. Example: *don't → do not*. Tell students that we usually use the uncontracted form in writing and the contracted form in speaking.
- Write the following on the board:
  Right: He doesn't work or study on weekends.
  Wrong: He doesn't work or doesn't study on weekends.
- Read the note with the class.

Note 7 *(Exercises 3–4)*

- Model the conjugation of each verb. For *have*, take an object out of your pocket or bag and say, "I have a(n) _____." Call one or two students to the front of the class to do the same. Say to one student, "You have a(n) _____." Then turn to the class and say, "She/he has a(n) _____." Repeat, but have students form the sentences.
- For *do*, make sentences about your routine: "Every day, I do the dishes. On Saturday I do the laundry. In the evening I do homework." Ask a student, "Do you do the dishes every day? When do you do the laundry?" Then ask the class, "Does Jaime do the dishes every day? When does Jaime do the laundry?"
- Repeat the procedure with *go*.
- Sum up by writing the pronouns on the board: *I, you, he,* etc. Include the plural. Elicit the forms of each verb from the class. Write them on the board, or have a student do it. Underline the irregular spelling of the third-person forms.

Note 8 *(Exercises 2, 4)*

- With the class, quickly recite the conjugation of the *be* verb.
- To reinforce the spelling of the third-person singular, give students a quick spelling quiz. Include the four irregular verbs and regular verbs with both *-s* and *-es* endings. Say a sentence with each verb, then repeat the verb. Example: "Robert goes to school every day. Goes."

Focused Practice (pages 73–75)

Exercise 2

flea market: a market, usually in the street, where old or used goods are sold

chain store: one of a group of stores owned by the same company and having the same name

Exercise 3

window shopping: the activity of looking at goods in store windows without intending to buy them

Exercise 4

designer clothes: clothes made by a well-known and fashionable designer, such as Calvin Klein

part-time: taking only a few hours each day or week

sounds: a verb used instead of *is* when someone wants to express an opinion

Exercise 5

manufacturers: the companies that make things such as clothes and cars

emergency: an unexpected and dangerous situation that you must deal with immediately

Communication Practice (pages 75–77)

Exercise 6

Before students listen, review the three pronunciations of *-s*. Remind students to put their hands on their throats to reinforce the /z/ sound.

Exercise 7

Follow the instructions in the text. Then have two pairs of students sit together. The students in one pair should say their sentences for the other pair.

Exercise 8

Follow up by having students make sentences about clothes and customs from their countries or their favorite holiday.

Exercise 9

Questions to generate ideas and elicit vocabulary:
- Who has an interesting job?
- Where does this person work?
- What time does he or she get up?
- How many hours does he or she work?
- What does this person like about his or her job?
- What doesn't he or she like?
- Is this person happy in his or her job?

Further Practice

Play a game called "Two Truths and a Lie." Give each student a 4 × 6-inch index card. Tell students to write three facts about themselves on the card. Two facts must be true; one must be a lie. Have students get up and circulate. They should show their cards to each other. After students read a classmate's card, they should put their initials next to the statement they think is a lie. At the end, each student reads his or her sentences to the class, says which sentence most people thought was a lie, and tells which one actually is a lie.

Movie talk. Show the movie *Groundhog Day* to reinforce the simple present tense. In the film a TV weatherman, played by Bill Murray, is forced to cover the Groundhog Day ceremonies in a Pennsylvania town for the fifth year in a row. But this year an amazing thing happens after he finishes the report: When he wakes up the next morning, ready to leave, he learns that it is February 2 again. The same thing happens the next day, and the next, and the next. . . . It is not necessary to watch the entire film, although students with even the most basic level of English can understand and enjoy it. Teachers can show the main character re-living Groundhog Day enough times (three or four) to establish that almost nothing changes from day to day. At that point the teacher can ask questions to elicit the simple present regarding the character's clothing, routine, and so forth.

The Simple Present: Yes/No Questions and Short Answers

UNIT 9

Unit Overview

Students will learn:
• simple present questions with *do* and *does*
• short answers

Grammar in Context (pages 78–79)

Vocabulary

bother: to annoy someone

neat: carefully arranged and not messy

messy: disorganized, dirty

talkative: not quiet

Comprehension Questions

• Does Dan smoke? Does Jon smoke? *(No. No.)*
• Who wakes up early? *(No one does.)*

• Is Dan neat? Is Jon neat? *(Yes. Yes.)*
• Do Dan and Jon listen to loud music? *(Yes.)*

Discussion Topics

• Ask students about good ways to find roommates.
• Find out if it is usual or customary for students to move in with people they don't know, as it is in the United States.

Grammar Presentation (pages 79–80)

Identify the Grammar

Do you smoke?
Does smoking bother you?

Grammar Charts

• Read the sentences from Identify the Grammar. Then point to the sentences and ask questions to elicit the structure. Examples:
—What's the verb in this sentence? *(smoke, bother)*
—What's the subject? Is it singular or plural? *(you, singular; smoking, singular)*
—Which word has *-s?* Why? *(Does. Smoking is third-person singular.)*
• Drill: Write a verb on the board, such as *learn.* Say a pronoun. The class says the question. Example:

TEACHER: We.

CLASS: Do we learn?

TEACHER: She.

CLASS: Does she learn?

• Model the short answers:

TEACHER: Ask me if I smoke.

CLASS: Do you smoke?

TEACHER: No, I don't. Ask me if I stay up late.

CLASS: Do you stay up late?

TEACHER: Yes, I do.

• To model the third-person short answer, call up two students to the front of the class. Example:

TEACHER: William, ask Bella if she likes rock music.

WILLIAM: Do you like rock music?

BELLA: Yes, I do / No, I don't.

TEACHER: Class, does Bella like rock music?

CLASS: Yes, she does / No, she doesn't.

Grammar Notes

Note 1   *(Exercises 2–4)*
This information is covered in Grammar Charts. To reinforce it, ask students to read the explanation and the examples.

Note 2   *(Exercises 2–4)*
• Read the explanation and examples.
• Do a transformation drill with the short and long forms. Repeat the procedure from the fourth step in the Grammar Charts, but have the class respond with the long form.
Example:

TEACHER: William, ask Bella if she likes rock music.

WILLIAM: Do you like rock music?

BELLA: Yes, I do / No, I don't like rock music.

TEACHER: Class, does Bella like rock music?

CLASS: Yes, she likes rock music. / No, she doesn't like rock music.

Note 3   *(Exercise 3)*
• Copy the four sentences from the note on the board, but do not cross out the mistakes. Point to each sentence and ask the class, "Is this correct or incorrect?" Have students fix the incorrect sentences.
• If students are having difficulty, quickly review the conjugation of *be*. Say the pronouns. The class should respond with the matching verb form.

→ For additional practice, see the Supplementary Activities on page 126.

Focused Practice *(pages 80–83)*

Exercise 1
alike: similar

midnight: 12 o'clock at night

Does it matter?: Is it important?

Exercise 2
Internet access: connection to the Internet by means of a service provider

designer clothes: clothes made by someone who is famous for designing fashionable things

Exercise 3
dormitory: a large building where students live at a college or university

Exercise 4
fluently: very well

relatives: members of one's family

conductor: the person who leads a group of musicians or singers

Communication Practice *(pages 84–86)*

Exercise 6
• Before students listen, have students read the directions and form model sentences about Gloria. (Example: *Gloria likes parties.*)
• After listening, take a class vote. Find out how many students think Andrea and Gloria are a good match. Ask them why.

Exercise 7
Give students the following instructions:
• Stand up and walk around. Talk to your classmates.
• Ask the questions from the chart.
• Find someone who says yes. Write the person's name. Then talk to a different person.
• Tell the class how your classmates responded.

Exercise 8
Variation: Have students walk around the room. When they find someone who has an item, they should write that person's name next to the item.

Exercise 9
To extend this activity, have students switch partners and role-play again with a different conversation.

Exercise 10
Questions to generate ideas and elicit vocabulary:
• How do you feel about your language school?
• Are you from a small town or a large city?
• Do you love to study?
• Do you like TV?
• Are you neat or messy?
• When do you usually go to bed?
• When do you wake up in the morning?

Further Practice
Play "What's My Line?" The purpose of this game is to guess someone's profession. One student thinks of a profession. (You may want to reproduce the list of unusual jobs from the Unit 2 Grammar Out of the Box.) The class asks *yes/no* questions. For example:

- Do you wear a uniform?
- Do you work outdoors?
- Do you work alone?
- Do you work with food?

The class has only three chances to guess the student's occupation. (This is to prevent the class from asking repeatedly, "Are you a carpenter? Are you a dogcatcher?" and so on.) Encourage students to gather as much information as possible about the job before guessing what it is. If they guess incorrectly, they lose. This game can also be played in small groups.

 **OUT OF THE BOX** . . . . . .

Song cloze. Many songs contain questions with *Do* or *Does*. Select one that is appropriate for your students. (Beatles songs are always popular, e.g., "I Get By with a Little Help from My Friends" or "Do You Wanna Know a Secret?") A general procedure for using songs in language teaching is as follows:

1. Read the lyrics yourself to discover the theme of the song. In class, ask students pre-listening questions about the theme.
2. First listening: Play the song. Afterward, ask students what they heard and what they understood. Write everything on the board. Then have students look at what you've written and try to figure out what the song is about.
3. Second listening: Prepare a cloze version of the song lyrics. Take out all occurrences of *Do* and the following verb. Students listen and fill in the blanks.
4. Go over the answers to the cloze. This is a good time to answer students' questions about vocabulary.
5. Third listening: Students read the complete lyrics and sing along.
6. Follow-up: Discuss the theme or story of the song.

Other old songs containing *Do:*

"Do You Wanna Dance?" by the Mamas and Papas

"Do You Believe in Magic?" by the Lovin' Spoonful

"Do You Remember?" by Phil Collins

"Do You Love Me?" from the play *Fiddler on the Roof*

"Do You Like to Boogie Woogie?" by Madonna

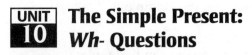 **The Simple Present: *Wh-* Questions**

Unit Overview

Students will learn:
- *Wh-* questions with *do* and *does: Where do you sleep?*
- *Wh-* questions about the subject: *Who dreams?*
- short answers and long answers

Grammar in Context (pages 87–88)

Vocabulary

expert: someone with special skills or knowledge of a subject

what's more: in addition, also

nightmares: bad dreams

creative: good at thinking of new ideas or things

Comprehension Questions

- Who is Helena Lee? (*The author of* Sleep and Dreams.)
- Why do people dream? *(Maybe to help us understand our feelings.)*
- Does everyone dream? *(Yes.)*
- Do animals dream? *(Yes.)*
- What dreams do people remember? *(unusual ones)*
- What is the meaning of a dream you have again and again? *(It has special meaning. You have to think about it.)*
- When do people dream? *(During REM sleep.)*
- Why is REM sleep important? *(Without it we can't remember or think clearly.)*

Discussion Topics

- Ask students if they believe animals dream. Ask if they have ever seen a dog or cat's eyes moving while the animal was sleeping.
- Ask if anyone has ever had a repeating dream. Ask what they think the dream means.

Grammar Presentation (pages 89–90)

Identify the Grammar

Question	Long Answer	Short Answer
What dreams do they remember?	People remember their unusual dreams.	Unusual ones.
When do people dream?	They dream during deep sleep.	During deep sleep.
Why do we need it [REM sleep]?	We need REM sleep because without it, we can't remember or think clearly.	Without it, we can't remember or think clearly.
Who dreams?	—	Everyone dreams.

Grammar Charts

- Reproduce the table above on an OHP slide. For questions with *Do*, use a contrasting color for the *Wh-* words and for the words in the long answer that answer the question. For example:
  When do people dream? They dream during deep sleep.
  For the last question, color *Who* and the answer, *Everyone.*
- Ask questions about questions with *Do* and the corresponding answers. Point to each *Wh-* word, read the question, and ask the following:
  —Which words answer the question? *(because we have machines; unusual dreams; during deep sleep; without it, we can't remember or think clearly)*
  —Are these words the subject or the object of the answer? *(object)*
  —Which word repeats in every question? *(do)*
- On the board, write *When, Where, What, Why, Who(m).* Choose a topic such as a member of your family, your pet, or a movie star. Have students form questions with each *Wh-* word + *do.* Answer each question with a long answer, or have another student do the same.

Example:
TEACHER: My dog.
A: When does your dog sleep?
TEACHER: He sleeps all afternoon and all night.

- Point to the question "Who dreams?" Point to the answer. Ask the following:
  —Which word answers the question? *(Everyone)*
  —Is it the subject or the object of the answer? *(subject)*
  —Does the question use *Do? (No.)*
- Practice a few subject-pattern questions and answers about the class. Example:
TEACHER: Who comes from Turkey?
CLASS: Didem comes from Turkey.
TEACHER: What happens every morning at 9 A.M.?
CLASS: Our class starts every morning at 9 A.M.

Grammar Notes

Note 1 *(Exercises 2–3)*
- Pick a context to use for drilling object-pattern questions. A good one is students' daily habits or schedules.
- To drill, provide a core sentence. Then prompt students with *Wh-* words. One student forms the question. Another student answers with the short answer. Example:
TEACHER: Javier goes to sleep at 11 P.M. When.
A: When does Javier go to sleep?
B: At 11 P.M.
TEACHER: Javier does his homework in the library. Where.
A: Where does Javier do his homework?
B: In the library.
- Have students ask and answer questions about each other's habits. First model the activity with a student. Then circulate as students talk in pairs.

Note 2 *(Exercises 2–4)*
- To drill subject-pattern questions, prepare a list of general-knowledge questions beginning with *Who* or *What.* Example:
  —What is a panda?
  —Who lives in the White House?
- Ask the questions. Students should respond with long answers.

- Reverse the procedure. Provide answers. Students should ask the questions. Example:

  TEACHER: Oranges grow in Florida.

  CLASS: What fruit grows in Florida?

- Put students in pairs again. Have them ask questions about who does what in their home. *(Who washes the dishes? Who makes the beds?)*
- Copy the wrong sentences from the note on the board. Ask students to correct the errors.

Note 3 *(Exercises 2–4)*

- Model the way in which questions with *who* and *whom* are formed. Demonstrate the transformations, making them as visual as possible:
  - On the board, write a subject-verb-object sentence. Both subject and object must be people, e.g., *John loves Mary.*
  - Cross out the subject, replace it with the word *Who*, and add a question mark:

    ~~John~~ loves Mary.

    Who loves Mary?
  - Write the sentence again. Cross out the object and replace it with *whom*. Draw an arrow to show the fronting of *whom*. Add *does*.

    John loves ~~Mary~~.

    John loves whom.

    Whom John loves?

    does

    Whom ↑ *John love?*

- Provide several sentences and have students form subject-pattern sentences. Example:

  TEACHER: Nati sings in the shower.

  CLASS: Who sings in the shower?

- Provide sentences and have students form object-pattern sentences. Example:

  TEACHER: Nati lives with her aunt.

  CLASS: Whom does Nati live with?

- Prepare two handouts for students to use in drilling each other. Each handout should have six to eight items and a mix of subject- and object-pattern sentences. Students read questions to their partners, then check their partner's answers. Example:

Student A

Read this to your partner:	Check your partner's answer:
1. Ilana daydreams about her boyfriend. (Who)	1. Who daydreams about her boyfriend?
2. Ilana daydreams about her boyfriend. (Whom)	2. Whom does Ilana daydream about?

Focused Practice (pages 90–93)

Exercise 1

night owl: a person who likes to stay up late at night

early bird: a person who likes to get up early

alarm: a clock that makes noise in order to wake someone up

daydream: to think about nice things so that you forget what you should be doing

breakfast bar: a fast-food item, shaped like a candy bar, that is eaten instead of a meal

Communication Practice (pages 93–95)

Exercise 7

Have students fill out the *You* column by themselves. Then put them in pairs to ask their partners the questions.

Exercise 8

Students should get up and circulate in order to do this activity.

Exercise 9

Put students in pairs. Each student should read his or her dream before they begin talking.

Further Practice

Prepare a series of general-information questions and answers. Each question and each answer should be on a separate slip of paper. Sample questions:

Who lives in the Vatican?

What language do they speak in Brazil?

When do kangaroos sleep?

Have students mingle. Those with questions search for the matching answer. As soon as students find each other, they sit down.

GRAMMAR OUT OF THE BOX ......

Trivial pursuit. Prepare two lists of general-knowledge questions. Each list should have six to eight questions. The game Trivial Pursuit is a good source of ideas. Divide the class into two groups. Give each group one of the lists. First, students should try to answer the questions. Then they write three or four new questions. Tell them to be sure they know the answers to the questions. The two groups should quiz each other. Students should take turns asking and answering the questions. Teams get one point for each question they answer correctly.

When, What + Noun; Prepositions of Time; Ordinal Numbers

UNIT 11

Unit Overview

Students will learn:
- how to form questions with *When is* and *What* (day/time)
- prepositions of time: *in December, on Wednesday, at 7:30*
- ordinal numbers

Grammar in Context (pages 102–103)

Background Notes

In the United States, elections for the president are held every four years. The election always takes place on the first Tuesday after the first Monday in November of an even year. Election Day is an official holiday in some states. The new president takes office on January 20th following the election.

Comprehension Questions

- Do the speakers go to school on election day? *(no)*
- When is Election Day? *(the first Tuesday after the first Monday in November)*
- Is it possible to have Election Day on the second Tuesday in November? *(yes)*

Discussion Topics

- Ask students what kind of leader their country has (president, king, premier, prime minister). Ask how this person is chosen.
- Ask whether students have ever voted.

Grammar Presentation (pages 103–105)

Identify the Grammar

When is it?
What day is Election Day?
It's the first Tuesday after the first Monday in November.

Grammar Charts

- Make several statements about calendar events in the United States. Then ask students about the same event in their countries. As you say one of the target grammar points, point to it or underline it in the example sentences on the board. Examples:

TEACHER: In the United States, Independence Day is on July 4. When is Independence Day in [Peru]?

A: In [Peru], Independence Day is on

_____.

TEACHER: In the United States, summer is in June, July, and August. When is summer in [Nigeria]?

B: In Nigeria, summer is in December, January, and February.

- Focus on *in/on/at*. As an example, speak about an appointment: "I have a dental appointment this week. My appointment is on February 12. It's on Tuesday. It's at 3 o'clock in the afternoon."
- Ask several students about appointments they have.

Grammar Notes

Notes 1–2 *(Exercises 2, 4)*
- Have students look at the expressions in Note 2.
- On the board, write four or five appointments, engagements, or obligations you have this week. Use the list to model the questions and answers in Notes 1 and 2. Example:

STUDENT: When is your dental appointment?

TEACHER: It's on Thursday at 3 in the afternoon.

• Put students in pairs. Have them repeat the procedure.

Note 3 *(Exercises 2–4)*

• Explain the difference between ordinal and cardinal numbers.
• Write your birthday on the board, e.g., *January 18.* Point and say, "My birthday is January 18th." Call a student to the board to follow your example. Stress the contrast between what we write and what we say.
• Have students repeat the above steps in pairs.
• Do a quick dictation. Say a date and have students write it. For example, say "November 23rd." Students should write *November 23.*

→ For additional practice, see the Supplementary Activities on page 126.

Focused Practice (pages 106–109)

Exercise 2
lunar: relating to the moon

leap year: in the United States, a year when February has 29 days instead of 28, which happens every four years

Exercise 5
fireworks: objects that burn or explode to produce colored lights and noise in the sky

Communication Practice (pages 109–111)

Exercise 6
Before students listen, have them look at the sentences with blanks and try to guess what the conversation will be about. *(It's about a misunderstanding about the location of a party.)*

Exercise 8
A variation on this activity is to bring in two calendars, one for the current academic term and one for the previous one. Give a different calendar to each student and have them take turns making statements about school holidays and events. Example:

A: This term the school party is on May 31.

B: Last term the school party was on March 14.

Exercise 9
Have students work in small groups. They should read the example, then discuss the questions until they feel ready to write.

Further Practice
Have students consult their calendars and find a time when they can get together with a classmate to study for an exam. Copy a page from a Week at a Glance or another calendar. Make a copy for each student. Have students fill in their schedules for the week, including time spent in class, appointments, dates, etc. Tell students it is fine for them to make up activities if they don't have many actual obligations. Put students in pairs. They cannot look at their partner's calendar. They should ask questions until they find a time to get together. Have each pair of students report to the class when they will meet.

GRAMMAR OUT OF THE BOX ......

Let's go to the gym. Bring in a schedule from a gym. Put students in pairs. Have them role-play a conversation in which two friends look at the schedule and choose a class they can take together. To help students get started, write the beginning of a model dialogue on a handout or on the board. For example:

A: *I hate to exercise. I don't want to go to the gym.*

B: *I don't like to exercise either. Hey! I have an idea! We can exercise together.*

A: *Great idea! Let's look at the schedule and find a class we can take together.*

This activity can also be done with a *TV Guide.* Students look at the schedule and choose a show that both of them want to watch.

UNIT 12 Possessive Nouns and Possessive Adjectives; Questions with *Whose*

Unit Overview

Students will learn:
• singular and plural possessive pronouns *(his, their)*
• possessive nouns with apostrophes
• questions and answers with *Whose*

Grammar in Context (pages 112–113)

Comprehension Questions

- Whose paper is excellent? *(Kim's)*
- Whose paper is good? *(Juan's)*
- Whose paper needs work? *(Boris's)*
- Does Boris's paper have a grade? *(no)*

Discussion Topics

- Ask students how their last composition was—excellent, good, or "needs some work."
- Ask the class if they think good handwriting is important.

Grammar Presentation (pages 113–115)

Identify the Grammar

Whose composition is this?
It's my composition.
It's Kim's composition.

Grammar Charts

- Say to the class, "My mother's name is _____." Turn to a student and ask, "What's your mother's name?" The student should answer and continue in a chain for eight to ten turns. After that, substitute the word *father* and repeat.
- Now that students have heard the form, write on the board:
  My mother's name is _____.
  My father's name is _____.
  You can add the names of other family members as well. Underline the possessive. Circle the apostrophe. Use different colors if possible.
- Write these sentences on the board.
  The women's room is on the second floor.
  Where is the men's room?
  My parents' house is in Chicago. Where is your parents' house?
  Very conspicuously, insert the apostrophe following the plural possessives. Point to the singular possessives and ask, "How many mothers do I have? How many fathers? And in this sentence, how many women are there? How many men? How many parents do I have?"
- Have the class look at the chart called Possessive Adjectives. Call on students in turn to read each line.

- Do a substitution drill as follows:

  Teacher: I'm a teacher. My name is Alexa. You.

  Class: You are a teacher. Your name is Alexa.

  Teacher: He [pointing to a student].

  Class: He is a student. His name is Song Goo.

- Walk around the room and pick up objects from students' desks. As you pick up each object, say "Whose _____ is this?" The class should respond, "It's _____'s _____." *(It's Lena's book.)*

→ For additional practice, see the Supplementary Activities on page 127.

Grammar Notes

Note 1 *(Exercises 2–3, 5–6)*
Have a student read the note. Explain the difference between a possessive noun *(Kim's)* and a possessive adjective *(her)*.

Note 2 *(Exercises 2, 5–6)*
- Use an OHP to illustrate these rules. Write the three examples from the book on the OHP slide. Don't write the apostrophes. Read the sentences out loud and have students tell you where to insert the apostrophes.
- Write four or five more sentences. Call students up to insert the apostrophes.

Note 3 *(Exercises 3, 5–6)*
Using the same slide as for Note 2, cross out all the subjects. Call students up and have them write in possessive adjectives instead. Example:
Their
~~My parents'~~ house has four bedrooms.

Note 4 *(Exercises 5–6)*
- Write contrasting pairs of sentences (below) on an OHP slide. Don't write the apostrophes.
  Beckys not home.
  Beckys sister has a horse.
  Its a nice day today.
  I have a pet fish. Its name is Goldy.
- For each sentence, ask the class:
  —What is the subject?
  —What is the verb?
  —Which word is a possessive adjective?
  —Do we need an apostrophe?

Note 5 *(Exercises 4–5)*
- Hold up an object and ask, "Whose _____ is this?" Then ask, "How do you spell *whose*?" Write the first question on the board.

- Ask, "Who's absent today? How do you spell *Who's*?" Write *Who's absent today?* on the board. Point to each sentence and once again ask, "What is the subject? What is the verb? Which word is a possessive adjective? When do we use an apostrophe?"

→ For additional practice, see the Supplementary Activities on page 127.

Focused Practice (pages 116–120)

Exercise 1
pharmacist: someone who is trained to prepare drugs or medicines for patients

occupation: a job or profession

Exercise 3
translator: someone who changes speech or writing into a different language

interpreter: someone whose job is to change spoken words from one language into another

fur: the soft hair of some animals, such as cats

calculator: a small machine that can add, multiply, and divide numbers

Exercise 5
cancel: to say or decide that something you have planned will not happen

scarf: a long, narrow piece of cloth worn around the neck or head

locker room: the room in a gymnasium where people shower and change clothes

Exercise 6
accountant: someone whose job is to keep and check financial accounts, prepare financial reports, and calculate taxes

travel agent: someone who makes travel arrangements and organizes vacations for people

film producer: someone who has general control of the preparation of a movie but does not direct the actors

Communication Practice (pages 120–121)

Exercise 8
Before students listen, model the pronunciation of *Maria* and *Maria's*. Instruct students to listen for the final /z/ sound. Review the difference in meaning between *Maria's* and *Marias*.

Exercise 10
- Have students fill in the blanks and compare answers with those of a classmate.

- Students can ask and answer the questions in groups or as a whole class. Be sure to monitor the pronunciation of *Who's*. It should sound the same as *Whose*.

Exercise 11
Questions to generate ideas and elicit vocabulary:
- *Who(m) do you want to write about?*
- *How is this person related to you?*
- *What's this person's job?*
- *Where does he or she live?*
- *What's this person like? (Describe person's character or behavior.)*
- *What is special about this person?*

Further Practice
A lot can be done with family trees. Have Student A write a list of names of people in his or her family. The list should include people from three generations. Student B receives a blank family tree. (These can be downloaded from the Internet. Alternately, Student B can draw on a blank piece of paper.) Student B asks questions about the people on Student A's list and places the people in the proper place on the family tree. Example:

A: Who's this? [pointing to a name]

B: It's my grandmother.

A: Is she your father's mother or your mother's mother?

B: She's my mother's mother.

Students switch roles and repeat.

GRAMMAR OUT OF THE BOX . . . . . .

Skit. Have students role-play the following skit. Tell the class to imagine that they are in a crowded theater. A couple comes in late and finds another couple sitting in their seats. They call the usher to help them sort it out. If possible, set up chairs in several rows. Assign the roles seen in the script, and have students sit in front, behind, etc., according to their roles.

LINDA: John, they're sitting in our seats.

JOHN: Excuse me, you're sitting in our seats.

GEORGE: No, we're not. They're ours.

MAN BEHIND: Shh!

JOHN: They're not yours. My ticket is for seat 101. My wife's seat is 102. You're sitting in 101 and 102.

WOMAN BEHIND: Please!

MAN BEHIND: Where's the usher?

LINDA: Yes, where *is* the usher?

MAN BEHIND: Shh!

WOMAN IN FRONT: Shh!

USHER: What is it?

LINDA: They're sitting in our seats.

USHER: Where are your tickets?

JOHN: Here's mine. This is my wife's.

PEOPLE: Shh!

JOHN: Her seat is 102. Mine is 101.

USHER [TO GEORGE]: May I see your ticket?

GEORGE: These are our seats.

USHER: Where's your ticket?

GEORGE: Here.

USHER: And your wife's?

GEORGE: Here!

PEOPLE: Shh!

USHER: You're in the wrong seats. Your tickets are E101 and 102. These seats are D101 and 102. Their tickets are D101 and 102.

GEORGE: Well, who's sitting in my seat? Look at his ticket.

PEOPLE: Shh! Please!

USHER: May I see your ticket?

MAN BEHIND: Here.

USHER: Your ticket is for Row F. You're sitting in Row E.

PEOPLE: Shh, groan, etc.

UNIT 13 — This/That/These/Those; Questions with *Or*

Unit Overview

Students will learn to use *this, that, these,* and *those* in the following ways:
• as pronouns: *This is a beautiful photo.*
• as adjectives: *This photo is my favorite.*
• to refer to people, places, and events
Students will also learn how to form choice questions with *or: Would you like coffee or tea?*

Grammar in Context (pages 122–123)

Background Notes

Bryce Canyon National Park is located in south-central Utah. It is relatively small compared to other well-known parks in the western United States such as Yosemite or the Grand Canyon, but its spectacular rock formations are unique.

Vocabulary

rock formations: groups of rocks that appear in particular shapes or groups

canyon: a deep valley with very steep sides of rock

Comprehension Questions

• Where was Guillermo? *(Bryce Canyon National Park)*
• Where is Bryce? *(in Utah)*
• How many photos does Guillermo have? *(over 200)*
• What is a hoodoo? *(a rock formation)*
• Where is Fairyland Canyon? *(near the park entrance)*
• Where is Guillermo going in September? *(the Canadian Rockies)*
• Who is going with him? *(Maria)*

Discussion Topics

• Ask students if they have ever seen rock formations like hoodoos. Ask if they would like to visit Bryce.
• Ask if they have ever traveled on horseback or if they would like to do so.

Grammar Presentation (pages 123–125)

Identify the Grammar

PRONOUNS
This is me in front of a hoodoo.
That's an amazing photo.
These are my best photos.
What are those?

ADJECTIVES
I like this picture.
Is it really you on that horse?
These hoodoos come in different shapes.

Grammar Charts

Note that although the text does not use the word *demonstratives,* you may find it useful to introduce this term for purposes of reference later in the lesson.

• Write the sentences from Identify the Grammar on the board. Read the example sentences to the class and underline all occurrences of *this, that, these,* and *those.*

- Ask questions to elicit the grammar:
  - —What's the subject of this sentence?
  - —What's the verb?
  - —Is *this* singular or plural?
  - —Is *these* a pronoun or an adjective?

→ For additional practice, see the Supplementary Activities on page 127.

Grammar Notes

Notes 1–3 *(Exercise 2)*
- Show a few photos of well-known people. Ask the class, "Who's this?" Elicit the answer, "That's _____." Repeat with plurals. Emphasize the use of *this/these* when you're holding the photo in your hands, but emphasize *that/those* when students respond. Then ask the class, "Do we use *this* and *these* [demonstratives] to talk about people?" *(yes)*
- Bring in some kitchen utensils. It's fun to use odd items such as a garlic press or a corkscrew. Hold up one and ask, "What's this?" *(That's a fork.)* Repeat with plurals: "What are these?" *(They're scissors.)* Then ask the class, "Do we use *this* and *these* [demonstratives] to talk about things?" *(yes)*
- Follow by asking a student to read Notes 1–3 out loud.

Note 4 *(Exercise 2)*
In this case it is useful to read the note first. Have students read the explanation and the examples. To reinforce, ask a mix of opinion questions and have students answer. Examples:
- Is this language course expensive?
- Marco, you went to a different language school before this one. Was that school expensive?
- Thirty years ago nobody had computers, cell phones, or palm pilots. Do you think life was easier or harder in those days?
- Do you like women's fashions these days?

Note 5
This note reinforces information that has already been presented. Have a student read it. Do a transformation drill using objects in the room. Example:

TEACHER: This is my grammar book.

STUDENT: This grammar book is heavy.

Note 6 *(Exercise 3)*
- Write a list of pairs of related objects on the board. Examples:
Coke, Pepsi
dogs, cats

beef, chicken
blue, green
hot weather, cold weather
swimming, jogging
- Model a question and have a student answer. Then cue the student to ask a similar question and another student to answer. Continue in a chain around the room. Example:

TEACHER: Andrei, do you prefer Coke or Pepsi?

ANDREI: I prefer Coke.

TEACHER: Dogs or cats.

ANDREI: Shula, do you prefer dogs or cats?

SHULA: I prefer cats.

Focused Practice (pages 125–127)

Exercise 1
ranger: someone who is in charge of protecting a forest or park

Exercise 3
stick: a long, thin piece of wood that has fallen or been cut from a tree

trail: a path across open country or through a forest

Exercise 5
flashlight: a small electric light that you can carry in your hand

Communication Practice (pages 127–128)

Exercise 6
Before students listen, demonstrate the difference in vowel quality between *this* /ɪ/ and *these* /iy/. Also remind students to listen for the *-s* ending on plural nouns.

Exercise 7
If all the students in the class have the same first language, have the students teach you.

Exercise 8
Questions to generate ideas and elicit vocabulary:
- What is the place in your picture?
- Where is it?
- Why is it famous?
- Does it have famous animals or plants?
- Does it have famous buildings?
- Is the food good?
- Are the people friendly?
- Do many tourists go there?

Further Practice

Have students bring in photographs of a vacation or special occasion. Divide the class into two groups. One group remains seated and prepares a display of the photos at their desks. The other group gets up, walks around, looks at the photos, and asks questions about the people and places using *this, that, these,* and *those.* At a signal from the teacher, the groups switch.

... OUT OF THE BOX ......

Restaurant role play. Students will role-play a conversation between a waiter and a customer in a restaurant. Bring in real or make-believe restaurant menus. Lunch menus are better because they are generally shorter and simpler than dinner menus. Make copies of the menu for all the students. Spend time reading the menu and answering students' questions. Do a model role play with one of the students. Take the role of the waiter to demonstrate the kinds of questions that servers typically ask:
• Would you like soup or salad?
• Would you like Thousand Island, French, or Italian dressing?
• Would you like coffee or tea?
• Would you like cheese on that?
Put students in pairs and have them do a similar role play. First have them practice by themselves. Then have each pair perform their role play for another pair. Finally, call on a few pairs to do their role plays in front of the whole class.

UNIT 14 *One / Ones / It*

Unit Overview

Students will learn to use *one, ones,* and *it* in a variety of contexts:
• *one* in place of *a(n)* + noun or noun phrase:
  A: Do you have a car?
  B: Yes, I have *one.*
• *one* or *ones* after an adjective in place of a singular or plural count noun:
  He has two black cats and a white *one.*
• *one* after *this* or *that:*
  A: Which hat do you like?
  B: That *one.*

• *it* instead of *the* + noun:
  A: Where's the milk?
  B: *It*'s in the refrigerator.
• *it* in place of a possessive pronoun:
  A: Where's my purse?
  B: *It*'s on the chair.
• *it* in place of *this* or *that* and a singular count noun:
  A: Where's that magazine?
  B: *It*'s on the coffee table.

Grammar in Context (pages 129–130)

Background Notes

In the United States, there are gift cards for almost any occasion. Nearly all stores, even many supermarkets, offer customers the option of buying gift cards instead of merchandise.

Nationally, an estimated $45 billion is spent on gift cards or certificates, according to the National Association of State Treasurers. Of that, roughly 10 percent goes unredeemed, according to the group.

Vocabulary

pocket: a small bag sewn into pants, coats, or other clothes where you can put keys, money, and other objects

hood: the part of a coat or sweatshirt that you can pull over your head

R & B: rhythm and blues—a type of popular music that is a mixture of blues and jazz

Comprehension Questions

• How many sweatshirts does the man look at? *(three)*
• What does the first sweatshirt say? *(Don't worry. Be happy.)*
• What does the second sweatshirt have? *(pockets)*
• What does the third one have? *(a hood)*
• What kind of music does the shopper's friend like? *(R & B)*
• Does the shopper buy the Beyoncé CD? *(no)*
• What does the shopper buy in the end? *(a gift card for $25)*

Discussion Topics

• Ask students if they have bought a gift for someone lately. Who was it, and what did they buy?
• Ask students if they enjoy shopping for gifts.

Grammar Presentation (pages 130–132)

Identify the Grammar

EXAMPLE 1
A: I want a large sweatshirt.
B: Here's one.

EXAMPLE 2
How about these sweatshirts? This one has pockets and that one has a hood. The ones with hoods are on sale.

EXAMPLE 3
A: Here's Beyoncé's latest.
B: I think she has it.

Grammar Charts

- Ask questions to focus students' attention on the meaning of one and it.
- In the first example above, point to one. Ask, "What does one mean?" (a large sweatshirt) Reinforce by writing:

    one = a large sweatshirt

- Underline a large sweatshirt. Next to it, write a + adjective + noun.
- For the second example, collect several sweatshirts from students. (Other objects will work as well.) Lay them on your desk. Point to them and say, "How about these sweatshirts?" Hold up one and say, "This one has pockets." Point to one on the desk and say, "That one has a hood." To reinforce, once again raise the one in your hand and say, "This one." Point to the one on your desk and say, "That one." Make a pile of several sweatshirts and say, "The ones with hoods are on sale." Make a sweeping motion with your arm to indicate you mean all the sweatshirts in the pile.
- Ask the class questions about the second example above:
  —What does one mean in this one? (It means a sweatshirt with pockets. It is close to the speaker.)
  —What does one mean in that one? (It means a sweatshirt with a hood. It is not close to the speaker.)
  —What does ones mean? (all the sweatshirts that are on sale)
  —With plural nouns, do we use one or ones? (ones)
- In the last example, point to the word it. Ask the following:
  —What does it mean? (Beyoncé's latest CD)
  —Is Beyoncé's a noun or a possessive adjective? (possessive adjective)

—After a question or statement with a possessive adjective, do we use one or it? (it)

Grammar Notes

Notes 1–2 (Exercises 2–4)
- Use diagrams to classify the information in the notes. For Notes 1–2, draw the following on the board:

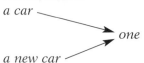

- Illustrate by having students read the examples in the notes.

Note 3 (Exercises 2–4)
- Tell the class that you met a couple who are getting married and they gave you a list of items they need. Write the list below (or a similar one) on the board or on an overhead transparency:

> 1. Tablecloths: 2 white, 1 blue
> 2. Towels: bath towels, hand towels, kitchen towels
> 3. Vases: 1 tall, 1 medium
> 4. Drinking glasses: 8 water, 8 juice
> 5. Cookbooks: Italian, vegetarian
> 6. Picture frames: 2 large, 5 small

- Review the list and ask the class who will buy each item. Students should respond with one or ones. Example:

  TEACHER: Who wants to buy the tablecloths?

  A: I can buy the white ones.

  B: I will get the blue one.

- As students volunteer to buy items, write their names on the board or transparency next to the items. Students can then form sentences like the following: Sue and Ming will buy tablecloths. Sue will buy the white ones. Ming will buy the blue one.

→ For additional practice, see the Supplementary Activities on page 128.

Note 4 (Exercises 2–4)
- Collect pairs of items from students: watches, notebooks, sunglasses, cell phones, jewelry.
- Hold up pairs of items. Ask a student, "Which one do you like?" The student will point and say, "I like that one." Give the item to that student. Repeat with the other items.

- In the end, all the items should be distributed to students who are not their owners.
- Have the students who donated the items stand up. The students holding the donated items should remain seated.
- Seated students should hold up their items and take turns asking, "Whose _____ is this?" The owner of the item should say, "It's my _____," walk over, retrieve the item, and return to his or her seat.

Notes 5–7   *(Exercises 3–4)*
- Summarize the rules with a diagram like the following (the general rule is that definite nouns are replaced by *it*):

the card
your card ——▶ *it*
that card

- Have each student write a list of six electrical appliances that he or she owns. Examples: electric shaver, lamp, computer, toaster oven.
- Have students sit in pairs and exchange lists. They should ask and answer questions as follows:

A: Where's the/your electric toothbrush?

B: It's in the bathroom.

Note 7
- This rule is demonstrated in the last step of the Note 4 activity. To reinforce it, write the following on the board and have a student come up and fill in the blanks:
Whose watch is this?
_____ *is Joseph's.* [This watch]
_____ *Joseph's watch.* [It's]
- Conclude by reading the rule and examples in the text.

Focused Practice (pages 132–134)

Exercise 1
blouse: a woman's shirt

belt: a band of leather or cloth worn around the waist

necklace: a piece of jewelry worn around the neck

Exercise 3
get rid of: to remove something or someone from a place

recognize: to realize that you know a person or thing because you have seen the person or thing before

conductor: someone who is in charge of a train

lend: to let someone temporarily borrow money or something that belongs to you

Exercise 4
shelf: a long, flat board attached to a wall or bookcase to hold objects

Exercise 5
counter: a flat, table-like surface

Communication Practice (page 134)

Exercise 6
Before students listen, choose one or two of the family members on the list and ask the class, "What kind of gift is good for this person?"

Exercise 7
Define the terms *handmade* and *practical.* Tell the class the kinds of gifts you like to give or get.

Exercise 8
Questions to generate ideas and elicit vocabulary:
- Whom did you give the gift to or receive the gift from?
- What was the gift you gave or received?
- Why did you give or receive this gift? Was it a birthday gift or other occasion?
- Why was this a special gift?

Further Practice
Play a matching game. In this game, each student receives an index card with a household item written on it, such as dinner fork, bath towel, frying pan. The student must find another student or students who have the same item. The game is played twice. The first time, you will need pairs of matching index cards. There should be enough cards so that each student receives one. Mix up the cards and hand them out in random order. Have students get up and search for the person who has the card that matches theirs. They should use the following language (remind the class that the first speaker must use *it*):

A: I need a green bath towel. Do you have it?

B: Yes, I have it. / No, I don't have it.

Play the game a second time. This time make three matching cards of each item and hand them out. Students will need to change their question slightly:

A: I need a green bath towel. Do you have one?

B: Yes, I have one. / No, I don't have one.

In both versions, when students find their partner or partners, they should sit down.

GRAMMAR OUT OF THE BOX ......

Choosing a birthday present. Bring in a variety of catalogues: clothing, cars, gardening, furniture, housewares. Try to have one catalogue for every four students. Tell the students your (or your spouse's, or another person's) birthday is coming soon, and the students' task is to look through their catalogue and select a gift. Model the language students will need. Write some of the sentences on the board, or instruct students to look at the Grammar Charts on pages 130–131. Example:
Do you think she will like this one or that one?
This one is nice.
The red ones are good for her.
Where will she put it?
What will she do with it?
I don't think it's good for her.

Present Progressive: Affirmative and Negative Statements

UNIT 15

Unit Overview

In this unit students will learn:
• the form of affirmative and negative statements in the present progressive
• the meaning and use of the present progressive

Grammar in Context (pages 142–143)

Background Notes
• In the United States, both children and adults enjoy yo-yos. There are yo-yo competitions for people of all ages.
• The Ferris wheel was invented by bridge maker George Ferris. He got the idea from looking at the structure of a merry-go-round. The wheel at the 1893 Chicago World's Fair was 264 feet (80.5 meters) tall.

Vocabulary

video arcade: a special room or small building where people go to play video games

vending machine: a machine that sells candy, drinks, cigarettes, and other goods

yo-yo: a handheld toy that is made of two joined circular parts that go up and down a string as you lift your hand up and down

Comprehension Questions
• What are Marcus and Julius playing with? *(yo-yos)*
• How tall is the Ferris wheel? *(as tall as a 25-story building)*
• What kind of television do Sue and Ralph Miller have? *(a color TV)*
• Where is Cozumel? *(Mexico)*
• What is Pac Man? *(a video game)*
• What can you do with a camera phone? *(send photos)*
• How is Yumi paying for her food? *(her cell phone)*
• How old are yo-yos? *(over 2,000 years old)*

Discussion Topics
• Ask students which of the events from the reading occurred in their lifetime or which events they remember.
• Look at each picture and have students raise their hands if they have done each activity (play with a yo-yo, ride a Ferris wheel, etc.).

Grammar Presentation (pages 143–144)

Identify the Grammar
Marcus and Julius <u>are playing</u> with yo-yos.
They're <u>flying</u> to Cozumel.
Berta <u>is sending</u> her photo to her boyfriend.
Yumi <u>isn't using</u> coins.

Grammar Charts
• Write the example sentences above on the board and read them out loud. Have the students repeat after you.
• For each sentence, ask the class what the verb is. Underline it. *(are playing, are flying, is sending, isn't using)*
• Ask the following:
  —How many words are in the affirmative verbs? *(two)*
  —How many are in the negative? *(three—is not using)*
  —What letters do we attach to the end of verbs in the present progressive? *(-ing)*
• Erase the verbs and replace them with blanks. Call up students to fill in the missing verbs.
• Drill the conjugations. In the affirmative, say a verb and a pronoun. Students say the complete verb. Encourage them to use contractions. Example:

TEACHER: Play. I.

CLASS: I'm playing.

TEACHER: You.

CLASS: You're playing.

• Provide an affirmative verb. Students transform it to the negative. Encourage students to use contractions. Example:

TEACHER: She is reading.

CLASS: She isn't reading.

Grammar Notes

Note 1   *(Exercises 2–4)*

• Walk around the room. As you walk, narrate what you see students doing, using the present progressive: "Akira is drinking coffee. Sofia is looking for something in her bag."
• Ask the class, "When are these things happening?" *(now)* On the board, write *now, right now, at this moment.* Repeat some of the sentences with each of these phrases: "Akira is drinking coffee now. At this moment, Shayna is looking out the window."
• Elicit similar sentences from students.
• Walk around again. This time make sentences with non-action verbs. Examples:
 —I'm thirsty. I want some of Akira's coffee.
 —I don't see Lana. Where is she?
 —How much does this dictionary cost?
• Elicit the rule about non-action verbs by asking questions: "I'm thirsty. What do I want? Can I say *I am wanting*?" *(no)*
• Select students to read the note and the examples. Ask students to form a few more sentences with non-action verbs such as *need, like, hear, cost,* and *have.*

Note 3   *(Exercise 4)*

• Write on the board:
 Linda is eating.
 She's reading the newspaper.
 Linda is eating and reading the newspaper.
• Pantomime a series of actions that lead up to a product or result. For example, pantomime brushing your teeth.
• As you act, students should say what you are doing, forming sentences like the model on the board. *(You are turning on the water. You are putting toothpaste on your brush and brushing your teeth.)*
• Call up several students to pantomime.

Note 4   *(Exercise 4)*

• Draw a simple timeline on the board like the one in Note 4 on Student Book page 144.
• Tell a simple story that illustrates the extended meaning of *now,* e.g., *this moment, this week, this month, this year.* Use contractions. For example:

"My cousin is a computer designer. He normally lives in Italy, but this year he's living in the United States. He's studying at _____ University. He's on vacation this week, so he's visiting me. Right now he's at the _____ Museum."

• As the meaning of *now* expands, add lines to the diagram, like this:

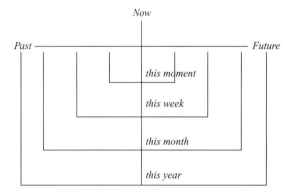

• Put students in pairs. Each student makes four sentences, saying what he or she is doing right now, this week, this month, and this year. Encourage them to use contractions.

Focused Practice (pages 144–147)

Exercise 2

BlackBerry®: A handheld device that combines a personal computer and mobile phone

Exercise 3

meditate: to make yourself feel calm by being silent and still and thinking about one thing, such as a sound or a religious idea

Exercise 4

ironing: the activity of making clothes smooth by using heat

founder: a person who starts something

fad: something that is very popular for a short period of time

Exercise 5

tai chi: an ancient Chinese discipline of meditative movements practiced as a system of exercises

stroller: a chair on wheels in which a small child sits and is pushed along

Communication Practice (pages 148–149)

Exercise 6

Before students listen, have students read the questions and guess what time of day it is and where each person is.

Exercise 8

Questions to generate ideas and elicit vocabulary:
- Where are you?
- What time is it?
- What are you doing?
- What are people around you doing?
- What are they wearing?
- What else is happening (or not happening)?

Further Practice

Find a photo or drawing that shows a large number of things happening. Put students in groups of three and make enough copies so that each group gets one copy. Hand out the picture face-down. At a signal from you, students turn over the picture and study it without talking for one minute. At another signal from you they turn the picture over once again. Working in groups, students write sentences in the present progressive about the things that are going on in the picture. Give them a time limit. When time is up, go around the room and have students say their sentences. Allow students to see the picture again. If you wish to make this into a competition, then the group that remembered the most activities is the winner.

GRAMMAR OUT OF THE BOX......

Video true/false. Divide the class into two groups. Send one group out of the room. The group that stays in the room watches a short (1–2 minute) segment of a movie or TV show with the sound turned off. Then students write five to six true or false statements about the action in the video, using the present progressive. Write the statements on the board. Bring the second group back into the room. Have them watch the same video segment and state whether each statement is true or false. Have them correct all false statements. Repeat the process, switching groups.

UNIT 16 — The Present Progressive: Yes/No and Wh- Questions

Unit Overview

Students will learn how to form questions in the present progressive tense:
- *yes/no* questions: *Are you working?*
- *Wh-* questions about the object: *What are you watching?*
- *Wh-* questions about the subject: *What's happening?*

Grammar in Context (pages 150–151)

Background Notes

I Love Lucy was a hugely popular television comedy that ran in the United States from 1951 to 1957. Reruns of the show can still be seen today. It starred Lucille Ball as the wife of a Cuban bandleader Ricky Ricardo, played by her real-life husband Desi Arnaz. In the show, Ricky tries to make it in show business while Lucy constantly gets into some kind of hilarious trouble.

Vocabulary

cough: to make short, loud sounds with the throat, caused by air suddenly coming out when a person is sick or choking

catching a cold: getting a cold

Comprehension Questions

- Where is Abby? *(She is home.)*
- What's Abby doing? *(She's watching* I Love Lucy *on TV.)*
- What are Lucy and Ethel doing? *(They're working at a chocolate factory.)*
- Is the show funny? *(Yes)*
- Does Greg like *I Love Lucy? (No.)*
- Who's catching a cold? *(Greg is.)*

Discussion Topics

- Ask students if they have ever seen *I Love Lucy.*
- Ask about popular comedies in students' countries or first languages.

Grammar Presentation (pages 152–153)

Identify the Grammar

How're you feeling?
Are you reading?
What are you watching?
What's happening now?

Grammar Charts

1. Write the examples from Identify the Grammar on the board. Read them and have the students repeat. Ask the class to identify the subject and verb in each sentence. Underline the subject once and the verb twice.

2. Write a *yes/no* question in large letters on an overhead transparency. Cut the sentence into individual words. Mix them up. Call up a student to arrange the words in the correct order. Repeat with two to three more sentences.

3. Drill the form of *yes/no* questions. Have students change statements into questions as follows:

   TEACHER: I'm standing.

   CLASS: Am I standing?

   TEACHER: You're reading.

   CLASS: Are you reading?

4. Repeat the step 2 procedure using cut-up *Wh-* questions.

5. Drill the form of object-pattern *Wh-* questions. Begin with a *yes/no* question. Cue students with a *Wh-* word. Have them form the new question. Example:

   TEACHER: Are you reading? What.

   CLASS: What are you reading?

   TEACHER: Are you going? When.

   CLASS: When are you going?

6. Repeat the procedure from step 2 using subject-pattern questions. To make it a little more challenging, cut up two questions and have a student sort them out.

7. Drill as in steps 3 and 5. Provide a statement and have students transform it into a question. Example:

   TEACHER: Sarah is writing a composition. Who.

   CLASS: Who is writing a composition?

   TEACHER: Something is burning. What.

   CLASS: What is burning?

→ For additional practice, see the Supplementary Activities on page 128.

Grammar Notes

Note 1   *(Exercises 2–4)*
Have students read the note and examples. Ask students to write three or four new examples.

Note 2   *(Exercises 3–4)*
• Have students think of one person who is very special to them. Put them in small groups, and explain that they will ask and answer questions about their classmates' special persons.
• Write the following on the board:
Who is . . .
Why is . . .
What is . . .
Where is . . .
When is . . .
• Model the activity with a student. Ask, "Who's your special person?" Then ask *Wh-* questions about the person using the cues on the board. Examples: "Where is _____ living now? Who is _____ living with? What is _____ studying?"

Note 3   *(Exercise 4)*
To practice subject-pattern *Wh-* questions, ask about students' relatives and friends in different time zones. Ask questions like the following:
• Who is sleeping now?
• Who is eating?
• Who is getting up?

Focused Practice (pages 153–156)

Exercise 2
TV Guide: a weekly magazine that provides information about television programs

cable TV: television programming available by subscription; programs reach homes by means of a cable attached to a special antenna

Exercise 3
ahead of: in front of

No kidding! An exclamation of surprise

autograph: a famous person's name written in his or her own writing

Exercise 5
chef: a skilled cook

lasagna: an Italian pasta dish made with cheese and meat or vegetables

sauce: a thick liquid that is served with food to give it a particular taste

Communication Practice (pages 156–158)

Exercise 6
Before students listen, have students predict possible ways to fill in the blanks.

Exercise 7

- Clarify the directions for this activity. *Look at the programs on channels 2 and 4* refers to the bulleted items on the page that begin with CHANNEL 2 and CHANNEL 4.
- Look at item 1. Read the sentences and model the questions Student A will ask:
  1. Where is the man lying?
  2. Who isn't breathing?
  3. What are the man's wife and housekeeper doing?
  4. What is the family friend doing?
  5. What are the big men wearing?
  6. What are the big men doing?
  7. What is a tall man carrying?
- If necessary, model Student B's questions as well. See page 186. Student B's questions are:
  1. Who is sitting at a desk?
  2. What is she wearing?
  3. What is she talking about?
  4. Where are they having dessert?
  5. Who is smiling?
  6. Who is throwing a pie in her husband's face?

Exercise 8

Model the conversation with a student. Then have students do the activity in pairs.

Further Practice

Ask the class for names of television programs they enjoy watching. Write the names of the programs on the board. Have students in pairs role-play the conversation from Exercise 8, using one of the programs listed on the board. This time, however, they should not use a script.

OUT OF THE BOX ......

TV talk. Episodes of *I Love Lucy* can be rented at video stores. Select one or more episodes and watch them with the students. To practice the present progressive, try one of the following activities:

- Stop the tape every few minutes. Ask questions about what is happening and have students answer.
- Tell half of the students to put their heads down on their desks so that they cannot see the television. The other half watch short segments from the program with the sound turned off and narrate what is happening. Switch roles.

UNIT 17 The Imperative

Unit Overview

Students will learn:
- the affirmative and negative forms of imperatives
- the use of the imperative in directions, orders, advice, warnings, and polite requests

Grammar in Context (pages 159–160)

Background Notes

Reader's Digest is a general-interest family magazine published monthly. In 2004 it had a U.S. circulation of 44 million readers a month. The magazine was founded in 1922 by DeWitt Wallace.

Vocabulary

address: to mail or send

section: one of the parts that something is divided into

current: happening, existing, or being used now

Comprehension Questions

- How much can you win if *Reader's Digest* prints your story? *($300)*
- How long can your story be? *(100 words)*
- Does *Reader's Digest* return stories? *(No, they don't.)*

Discussion Topics

- *Reader's Digest* is published in many languages. Ask if students have seen or read it.
- Ask if students have a funny story to send to *Reader's Digest.*

Grammar Presentation (page 161)

Identify the Grammar

Write a true story.
Don't write more than 100 words.

Grammar Chart

- Write the two examples of the target grammar from the reading on the board. Ask students to identify the verb in each case. Teach the term *imperative.*

- Ask, "What is the subject in each sentence?" Explain that the subject is *you*, but we don't say it.

Grammar Notes

Note 1   *(Exercises 2–3, 5)*
- Read the note and make sure students understand the term *base form*.
- Demonstrate a few imperatives with simple commands such as *stand up, sit down, close your eyes, don't talk, don't write*.
- Call on several students to demonstrate more imperatives.

Note 2   *(Exercises 2–3, 5)*
- Copy each use of the imperative and each example onto an overhead transparency. Cut them into strips. Mix them up and project them. Call up one or more students to match the uses and the examples.
- Divide students into five groups. Assign one use to each group. Instruct students to come up with five additional examples of the imperative to illustrate their assigned use. At least two examples must be negative.
- One representative from each group should read the examples to the class. Listeners can repeat the sentences.

Note 3   *(Exercises 2–3)*
Do a quick transformation drill. Provide an affirmative command and have students change it to the negative. Then do the opposite.

→ For additional practice, see the Supplementary Activities on page 128.

Note 4   *(Exercises 2–3)*
- On the board, write:
  Right: Ask for directions.
  Wrong: You ask for directions.
- Draw an *X* through *You*. Ask a student to restate the rule.

Note 5   *(Exercises 2, 4)*
- Read the note.
- Play a version of Simon Says: One person gives commands which listeners must follow only if he or she says "Simon says." In this version, commands should also use *please*, such as: "Simon says please touch your nose." If the speaker says "Simon says . . . please," listeners must follow the command. On the other hand, if the speaker leaves out "Simon says . . . please," listeners should not move. Anyone who performs the command is "out."

Focused Practice (pages 162–165)

Exercise 2
bandage: a long piece of cloth used to cover and protect a wound

an empty stomach: how the stomach feels when a person is hungry

vinegar: a sour-tasting liquid made from wine, usually used in salad dressings

Exercise 5
entry: an application for a contest

Communication Practice (page 166)

Exercise 7
- As a follow-up, play the game telephone. Have the class sit in one or two big circles, depending on the size of the class. Choose one student or find a volunteer from each circle to begin the telephone chain by whispering a message into his or her neighbor's ear. The message should include who called and three imperative statements. For example, "Juan called. Pick the shirts up at the cleaner. Buy some milk at the store, and put gas in the car."
- The message gets whispered from student to student, all the way around the circle.
- The last person in each circle tells the whole class what the message is.

Exercise 8
- Have a brief discussion to generate ideas for the ad. Ask the class:
  —Why did you choose this school?
  —What do you like about it?
  —What is the best thing about this school?
- Bring in colored paper, pencils, crayons, and markers. Put students in groups to make their posters.

Exercise 9
Questions to generate ideas and elicit vocabulary:
- Where is Carol's building?
- Where is the bakery/school/supermarket/drugstore?
- How do you get to the bakery from Carol's building?

Further Practice
Tell students that several people have complained that they think your rules are too strict. Therefore, you are giving students the opportunity to create new classroom rules. Put

students in small groups. Give them an overhead transparency or a large sheet of paper on which to write. Write a few examples on the board to get them started: *Don't write your name on your paper. Talk when the teacher is talking.* Have students share their rules with each other. Consider setting aside a day or part of a day for students to follow their new rules. Students who disobey will be punished!

OUT OF THE BOX......

Recipes. If possible, demonstrate a simple recipe, such as salad dressing or a peanut butter and jelly sandwich, for the class. Bring in all the necessary tools and ingredients. Call a student to the front of the class and have the student prepare the recipe according to your instructions. Bring in examples of simple recipes. Have students read and discuss them. Have students prepare a class recipe book. Students write out the recipes for a dish from their country or another dish that they like. Encourage them to illustrate their recipes. If possible, students can prepare the dish at home and bring it to class for everyone to taste.

UNIT 18 *Can/Could*

Unit Overview

Students will learn:
- the form and use of *can / can't* for ability and possibility
- the form and use of *could / couldn't* for past ability

Grammar in Context (page 167)

Background Notes

African Gray parrots live in the tropical forests of central Africa. In the past they were hunted for food and for their red tail feathers. Nowadays wild parrots are a protected species. Only animals bred in captivity are sold as pets.

Vocabulary

genius: a person of exceptional intelligence or ability

invent: to make, design, or produce something for the first time

ape: a large monkey, such as a gorilla

puzzle: a game or toy with a lot of pieces that you have to fit together

Comprehension Questions

- How many words can N'kisi say? *(almost 1,000)*
- What does he do when he doesn't know a word? *(He invents one.)*
- Where does he live? *(in New York City)*
- Who is his teacher? *(His owner, Aimee Morgana)*
- Which animals can think at high levels? *(parrots, apes, chimpanzees)*
- What are some "tricks" that African Gray parrots can do? *(easy puzzles, say 'good night' when you turn off the lights at night, say 'good-bye' when you put your coat on)*

Discussion Topics

- Discuss why birds are / are not good pets.
- Talk about different ways that animals communicate.

Grammar Presentation (pages 168–169)

Identify the Grammar

Everyone knows parrots <u>can talk</u>.
Most parrots <u>can't "really" express</u> ideas.
He <u>couldn't talk</u> much at first.
At first, he <u>could</u> only <u>say</u> a few words.

Grammar Charts

- Ask the following questions to elicit information about the form of *can, can't, could,* and *couldn't:*
  —What are the meaning and time of *can* and *can't*? *(ability in the present)*
  —What are the meaning and time of *could* and *couldn't*? *(ability in the past)*
  —What form of the verb is used with modals? *(base form)*
  —Where do modals go in statements? *(before the verb)*
  —Where does the modal go in *yes/no* questions? *(before the subject)*
- Point out the rules governing the pronunciation of these modals:
  —*Can* and *could* are unstressed. The verb following them is stressed.
  —*Can't* and *couldn't* are stressed, and so is the verb that follows them.

Grammar Notes

Note 1
- Make three or four sentences about things you can do very well. Be sure to model correct pronunciation. Examples: "I can speak French. I can sing. I can make chicken soup."
- Ask the class, "How about you?" Then go around the room in a chain, each student saying one thing he or she does well.

Note 2 *(Exercise 2)*
Repeat the procedure from Note 1, but have students form negative sentences.

Note 3 *(Exercise 3)*
- Make a handout with two lists of verbs, like the following:

Student A	Student B
swim whistle touch your toes without bending your knees	ski play piano speak Chinese

- Put students in pairs and have them use the lists to interview one another. They should answer truthfully. Example:

A: Can you swim?

B: Yes, I can. Can you ski?

- As an optional follow-up, go around the room and have each student make a sentence about his or her partner, as follows: "Aki can swim, but he can't whistle."

Note 4 *(Exercise 4)*
- Put the following chart on an overhead transparency or a handout:

	NOW	THEN
1.	can	could
2.	can't	couldn't
3.	can't	could
4.	can	couldn't

- Have students sit in small groups.
- Instruct students to form sentences using the cues in the chart. For example, their first sentence should be about something they can do now and could do in the past. (Choose a past time such as "when you were a child,"

"five years ago," or "before you came to this country.")
- Follow up as in the last step of Note 3.

Note 5 *(Exercise 4)*
- Use the handout from Note 3, but instruct students to use *could*. Give them a past time to talk about, as in Note 4, step 3.
- Have students work with different partners.
- Follow up as in previous notes, if desired.

Focused Practice (pages 169–171)

Exercise 4
hunter: an animal that catches other animals for food

mice: the plural of *mouse*

gesture: a movement of the head or other body part that expresses meaning

watchdog: a dog that protects someone's property

trick: something you do to surprise someone or to make other people laugh

team: a group of people who compete against another group in a sport or game

Communication Practice (pages 171–173)

Exercise 6
Before listening, rehearse the directions using the example. Write another example on the board and practice if necessary.

Exercise 7
As an optional follow-up and expansion, teach students the phrase *I can't _____, but I would like to someday.* Have them write sentences using the phrase and share them with a partner. Then have the students report on their partners' desires.

Exercise 8
As an added challenge, have students write three more questions for homework. Select three questions from those the students write and play the game again.

Exercise 9
If students need an alternative topic, ask them to write about an animal they find interesting.

Further Practice
Write the names of 20–30 animals on slips of paper and put them in a box or hat. One student picks a paper out of the hat. The class asks the student questions using *can* about the

animal's abilities or what can be done with it. For example:
- Can it fly?
- Can you eat it?
- Can it live underwater?
- Can you see it on a safari?
- Can you use it to make clothes?
- Can you carry it?

The student who guesses the animal picks next.

 OUT OF THE BOX ......

Superheroes. Bring in a variety of superhero comic books, such as *Batman, Superman,* or *Spiderman.* Put students in groups and let them read the books. Afterward students should talk about the hero's special abilities. *(Superman can fly. He can leap over tall buildings. He can stop a train.)* Another possibility is to view a movie featuring a well-known superhero, such as *Spiderman.* Have students discuss the hero's abilities and decide which superpowers they would like to have.

 UNIT 19

Suggestions: *Let's, Why don't we . . . ?, Why don't you . . . ?,* Responses

Unit Overview

Students will learn to make and respond to suggestions including:
- suggestions using *Let's, Let's not,* and *Why don't we . . .*
- suggestions to another person using *Why don't you . . .*
- expressions for agreeing and disagreeing with suggestions

Grammar in Context (pages 174–175)

Background Notes

Snuba® is a shallow-water diving system that combines snorkeling and scuba diving. Snuba divers breathe underwater by means of a 20-foot airline connected to a standard scuba tank. The tank sits on a raft on the surface. There is no heavy diving gear.

Vocabulary

snorkeling: a water sport in which swimmers use a tube to breathe air when the face is underwater

scuba: the sport of swimming underwater while breathing from a container of air on your back

tank: a container for air, worn by swimmers while scuba diving

brochure: a thin book that gives information or advertises something

Are you game?: Are you willing to do something dangerous, new, or difficult?

disposable: intended to be used once or for a short time and then thrown away

Comprehension Questions
- How's the weather? *(perfect)*
- What is Snuba®? *(It combines snorkeling and scuba diving.)*
- Can children go Snuba diving? *(Yes, children over eight)*
- What is Shira going to buy? *(a disposable underwater camera)*
- Who is going to get information about Snuba diving? *(Arda and Rodica)*

Discussion Topics
- Ask if students would like to try Snuba® diving.
- Talk about other sports that students enjoy watching and playing.

Grammar Presentation (pages 175–176)

Identify the Grammar

SUGGESTION	RESPONSE
Let's go snorkeling again.	Yeah.
Why don't we try scuba diving?	I have a better idea.
Let's go Snuba® diving.	Sure. Why not?
Why don't you get the camera?	OK.

Grammar Charts
- Write the examples of the target grammar from the reading on the board. Then read them out loud and underline the expressions of suggestion. Ask the following questions to focus students' attention on the target structures:

—What do I say to make a suggestion for you and me? (Let's / Why don't we)

—What does the apostrophe -s mean in Let's? (us)

—Which form of the verb do we use after Let's? (base form)

—What do we say to give a suggestion to another person? (Why don't you)

• Ask the following questions:

—What do we say if we agree with the suggestion? (yeah, sure, why not, OK)

—What are some other things you can say? (That's a good idea, That sounds good)

—What can you say if you don't agree? (I have a better idea, I can't, No, I don't feel like it)

—What else? (I'm not sure, I don't think that's a good idea)

Grammar Notes

Note 1 *(Exercises 2–4)*

• On the board, create a two-column chart with the heads *Good* and *Bad*. Ask students to tell you the names of restaurants they like and don't like. List them in the appropriate columns.

• Provide a context such as the following: "It's the middle of the school term, and you've been working very hard. Let's take a break from studying and go out to lunch. Where should we go?"

• Initiate the following drill:

TEACHER [pointing to *Let's* and selecting a volunteer]: Yes, Peter?

PETER: Let's go to Mario's.

TEACHER [pointing to *Let's not* and calling on a different student]: What do you think, Leila?

LEILA: Let's not go to Mario's.

TEACHER: Why?

LEILA: It's too expensive.

• Repeat several times to reinforce the fact that we normally give a reason with *Let's not*.

Note 2 *(Exercises 3–4)*

• Call on students to read the note and examples out loud. Restate the fact that *Why don't we* has the same meaning as *Let's*.

• Have students work in pairs. Tell them they need to make plans together for the weekend. Give each pair a list of entertainment options; for example, *go to the movies, go shopping, go to a(n) Italian/Greek/Chinese/Sushi/Colombian*

restaurant. Ask students to use *Why don't we . . .* to make suggestions. Have students report their plans to the class. You may want to give them the phrase *We're going to . . .* to do this.

• To practice *Why don't you*, ask the class if anyone has a medical problem, such as upset stomach, headache, or insomnia. Call on a volunteer and give the student advice appropriate to the complaint. Example:

STUDENT: I have a headache.

TEACHER: Why don't you drink some water?

• Call on other students to give the student other suggestions (*drink coffee, take an aspirin, take a nap, get a massage*).

• Repeat with one or two more medical complaints.

Note 3 *(Exercise 4)*

Call on students to read the note and examples. Ask students to write three or four new examples.

→ For additional practice, see the Supplementary Activities on pages 128–129.

Focused Practice (pages 176–178)

Exercise 1

souvenir: an object you keep in order to remind yourself of a special place or occasion

Exercise 2

volcano: a mountain with a hole at the top out of which rocks, lava, and ash sometimes explode

Exercise 3

complain: to say that you are annoyed, unsatisfied, or unhappy about something or someone

receptionist: someone whose job is to welcome and help people at a hotel, business, or office

fitness room: a room in a hotel with exercise equipment for the guests to use

Exercise 4

pick up: buy

check out: to look at something in order to make sure it is good or acceptable

Communication Practice (pages 179–180)

Exercise 6

Before listening, have students look at the pictures and describe the activities they see.

Exercise 7

This activity can also be done with a small group of students sitting in a circle and making suggestions in a chain. After students finish the items in the Student Book, encourage them to add suggestions of their own.

Exercise 8

As an optional follow-up, have students report on what their partners will buy for each of the people. Have them give reasons for why their partner chose each gift, as this will expose students to new vocabulary. For example, "Hector is going to buy a T-shirt for his brother because his brother *collects* T-shirts."

Further Practice

Plan a class party or a class picnic. Work with the class as a whole to determine the location of the event, a budget, how money will be raised, and what committees (food, drinks, music, decorations) are needed. When making these decisions, students should use the language from this unit to make suggestions and agree/disagree with them. Divide students into committees to continue planning. Once again, make sure students are using the language from this unit. Have a great time!

An advice columnist. Collect advice columns, such as "Dear Abby," from newspapers, magazines, and the Internet. Select letters that students will be interested in discussing. Paste each letter on an index card. Paste the columnist's answer on the back. Put students in pairs. One student plays the role of the letter writer. The student should read the letter, retell it in first person, and ask his or her partner for advice. The other student should give advice using *Why don't you . . .* Example:

A: I have a problem. My neighbors never close their drapes in the evening. When I am sitting in my living room in the evening, I can see directly into their house. This makes me feel uncomfortable. What can I do?

B: Why don't you close *your* drapes?

UNIT 20
The Simple Past: Regular Verbs—Affirmative and Negative Statements

Unit Overview

In this unit, students will study the form and meaning of the simple past tense. The following structures are presented:
- affirmative and negative statements
- past time markers, such as *yesterday, ago, last [night]*

Grammar in Context (pages 188–189)

Background Notes

Sugarloaf is a steep mountain that dominates the landscape in the city of Rio de Janeiro, Brazil. Ipanema is a district located in the southern part of the city, famous for its rich, chic beach.

Vocabulary

unbelievable: amazing, great

out of this world: fantastic, wonderful

flight: a trip by airplane

bumpy: not smooth, uneven

body language: changes in your body position and movements that show what you are feeling or thinking

Comprehension Questions

- Where are Karen and Gene? How do you know? *(Rio de Janeiro)*
- What kind of game did they see? *(foot-volley)*
- What is Sugarloaf? *(a mountain)*
- What is a churrascaria? *(a barbecued meat restaurant)*
- How was their flight? *(bad, bumpy)*
- How is their room? *(beautiful)*
- How is their Portuguese? *(not good)*

Discussion Topics

- What do students know about Brazil?
- Would they like to take a vacation in Brazil? Why or why not?

Grammar Presentation (pages 190–191)

Identify the Grammar

We watched a foot-volley game.
They didn't miss the ball.

Grammar Charts

- Point to the example sentences and ask:
  —How do we form the regular past tense? *(by adding -ed)*
  —How do we form the negative? *(didn't + base form)*
- Have students look at the charts showing affirmative and negative statements. Recite a complete conjugation (*I walked, you walked, he walked,* etc.) in both the affirmative and the negative. Have students repeat. Then ask, "Does the form of the past tense change from singular to plural?" *(no)* "Is it the same for all persons?" *(yes)*
- On the board, write:
  yesterday   ago   last
- Model several sentences with these time expressions. Use a common verb such as *talk.* Examples: "I talked to my mother yesterday morning. I also talked to her two days ago. I didn't talk to her last week because she was out of town."
- Have several students form similar sentences. Useful verbs are *call, check e-mail, exercise, visit.*
- Do a transformation drill, from affirmative to negative and vice-versa, as follows:

  TEACHER: I talked to my mother.

  CLASS: I didn't talk to my mother.

  TEACHER: Alice called a friend.

  CLASS: Alice didn't call a friend.

  TEACHER: We didn't watch a movie.

  CLASS: We watched a movie.

  TEACHER: They didn't walk to work.

  CLASS: They walked to work.

Grammar Notes

Note 1   *(Exercises 4, 6)*
- Prepare a handout of regular verbs for students to use in this unit. Here are a few useful ones:

answer	help	study
arrive	hurry	travel
brush	learn	type
call	like	use
change	listen	visit
check (e-mail)	live	walk
decide	open	wash
enjoy	play	watch
exercise	rain	work
finish	relax	worry
happen	start	

- With the class, read Note 1. Hand out the list of verbs and elicit examples from the students of activities they did the day before.

Note 2   *(Exercises 2, 4, and 6)*
- Draw a three-column chart on the board or an overhead transparency. Add the headings as follows:

/d/	/t/	/ɪd/

- Read the examples from the note. Instruct students to listen for the ending of the verbs and to tell you which sound they hear. Write the verbs in the appropriate columns above. *(arrived /d/; landed /ɪt/; tried /d/; worked /t/; waited /ɪd/)*
- Tell students that first you are going to demonstrate the difference between /d/ and /t/. To begin, remind students of the difference between voiced and voiceless sounds, presented in Unit 8, in connection with the pronunciation of the *-s* ending. Have students put their hands on their throats and pronounce /s/ and /z/ as a reminder. Then have them pronounce /t/ and /d/. Ask, "Which sound is voiced?" *(d)* "Which sound is voiceless?" *(t)*
- Remind students that the pronunciation of the ending depends on the last sound of the word: *voiced + voiced, voiceless + voiceless.* Demonstrate with the examples from above: *arrive + /d/; try + /d/; work + /t/.*
- Using the handout of regular verbs in Note 1, elicit a few more verbs that belong in the first two columns, such as */t/: wash, watch, relax, help; /d/: change, happen, travel.* Remind students to keep their hands on their throats and feel the pronunciation of the last sound of each verb.
- To demonstrate the third ending, /ɪd/, write the following verbs on the board:
  need
  decide
  rent
  wait
  visit
  start
- Elicit the past-tense pronunciation from the students. Correct them if necessary. Write the verbs in the appropriate column on the board. Elicit the rule. *(We say /ɪd/ when a verb ends in /t/ or /d/.)*

Note 3 *(Exercises 4 and 6)*

This information was presented in Grammar Charts. To review, call on students to read the note and the examples.

Notes 4–5 *(Exercises 3–6)*

• Call on students to read these notes out loud.

• Reinforce the position of time markers by asking students to form a few sentences about what they did yesterday. For example, ask them to tell you what the class learned yesterday morning. Elicit an answer from a student, then transform it:

TEACHER: What did we learn yesterday morning?

A: We learned the past tense yesterday morning.

TEACHER: What's another way of saying it?

B: Yesterday morning we learned the past tense.

→ For additional practice, see the Supplementary Activities on page 129.

Note 6 *(Exercise 6)*

This information has already been presented several times. For reinforcement, call on students to read the note and the examples.

Focused Practice (pages 191–195)

Exercise 2

guidebook: a special book about a city or country that gives details about the place, usually for tourists

parade: a public celebration in which musical bands, decorated vehicles, and performers move down the street as people watch

comedian: someone whose job is to tell jokes and make people laugh

hug: to put your arms around someone in order to show love or friendship

Exercise 3

egg roll: a type of fried Chinese appetizer

Exercise 4

log: an official record of events

share: to have or to use something with other people

open: willing to accept new ideas or people

promise: to tell someone that you will definitely do something or that something will definitely happen

Exercise 5

on the road: traveling

Exercise 6

guided tour: a trip led by a professional who knows the place very well

crib: a baby's bed with bars on the sides

Exercise 7

magical: very enjoyable and exciting, in a strange or special way

Communication Practice (pages 195–197)

Exercise 8

Before listening, have students look at the questions and guess the context of what they are going to hear.

Exercise 9

An alternative way to do this exercise is to have students make negative statements if they didn't do one of the items on the list.

Exercise 10

Emphasize that there are no right or wrong answers in this exercise. Try to elicit an additional one or two situations to fit the example. *(A man and his wife arrived late to the opera. They didn't have time to park their car, so they asked the valet to do it. They were very late so the husband said, "Here's 20 dollars. Please park the car and keep the change.")*

Exercise 11

Questions to generate ideas and elicit vocabulary:

• What city do you know well?
• When did you arrive there?
• Where did you stay?
• How did you travel around?
• Did you enjoy the weather?
• Did you shop?
• Do you want to visit this city again in the future?

Further Practice

Have students prepare 3–4 minute presentations about a memorable vacation they have taken. Encourage them to bring photos, postcards, or mementos to illustrate their presentations. Students can present in front of the whole class or in small groups.

What just happened? In this activity, students look at unusual photos and tell the story of what happened just before the picture was taken. Collect magazine pictures showing people in unusual situations or with unusual expressions on their faces. Advertisements work well. Distribute the pictures to individual students, pairs, or small groups and have them come up with a story to fit the picture. Have students share their stories with the class. It is also possible to use one picture with the entire class and enjoy the variety of stories students come up with.

The Simple Past: Irregular Verbs—Affirmative and Negative Statements

UNIT 21

Unit Overview

In this unit, students will learn:
- the affirmative and negative form of *be* in the past tense
- the affirmative and negative form of some other common irregular past-tense verbs

Grammar in Context (pages 198–199)

Background Notes

There are thousands of Chinese folktales, which have survived for thousands of years through the oral tradition. The value of these tales lies in their folk wisdom and their display of Chinese values such as the triumph of justice over injustice, the supremacy of wisdom over sheer physical strength, and the loyalty of children to their parents. These values are passed from one generation to the next through the telling of folktales.

Vocabulary

peasant: a poor farmer who owns or rents a small amount of land

excited: happy, interested, or hopeful because something good has happened or will happen

run into: to hit someone or something while moving

misfortune: bad luck

border: the official line that separates two countries, states, or areas

Comprehension Questions

- Where did this folktale happen? (*China*)
- What did the farmer say when the horse appeared? (*You never know what will happen.*)
- What happened two days later? (*The horse ran away.*)
- How did the farmer feel? (*He didn't get excited.*)
- What happened a week later? (*The horse returned with three other horses.*)
- What happened to the peasant's son? (*A horse ran into him, and he hurt his leg.*)
- What happened a month later? (*Soldiers took all the young men to fight.*)
- What happened to the young men? (*They were all killed.*)
- What happened to the peasant's son? (*Nothing. He lived a long and happy life.*)

Discussion Topics

- Ask students what the farmer meant when he said, "You never know what will happen."
- Have students tell folktales from their cultures.

Grammar Presentation (pages 200–201)

Identify the Grammar

When the peasant's friends <u>saw</u> the horse they <u>said</u>, "How lucky you are!"
Two days later the horse <u>ran</u> away.
The peasant <u>didn't get</u> excited.
Exactly one week later the horse returned. And it <u>brought</u> three other horses.

Grammar Charts

- Write the examples of target grammar from the reading on the board. Call a student to the board.
- Ask other students to read each sentence and identify the verb. The student at the board should underline the verbs.
- For each affirmative verb, ask the class if it is regular or irregular. Ask if anyone knows the base form of the irregular verbs. (*saw—see, said—say, ran—run, brought—bring*)
- For the negative example, ask if there is any difference between regular and irregular verbs. (*no*)
- Review the conjugation of the past of *be*. See Unit 3, page 23 in the Student Book.

Grammar Notes

Note 1 *(Exercises 2–4)*

• Because there are so many irregular verbs, you will need a plan to help students learn them in manageable chunks. One way to do this is to choose several verbs a day for students to memorize and practice. You can choose the verbs from an alphabetical list, or you can present groups of verbs with the same morphology (e.g., the *-aught* verbs such as *teach* and *catch*).

• To begin, make a handout of the verbs in this chapter, which are compiled below:

be	find	see
become	give	sell
begin	go	sit
bring	have	speak
buy	know	stand
come	lose	take
do	make	teach
eat	meet	tear
fall	(re) build	understand
feel	ride	write
fight	run	

• Call on students to read Note 1 and the examples.

• Drill: Say the base form and the past form of the verbs on the handout. Students repeat.

• Do another drill. This time say only the base form. Students should say the past form. Then reverse the order.

• Put students in pairs. Have them drill each other. One student says the base form, and the other says the past.

Note 2 *(Exercises 2–4)*

• Have students read the note and the examples. Remind students that regular and irregular verbs are the same in the negative.

• Transformation drill: Say the base form. One student says the affirmative. Another student says the negative. Example:

TEACHER: Say.

A: Said.

B: Didn't say.

Note 3 *(Exercises 2–4)*

• Do a transformation drill. Alternate between persons and affirmative/negative as follows:

TEACHER: I was sick yesterday. He.

CLASS: He was sick yesterday.

TEACHER: Negative.

CLASS: He wasn't sick yesterday.

TEACHER: We.

CLASS: We weren't sick yesterday.

• Write a list of adjectives on the board. Put students in pairs or groups. Have them make true sentences about themselves using *was/wasn't*. Sample adjectives to use: *late, early, absent, sick, tired, worried, happy, cold.*

Note 4 *(Exercises 2–3)*

• Model the following sentence: "I was born on January 18. I was born in Los Angeles."

• Go around the room and have students repeat the sentence with their own birth dates and places.

Focused Practice (pages 201–204)

Exercise 1

award: a prize or money given to someone to show appreciation for something he or she has done

do well: to succeed

chemistry: the science that studies the structure of substances and the way they change and combine with each other

Exercise 2

go from rags to riches: to become very rich after starting your life very poor

founder: someone who starts a business, company, or organization

cofounder: someone who starts a business or company with someone else

fit in: to be accepted by other people in a group because you have the same background, attitudes, or interests

real estate: property in the form of land or houses

give up: to stop trying

rebuild: to start again from the beginning

Exercise 3

bilingual: able to speak two languages

powers: natural or special abilities to do something

attempt: the act of trying to do something

full-time: working or studying for the number of hours per week that work is usually done

best seller: a very popular book that many people buy

Exercise 4

cruise: a vacation in which you travel on a large ship

instead: in place of something or someone

Communication Practice (pages 204–205)

Exercise 6
Before listening, have students underline the verbs in Exercise 6 (*gave, made, tore, felt, said,* and *found*) and identify the base form of each. Make sure they know the meanings. Have them read each incomplete sentence in Exercise 6 and try to guess something about the story they are going to hear.

Exercise 7
A variation of this game is to play without taking notes. Students must rely on their memories.

Exercise 8
An amusing variation on this activity is to put students in groups and have them tell a chain story, with each student adding one sentence. For example:

A: I had a wonderful day yesterday.

B: First, I got up late and took a bath.

C: Then I went out to breakfast with my best friend.

D: We ate, talked, and drank coffee for two hours.

Exercise 9
As a follow-up, collect the students' autobiographies and put them together to form a short book. Make several copies for the students to check out and read overnight.

Further Practice
Have students write short stories. First, put students in pairs or small groups. Give each group a list of five irregular verbs. Within a time limit of five minutes, students must work together to compose one-minute oral stories using all their verbs. Repeat using different lists of verbs. (Note: If your teaching plan is to give students a small number of verbs to learn each day, this activity can be done daily.)

GRAMMAR OUT OF THE BOX . . . . . .

You never know what will happen. Have each student do a project on the theme "You never know what will happen." Students should choose the medium they prefer and tell a story with an unexpected ending. Stories can take one of the following forms:

- a written narrative, possibly illustrated
- an oral story
- a cartoon story
- a photographic essay
- a videotaped story

UNIT 22 The Simple Past: *Yes/No* and *Wh-* Questions

Unit Overview

Students will learn how to form past-tense:
- *yes/no* and *wh-* questions
- affirmative and negative short answers
- long answers

Grammar in Context (pages 206–207)

Background Notes
J.R.R. Tolkien is famous for having written *The Hobbit* and *The Lord of the Rings* trilogy. There are hundreds of websites and organizations devoted to his books.

Vocabulary
initial: the first letter of a name

grow up: to develop from a child into an adult

cousin: a child of your aunt or uncle

sweetheart: the person you love

imaginative: able to think of new and interesting ideas

retirement: the official act of stopping work, usually as one approaches old age

Comprehension Questions
- Was Tolkien's family South African? (*No, they were English.*)
- Why was Tolkien born in South Africa? (*His father was there on business.*)
- When did Tolkien start telling stories? (*when he had children*)
- What was Tolkien's job? (*He worked on the* New English Dictionary *and he was a teacher.*)
- When did he write *The Hobbit*? (*in the 1930s*)

Discussion Topics
- In what ways was Tolkien an unusual man? In what ways was he ordinary?
- Ask students who are familiar with *The Lord of the Rings* to describe the characters and to summarize the plot.

Grammar Presentation (pages 208–209)

Identify the Grammar

Where was Tolkien born?
When was Tolkien born?
Where did he grow up?
Did he grow up in South Africa?

Grammar Charts

- Write the examples of the target grammar on the board. Ask questions to focus their attention on the structures:
  - —What is the word order in *yes/no* questions in the simple past? (Did + *subject* + *verb*)
  - —What is the word order in *wh-* questions about the object? (Wh- *word* + did + *subject* + *verb*)
  - —What is the word order in *wh-* questions with *be?* (Wh- *word* + be + *subject*)
- Have students look at the last grammar chart and ask about the word order of *wh-* questions about the subject. (Wh- *word* + *verb* + *object*) Point out that the *wh-* word is the subject in these questions.
- Remind students that questions have the same word order in the present and in the past. Write contrasting sentences on the board:
  Does he have a dog?
  Did he have a dog?
  Where do you live?
  Where did you live?

Grammar Notes

Note 1 *(Exercises 2, 4)*
- To drill the form of *yes/no* questions, provide a kernel statement and have students transform it into a question. Use a mix of regular and irregular verbs. For example:

  TEACHER: I made a cake.

  CLASS: Did you make a cake?

  TEACHER: Alice lived in Alaska.

  CLASS: Did Alice live in Alaska?

- Have students write the name of their favorite English book or film on an index card. Put all the cards in a box, bag, or hat.
- Have a student draw one card out of the box, read it, and say, "I read/didn't read *The Hobbit*. [Candace], did you read *The Hobbit*?"
- The student should answer truthfully. For example:
  —Yes, I did. / No, I didn't.

—Yes, I read it, but I didn't like it.
—No, I didn't read it, but I want to.
- Then the student should draw another card out of the box and ask the next question.
- Continue in a chain until all students have asked and answered a question.

Notes 2–3 *(Exercises 3–4)*
- Before class, arrange for one student to help you with this part of the lesson. Ask this student to pretend to have been in an accident. The student can limp, or you can tie up the student's arm in a bandage.
- To begin, write *who, what, when, where, why, how, whom, how long* on the board.
- Say to the class, "Poor [Alex]. He had an accident. [Alex,] come up here." "Alex" should then limp up to the front of the class.
- Ask "Alex" *Wh-* questions about the accident. For example:
  —What happened?
  —Where did it happen?
  —Who was with you?
- Encourage the class to ask additional questions.
- Call up a pair of students to the front of the class. Have them role-play a similar situation. Again, encourage students to ask questions.
- Put students in pairs. Have them ask and answer questions about a true unusual event that happened to them. Walk around the room and note the errors you hear. After the students are finished talking with their partners, write sentences on the board with the errors you heard. Have students copy them and correct them for homework.

Note 4 *(Exercises 3–4)*
- Point out that short answers are the same in the present and past tenses except for the form of *do:*
- Do you live with your parents? *(Yes, I do / No, I don't.)*
- Did you live with your parents? *(Yes, I did / No, I didn't.)*
- For fun, teach students the proper stress and intonation of the expressions *uh-huh* (affirmative) and *uh-uh* (negative). Write these expressions on the board and draw arrows above them as follows:

uh-huh   *uh-uh*

Explain that these are common ways of indicating *yes* and *no* in American English.
- Have students ask you some simple *yes/no* questions and model the answers.

- Have students in pairs do the same. Encourage them to have fun with the questions and answers. For example:

A: Jana, do you love Brad Pitt?

B: Uh-huh!

Focused Practice (pages 209–212)

Exercise 2

storyline: the story or plot of a movie or book

review: a piece of writing that gives an opinion about a new book, movie, or concert

Exercise 3

bill: a written statement of the amount you have to pay for services such as telephone and gas

Exercise 4

agent: a person or company that represents another person, such as an artist, in his or her business or legal affairs

Communication Practice (pages 213–214)

Exercise 6

Before listening, have students look at the sentences and try to predict the questions Ali asks Berrin.

Exercise 7

Some students may not have grandparents or may not remember them. Tell them they may speak about any older person they know well.

Exercise 8

Questions to generate ideas and elicit vocabulary:
- Who is your favorite artist/writer/musician?
- Who is a famous artist/writer/musician from your culture?

Further Practice

Have students talk about important people in small groups. Repeat Exercise 7, but instead of talking about grandparents, have them ask and answer questions about one of the following:
- my favorite teacher
- a person who changed my life
- a very unusual person
- the person I love most
- my hero
- my best friend

GRAMMAR OUT OF THE BOX . . . . . .

The 5 W's. Journalism students learn that the first paragraph of a news story must answer five questions: *who, what, when, where,* and *why.* Make a handout like the following and give one to each student.

Title: _____

Who	What	When	Where	Why

Bring in short news stories. Give one to each student. Have students read their stories and summarize the important information by filling in the chart. Put students in pairs. Instruct them to ask questions about their partner's story until they understand everything that happened. They must ask a minimum of five questions. They may not look at their partner's notes.

Find someone with the answer. Prepare a series of general-information trivia questions and answers. Each question and each answer should be on separate slips of paper. Sample questions:
- Who lives in the Vatican?
- What language is spoken in Brazil?
- When do kangaroos sleep?

Students should mingle. Those with a question search for the matching answer. As soon as students find each other, they sit down.

UNIT 23 — There Is / There Are; Is There . . . ?/Are There . . . ?

Unit Overview

Students will learn:
- affirmative and negative statements with *There is (not) / There are (not): There isn't a restaurant on the second level.*
- contractions: *there's*
- *yes/no* questions: *Is there a bank nearby?*

Grammar in Context (pages 222–223)

Background Notes

The West Edmonton Mall is the largest mall in the world. Located in Edmonton, Alberta, Canada, it contains shopping and entertainment facilities, a hotel, and 110 eating establishments!

Vocabulary

one-of-a-kind stores: stores that are not part of a chain

specialties: food or products created especially for, and sold especially in, one type of store

attractions: special things for tourists to see and do

Comprehension Questions

• What shops can you find at the West Edmonton mall? *(Old Navy, Godiva Chocolatier, and one-of-a-kind stores)*
• What gives the mall an international flavor? *(Chinatown and Europa Boulevard)*
• How many eating places are there? *(over 110)*
• What attractions does the mall have? *(a water park, an amusement park, and an indoor skating rink)*

Discussion Topics

• Ask students if they enjoy going to malls. What is their favorite mall? Why do they like it?
• Ask if anyone has been to the West Edmonton Mall. If not, would they like to go? Is this a good place to take a vacation?

Grammar Presentation (pages 223–224)

Identify the Grammar

There are more than 800 stores.
There's Chinatown.
There isn't a better time to get away.

Grammar Charts

• Write the examples of the target grammar point on the board. Underline *There are*, *There's*, and *There isn't*. Say the phrases. Have students repeat them.
• Ask questions to help students notice the structures:
  —In the first sentence, what is the subject? *(stores)*
  —Is it singular or plural? *(plural)*
  —Do we use *there is* or *there are* with plural subjects? *(there are)*
  —What does the contraction *there's* mean? *(there is)*

—What is the subject in the second sentence? *(Chinatown)*
  —Is it singular or plural? *(singular)*
  —Do we use *there is* or *there are*? *(there is)*
  —How do we form the negative? *(there isn't)*
• To demonstrate the question form, give the students one minute to look around the room. Then tell them to close their eyes. Ask questions with *Is there* and *Are there*. For example: "Is there a calendar in our room? Are there any red floor tiles? Are there any photographs on my desk?"
• Call two volunteers up to the board. Have them write questions with *Is there* and *Are there* like the ones you just modeled. Elicit the answers from the class.

Grammar Notes

Notes 1–2   *(Exercises 1, 2, 4–7)*
• Call on students to read the notes and the examples.
• On the board or on an OHT, make a quick sketch of a room in your home. Draw the large pieces of furniture. Then model three or four sentences with *there is* and *there are*. As you speak, add these items to your sketch. For example:
  —There's a painting above the fireplace.
  —There are photos of my children on my desk.
  —There's a lamp next to the couch.
• Add items to your sketch. If you cannot draw well, write the words in the appropriate places on your sketch. Have students make sentences with *there is* and *there are*.

Note 3   *(Exercises 2–3, 6)*
• Using the same sketch of a room, form sentences with *there isn't* and *there aren't*. For example, "There aren't any flowers. There isn't a television."
• Elicit similar sentences from the students.

Note 4   *(Exercise 6)*
Do a short chain drill using *any* with *yes/no* questions. Ask about the students' homes as follows:

TEACHER: Are there any plants in your house, Jasmine?

JASMINE: No, there aren't.

TEACHER: Cats.

JASMINE: Are there any cats in your house, Enrique?

ENRIQUE: Yes, there are. / Yes, there's one.

→ For additional practice, see the Supplementary Activities on page 130.

Note 5 *(Exercises 3–4, 6)*

- Write the example sentences as a paragraph on an OHT. Replace *here, there,* and *their* with blanks. You may wish to add two or three more sentences to the paragraph in order to further illustrate the teaching point.
- Call students up and have them fill in the blanks. Correct and discuss any errors.
- Have students copy the paragraph but replace the information about Banff with information about another place. For example, students can write about Los Angeles and say that there are several amusement parks there.
- Have students exchange and correct each other's papers.

Note 6 *(Exercises 1, 5–6)*

- On the board, write: *There are, There's,* and *There isn't.*
- Read the example sentences in Identify the Grammar and point to the words on the board as you say them.
- Make up similar sentences with *There is/are.* Have students follow up with an appropriate response containing *It's, he's,* or *they're.* For example:
  —There's a cat on the porch. *(It's black and white.)*
  —There's a sweater on the floor. *(It's John's.)*
  —There's someone here to see you. *(He's waiting in the reception area.)*
  —There are two bottles of wine in the refrigerator. *(They're for the dinner party tonight.)*
  —There are two new students in Ms. Jackson's class. *(They're from China.)*

Focused Practice (pages 225–228)

Exercise 1
food court: an area in a shopping mall where there are many small restaurants

unisex: for both men and women

Exercise 3
placemat: a mat that you put on the table for each person who is eating to protect the table

fan: a machine that makes air move in order to make a room cooler

Exercise 6
aboriginal: indigenous, native

auction: a public meeting where land, animals, buildings, paintings, and other goods are sold to the person who offers the most money for them

Exercise 7
pepperoni: a strong-tasting red Italian sausage

broccoli: a green vegetable

tofu: a soft white food that is made from soybeans

curry: a yellow powdered spice

herring: a small fish

Communication Practice (pages 228–230)

Exercise 8
Before students listen, have them read the questions and guess the context of the conversation.

Exercise 9
For advanced students, you can make this activity more difficult by instructing them not to look at their partner's picture. They must then ask each other questions in order to get the information they need. For example:

A: Is there a shoe repair in your picture?

B: Yes. It's between the flower shop and the bakery.

A: In my picture it's between the flower shop and the supermarket.

Exercise 10
Have students get up and walk around to do this activity. Remind them that they can only write a person's name once.

Exercise 11
Questions to generate ideas and elicit vocabulary:
- What is the name of your shop?
- What can you buy there?
- Where is it?
- Who are the owners?
- Is it expensive?
- Why do you like it?

Further Practice
Using the entertainment section from your local newspaper, have students role-play a conversation about choosing an activity to do together on Saturday night. Put students in pairs. Tell them to pretend they are at home. Give the entertainment section to one of the students, who will read the paper while the other pretends to be engaged in a domestic activity such as cooking or ironing. The students must talk about actual events in the paper until they find one that they agree to do together. For example:

A: Where should we go on Saturday night?

B: Let's see. There are lots of interesting things to do. Do you want to see a movie?

A: Maybe. What's playing?

B: There's a French film festival at the Royal Theater.

A: No, I want to see something in English.

B: How about a play? There's a great comedy playing at the _____ theater.

A: I heard there aren't any tickets left. Maybe there's something at a smaller theater.

GRAMMAR OUT OF THE BOX ......

Mall maps. Find or draw maps of two malls. (Large malls have maps posted on their websites.) Make two shopping lists consisting of specific items that can be bought at a mall. For example:

Student A	Student B
a man's wool vest	Levi's blue jeans
miso soup	a straw hat
a book about	a teapot
New Zealand	a hamburger
rain boots	a tennis racket
vitamins for a dog	a Macintosh
a Turkish rug	computer

Put students in pairs. Give one of the maps and a shopping list to each student. Have students think of the type of shop that would sell the items on their lists and then ask their partner if there is such a shop at the partner's mall. For example:

A: I want to get some miso soup. Is there a Japanese restaurant at your mall?

B: Yes, there's one in the food court on the third floor.

Fun with a song. Rent the movie *West Side Story*. Do an Internet search to find the lyrics to the song "Somewhere." In class, summarize the movie plot. (*West Side Story* is a classic tragedy about two young people from clashing ethnic groups who fall in love against all odds.) Then show the scene in which the young lovers, Tony and Maria, sing "Somewhere." Hand out the lyrics to the class. Read and discuss them. Play the scene again. Encourage the students to sing along. Have a discussion. Ask students if they know of cases similar to that of Tony and Maria, either from their own experience or from other movies, books, or plays.

UNIT 24
Subject and Object Pronouns; Direct and Indirect Objects

Unit Overview

Students will review subject pronouns (*I, you, he, we,* etc.) and learn the object pronouns (*me, him, them,* etc.). They will also learn the following sentence patterns:
- subject + verb: *John slept.*
- subject + verb + object: *Maria teaches Spanish.*
- subject + verb + direct object + *to* + indirect object: *Anna gave a gift to her mother.*
- subject + verb + indirect object + direct object: *Anna gave her mother a gift.*

Grammar in Context (pages 231–232)

Background Notes

One way of interpreting the saying "Give a man a fish" is as follows: You can help people in the short term by giving them what they need. However, it's better to teach people the skills they need in order to take care of themselves in the long run.

Vocabulary

phrase: a group of words

Comprehension Questions

- What language is *ohayoo*? (*Japanese*)
- What language is *tudo bem*? (*Portuguese*)
- Where did Masako and Maria meet? (*at the library*)
- How is Masako teaching Maria Japanese? (*She says a phrase and Maria repeats it. Then she writes it down and Maria reads it and tries to memorize it.*)
- What did Maria give Masako? (*a tape*)
- What did Masako lend Maria? (*a Japanese phrase book*)
- What does *bonne chance* mean? (*"good luck" in French*)

Discussion Topics

- Have students teach the class a basic greeting in their language.

• Teach a variety of greetings in English, such as *Hello, How are you,* and *How's it going?* Explain that in English *How are you?* is a greeting. It is not a true question about someone's health.

Grammar Presentation (pages 232–234)

Identify the Grammar

Group 1
We greeted each other.
I'm teaching her Japanese.
Maria repeats it.
Yesterday Maria gave me a tape.

Group 2
I met her at the library last month.
She's teaching me Portuguese.
I say a phrase.
I write it down.
She reads it and tries to memorize it.
I can't remember anything.
I lent her a Japanese phrase book.
Don't confuse me.

Grammar Charts

1. Write the two groups of example sentences on the board or on an overhead projector transparency. Number the sentences for ease of reference.
2. Write the following grammar terms on the board:
   subject pronoun
   object pronoun
   direct object
   indirect object
3. Work with the examples from Group 1. Name and label the parts of the example sentences using the grammar terms above and explain as follows: "The subject pronouns are *We* (example 1) and *I* (example 2). A subject pronoun replaces a noun as the subject of a sentence. The object pronoun is *it* (ex. 3). Object pronouns replace a noun as the object of a verb. The direct objects are *each other* (ex. 1), *Japanese* (ex. 2), *it* (ex. 3), and *a tape* (ex. 4). Direct objects tell whom or what. Whom did we greet? We greeted each other. What am I teaching? I'm teaching Japanese. What did Maria repeat? She repeated it. What did Maria give me? She gave me a tape. The indirect objects are *her* (ex. 2) and *me* (ex. 4). Indirect objects answer the questions *to whom* or *to what*. To whom am I teaching

Japanese? To her. To whom did Maria give a tape? To me."
4. Now work with the sentences in Group 2. Call students up to the board or the OHP and have them label the parts in response to your questions:
   • What is the subject? *(I)*
   • Is it a noun or a pronoun? *(pronoun)*
   • What is the object? *(her)*
   • Is it a noun or a pronoun? *(pronoun)*
   • What is the direct object? For example, in sentence 2, what is she teaching me? *(Portuguese)*
   • What is the indirect object? For example, in sentence 2, to whom is she teaching? *(me)*
5. Go over the verbs in the last chart. Define them where necessary and elicit an example sentence for each verb. Example:

   TEACHER: *Hand* means to pass something from one person's hand to another person's hand. Who can give an example?

   STUDENT: Eva handed me a pencil.

→ For additional practice, see the Supplementary Activities on page 130.

Grammar Notes

Note 1 *(Exercises 3–4)*
Subject pronouns are taught in Unit 1. If review is needed, see the Unit 1 Grammar Charts on page 15 of this Teacher's Manual.

Note 2 *(Exercises 2–4)*
Do an oral fill-in-the-gap. Say sentences like the ones below. The class fills in the missing object pronoun at the end.
• There's a beautiful pair of shoes. I want _____ *(them).*
• You got a haircut! I like _____ *(it).*
• How do you do? I'm so glad to meet _____ *(you).*
• Was Jackie at the party? I didn't see _____ *(her).*
• I've never met my husband's cousins. I don't know _____ *(them).*
• We enjoyed meeting you. Next time you're in town, please come visit _____ *(us).*

Note 3 *(Exercise 4)*
• Have students read the note and the examples.
• Say a few phrases like the following. Students should say "right" or "wrong."
   —she and I *(right)*
   —Maria and Erik *(right)*
   —I and Maria *(wrong)*

Note 4 *(Exercise 4)*

• Make a handout or a transparency like the one below. Each column contains verbs that fit one of the sentence patterns in the note.

S + V	S + V + O	S + V + O + I
Maria taught.	Maria taught Portuguese.	Maria taught Portuguese to Masako.
sleep cry laugh disappear rise sneeze fall fly	e-mail pass read sell teach throw write drink eat win	give hand lend owe pass read sell show teach tell throw write

• Read Note 4 with the students.
• Call on students to compose additional example sentences using verbs from the lists.
• Put students in pairs or small groups and have them continue to form their own sentences. Encourage them to make true sentences based on their own experiences.

Note 5 *(Exercises 4–5)*

• Have students read the note and the examples.
• Compose sentences using verbs that take *to* (in the third column of the handout for Note 4). Write each sentence on a strip of paper. For example (use the names of your students instead of the names below):
  —Mary gave Jack the book.
  —The teacher handed Hiro a test paper.
  —I lent Peter my car.
• Hand out the strips to various students. Use them in a transformation/substitution drill as follows:

A [reads the sentence on his or her strip]:
   Mary gave Jack the book.

TEACHER: Who?

B: Mary gave the book to Jack.

C: Mary gave it to Jack.

D: The teacher handed Hiro a test paper.

TEACHER: Who?

E: The teacher handed a test paper to Hiro.

F: The teacher handed it to Hiro.

→ For additional practice, see the Supplementary Activities on page 130.

Focused Practice (pages 234–237)

Exercise 1
owe: to need to pay someone because he or she has allowed you to borrow money; also, to feel that you should do something for someone because he or she has done something for you

Exercise 4
borrow: to use something that belongs to someone else and give it back to him or her later. (Note: Students are often confused by the difference between *borrow* and *lend*. Illustrate with sentences such as the following: *I borrowed a dollar from Fanny. Fanny lent me a dollar.*)

Exercise 5
hand: to pass something to someone
rolls: small round loaves of bread for one person

Exercise 6
boxing: the sport of fighting while wearing big leather gloves
champion: the person or team that has won a competition, especially in sports

Communication Practice (pages 237–238)

Exercise 7
Before students listen, have them read the sentences and predict what will go in the blanks. Then have them listen and check their predictions.

Exercise 8
Help students prepare their talks. First, if they have trouble thinking of a topic, provide a few suggestions (see the Example). Second, have students prepare an outline of the steps in the activity or skill they want to teach. Help them with vocabulary and grammar. A third step is to put students in pairs to practice out loud before they speak in groups.

Exercise 9
Questions to generate ideas and elicit vocabulary:
• What was the teacher's name?
• What subject did he or she teach you?
• What grade (level of school) were you in?
• What other things were happening in your life at that time?
• Why was this person a good teacher?

- Why was this teacher special for you?
- Do you ever see or speak to this teacher now?

Further Practice

- On a handout or OHT, make a list of unusual items to be given as gifts. If you can find pictures of the items, that is even better. There should be a few more items than there are people in your class. Write the name of every student on a slip of paper. Hand out the slips so that each student has a mystery partner.
- Hand out or project the list. Students should pick an item to give their mystery partner as a gift, and they should prepare to explain why they chose that gift for that person. Provide the following model sentence: "I'm going to give a kitten to Leonardo because I know that he loves cats." Go around the room and have each student say his or her sentence. To elicit additional language, add the following step: As students hear about their gifts, they can either accept or reject them. To accept, they can simply respond, "Thank you very much." To reject, they can say, "Thank you, but [a reason]." For example, "I already have one/I don't have space for it/It's the wrong color."
- For further entertainment and language practice, hold a gift auction. Students can sell their gifts to the highest bidder. Write a model script for the auction on the board:

A: *My husband is allergic to cats, so I cannot keep this adorable kitten. Who would like to buy it?*

B: *I'll buy it for one dollar.*

C: *I'll buy it for two dollars.*

A: *Are there any other bids? Do I hear three dollars? No? OK. Two dollars going once, going twice, SOLD to [Student C] for two dollars.*

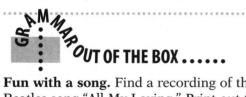

Fun with a song. Find a recording of the Beatles song "All My Loving." Print out the lyrics. Have students listen once. Ask what they heard and understood. Then hand out the lyrics and read them with the class. Explain vocabulary and answer questions. Play the song again, and have students sing along. Finally, have a discussion. Ask students if they have ever been far away from a person they loved, how they felt, and what they did to try to stay in touch with that person.

Count and Non-Count Nouns; Articles

Unit Overview

Students will learn about count and non-count nouns with articles and quantifiers in affirmative and negative statements. Charts include the following specific information:
- singular count nouns and articles
- plural count nouns and quantifiers
- non-count nouns and quantifiers
- the definite article

Grammar in Context (pages 239–240)

Vocabulary

invitation: a request that someone go somewhere or do something; the card that this request is written on

reservation: an arrangement that you make so that a place in a hotel, on an airplane, or at an event is kept for you to use

reviews: articles that give an opinion about a new book, play, movie, or concert

Comprehension Questions

- What do the speakers need to do to prepare for the party? *(They need to make the reservation, send invitations, and collect the money.)*
- How did the speakers get information about the restaurants? *(One of them read some reviews.)*
- How are the prices at Ali Baba? *(They are not bad.)*
- What is Speaker A going to do? *(Speaker A will make the reservation and send the invitations.)*
- What is Speaker B going to do? *(Speaker B will collect the money.)*

Discussion Topics

- Which restaurant do you prefer, Green Grill or Ali Baba?
- What is your favorite restaurant? Why do you like it?

Grammar Presentation (pages 241–243)

Identify the Grammar

	Affirmative	Negative
Singular Count Nouns	*a vegetable soup* *a reservation*	
Plural Count Nouns	*a few minutes*	*aren't many tables*
Non-Count Nouns	*music* *a little salt*	*isn't much meat or fish*

Grammar Charts

- On the board or on a transparency, make a chart like the one above of examples from the reading. Leave space for students to add more examples.
- Introduce the categories and examples. For instance, begin by saying that English has three types of nouns: singular, plural, and non-count (or uncountable). Say that *a, an,* and *the* are called articles. Words that tell how much or how many are called quantifiers.
- Ask students to identify the quantifiers in the chart (*a few, a little, many, much*).
- There are no examples of singular count nouns in negative sentences in the reading. Inform students that singular count nouns are the same in the affirmative and the negative.
- Have students go through the reading and find additional examples of each category. Call them up to the board or OHP to write the examples on the chart.
- Elicit additional examples from the students and add them to the chart.
- Have students find all the examples with *the*. List them on the board and have students identify the type of noun that follows each example: singular, plural, or non-count. Elicit further examples and list them on the board.

Grammar Notes

Note 1
- In a large box, collect 15–20 countable items. Include a few that begin with vowels, such as egg, onion, apple, envelope, and umbrella. Put in one of some items and more than one of other items. Plural items should be kept together in a clear plastic bag or with a rubber band.
- Have students read the note and the examples.
- Place the box on your desk and have students come up one at a time, reach in, pull out an object, and say what it is: "an egg/a wristwatch/two pens."
- Do a variation of the above activity. Put a blindfold on students before they reach into the box. Then, after they select an item, they should feel it and say what they think it is: "It's an egg." If they're unable to guess, the class can provide hints: "You can eat it. It comes from a chicken."

Note 2
- Make a full-page handout like the one below. Leave space in each cell for students to add items.

Liquids milk	Solid foods cheese	Particles[1] sugar
Natural elements wood	Natural phenomena and weather rain	Abstract nouns love
Gases air	Groups consisting of similar items jewelry	Activities and recreation golf swimming

[1]That is, substances made up of many tiny parts, such as dust, sugar, salt, hair, sawdust, grass, chalk, rice.

- Divide students into groups. Assign one category of non-count nouns to each. Students must come up with additional nouns to add to the chart.
- Have each group share its work with the class. Correct errors.

Note 3 *(Exercises 2–3)*

- Have students read the note and the examples.
- Write the following incomplete dialogue on the board:

    A: *For dinner last night I had* _____,
    _____, _____, *and* _____.

    B: *How was the* _____?

    A: *It was [spicy / sour / bitter / overcooked / undercooked / not fresh / delicious / sweet / good / fresh / wonderful].*

- Model, telling about your own experience:

    TEACHER: Last night for dinner I had chicken, rice, salad, and ice cream.

    CLASS: How was the chicken?

    TEACHER: It was a little dry.

- Put students in pairs or small groups. Have them follow the model and speak about a recent dinner.

Note 4 *(Exercises 2–3)*

Have students read the note and the examples. It may be helpful to put the following diagram on the board:

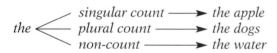

→ For additional practice, see the Supplementary Activities on page 131.

Note 5 *(Exercises 4–5)*

- Read the note and the examples with the class.
- Do a transformation drill. Students convert sentences with non-count and plural-count nouns from affirmative to negative and vice versa. For example:

    TEACHER: I had some orange juice.

    CLASS: I didn't have any orange juice.

    TEACHER: I didn't have any eggs.

    CLASS: I had some eggs.

- Ask students what they really ate for breakfast. Elicit affirmative and negative sentences, such as "I had some cereal. I didn't have any coffee."

Note 6 *(Exercises 5–7)*

- Have students read the note and the examples.
- Summarize the information in a chart. Draw the cells and headings on the board. Elicit the quantifiers from the students.

	Small amounts	**Large amounts**
Count	*[a few]*	*[a lot of, many]*
Non-count	*[a little]*	*[a lot of, (not) much]*

- To practice, put students in groups. Have them describe the contents of their refrigerator or closet using the quantifiers above. They can also use *some/any* and *a/an*. (*some milk, a few apples, a lot of Coke, a little cheese, a watermelon, not much ice cream*)

Note 7

- Have students read the note and the examples. Write a few more examples on the board:

    chicken
    a chicken
    noise
    a noise
    glass
    a glass

- This concept may be difficult for students to understand. Explain that the countable item refers to something that is a whole unit (a chicken), a single event (a noise), or an object (a glass). The non-count noun refers to a substance (chicken), phenomenon (noise), or material (glass) in general.
- Put students in pairs and assign one count/non-count noun pair to each. Challenge them to compose sentences using both the count and the non-count noun together. For example:

    —I love coffee, but my brother hates it. We went to a café and I bought a coffee for myself and a soda for him.

    —My son said he wants chicken for dinner tonight, so I went to the supermarket and bought a chicken, some rice, and some broccoli.

Focused Practice *(pages 243–247)*

Exercise 1

napkin: a small piece of cloth or paper used for cleaning your mouth or hands when you are eating

server: someone who brings you food in a restaurant; the main computer on a network that controls all the others

Exercise 2

album: a book in which you put photographs, stamps, and other items you want to remember

case: a container for storing something

Exercise 3

critic: someone whose job is to give judgments about movies, books, or other works of art

the tab: the bill for a meal or service

Exercise 5

trouble: problems that make something difficult

Exercise 7

in no time: very quickly

stop for: to pause during an activity to get something

Exercise 8

battery: an object that provides electricity for something such as a radio or car

Communication Practice (pages 247–249)

Exercise 9

Before students listen, have them try to guess what the problem in question 2 might be.

Exercise 10

In step B, it might be impractical to have all the students write their sentences on the board. As an alternative, students can write sentences on paper and work with a partner or group to compare sentences.

Exercise 11

Suggest that students add two or three sentences about items not found in the box.

Exercise 12

Questions to generate ideas and elicit vocabulary:
• What is the name of the restaurant?
• Where is it?
• What kind of food does it have?
• Which dishes are good? Which dishes are not good?
• How are the prices?
• How is the service?
• How is the atmosphere?
• Do you recommend this restaurant?

Exercise 13

Explain to students that the man is saying that the soup is old. *Soup of the day* normally refers to the fact that some restaurants feature a different type of soup on their menu every day of the week.

Further Practice

Have students write out the ingredients to a recipe they know, preferably one from their culture or country. They should try to use all the articles and quantifiers included in this lesson. Correct the students' recipes. Put students in pairs or small groups. Have them dictate the ingredients in their recipe to their partner(s). The partner(s) should write what they hear. At the end of the dictation, the writers should compare what they wrote with the original recipe list. The following simple recipes are provided for the benefit of students who don't know how to cook.

Chicken Soup	Pea Soup
10–12 cups water whole chicken, cleaned 2 onions, sliced 2 carrots, sliced 2 stalks celery, sliced 1 parsnip or zucchini (optional), sliced 1 clove garlic, crushed ½ teaspoon dry dill salt pepper	2 cups dried green peas 8–10 cups water 2–3 beef neck bones 1 onion, sliced 1 large carrot, sliced 1 clove garlic salt pepper
Put all the ingredients in a large pot. Heat the mixture to boiling, then turn the heat down to low and cook for 2–3 hours.	Put all the ingredients in a large pot. Boil, then cook on low heat for about 1 hour. To thicken, put some of the peas through a strainer or blender.

Cheese Omelette
2 eggs butter or margarine ½ cup grated cheddar cheese 1 chopped green onion salt pepper
Put the eggs in a bowl and mix them with a fork. Stir in the chopped onion and cheese. Put the butter or margarine in a frying pan on medium heat and let it melt. Pour in the egg mixture. Sprinkle with salt and pepper. Cook both sides of the omelette until firm.

Class potluck. Explain to students the American tradition of a potluck meal, in which each person brings one dish. Arrange to have a class potluck. Make a sign-up sheet with the following categories: drinks, soup, appetizer/salad, main dish, vegetable dish, paper goods (plates, napkins, etc.). Have each student sign up for one of the categories. Instruct students to prepare a card to go along with each food item. The card should list the ingredients of the dish.

The Simple Present and Present Progressive; Adverbs and Expressions of Frequency

UNIT 26

Unit Overview

Students will review the contrast between the simple present and present progressive tenses. In addition, they will learn:

• questions with *how often* and answers with adverbs of frequency (*always, often, never*) and expressions of frequency (*once a week, twice a month*)
• word order of adverbs of frequency in present-tense sentences with *be* and other verbs

Grammar in Context (pages 256–257)

Background Notes

Talk shows are very popular in the United States. On these radio programs, a host interviews a guest who is an expert in the topic of that day's program and accepts phone calls from listeners who want to ask a question or participate in the discussion. There are talk shows dealing with a wide variety of topics, such as politics, gardening, health, music, and psychology.

Vocabulary

psychologist: someone who is trained in the study of how the mind works and how mental problems can be treated

slob: a person who is very untidy

Are we in trouble? Do you think we will have a problem if we get married?

nut: a person who is a little crazy

dusting: cleaning the dust from something, usually furniture

polish: to make something shiny by rubbing it

Comprehension Questions

• What is Nita's complaint about Bob? *(He is a slob.)*
• What is Bob's complaint about Nita? *(She always cleans.)*
• How often does Bob clean his apartment? *(once in a while)*
• What is Nita doing right now? *(She is dusting and polishing the furniture.)*
• Do you think this couple can have a happy marriage?

Discussion Topics

• Are you a slob or a "nut" about neatness?
• Is it a serious problem in a marriage if one person is neat and the other person isn't?
• What can a couple do to avoid conflict if one is neat and the other isn't?

Grammar Presentation (pages 258–260)

Identify the Grammar

(Bob) <u>never cleans</u>.
(Nita) <u>always cleans</u>.
<u>Every day</u> *she cleans.*
How often do you clean your apartment? <u>Once in a while</u>.
I'm <u>almost never</u> there.
<u>Right now</u> *I'm dusting and polishing.*

Grammar Charts

• Write the examples from Identify the Grammar on the board. Call on students to read the examples. Have students name the tense—simple present or present progressive.
• To review the present progressive, point to the last sentence. Ask, "What is the verb?" *(dusting and polishing)* "What is the time?" *(right now)*
• Call on students to read the sentences in the box labeled **The Present Progressive** on page 258 in the Student Book. Cue the class with another verb, such as *drive,* and have students make sentences like the ones in the box. Repeat this procedure, if necessary, with other verbs.

- Turn back to the example sentences on the board. Ask questions to elicit those sentences:
  —How often does Bob clean?
  —How often does Nita clean?
  —How often do you clean?
  —When is Bob there?
- Underline each adverb and expression of frequency. Explain that *never* and *always* are adverbs of frequency. *Every day* and *once in a while* are expressions of frequency.
- Have students look at the two boxes on the top of page 259 in the Student Book. Say the expressions and have students repeat them after you.
- Ask questions to help students notice the placement of the frequency expressions:
  —Where do we say adverbs of frequency? (*after* be *and before other verbs*)
  —Where do we say frequency expressions like *every day*? (*at the beginning or the end of the sentence*)

Grammar Notes

Notes 1–2   *(Exercises 2–3, 5)*
- Call on students to read the notes and examples.
- Write the following sentences on the board:
  I usually drink coffee in the morning, but today I'm drinking tea.
  We always visit my mother during Christmas vacation, but this year we're going on a cruise instead.
- Ask, "Which tense do we use to talk about activities that are usual, habitual, or normal?" *(simple present)* "Which tense do we use to talk about something that is unusual or temporary?" *(present progressive)*
- Have students compose sentences similar to the ones on the board. To guide their thinking, write the following templates on the board:
  —*I usually _____, but today I'm _____.*
  —*Normally, I _____ on [Saturday], but this week I'm _____ on [Sunday].*
  —*In my country, I always _____, but while I'm in the United States, I'm _____.*
  —*Most of the time I like to _____ in the [morning], but today I'm _____ in the [evening] because _____.*
- Put students in small groups to share their sentences.

Note 3   *(Exercise 4)*
- Call on students to read the note and the examples.

- To practice, put students in pairs. Have them ask and answer questions with *How often . . . ?* Use the two lists of activities below, or make up your own.

A	**B**
talk to a child	pet a dog
change the oil in your car	listen to classical music
fall asleep in your clothes	eat walnuts
lose a contact lens	forget where you put your keys
wear sandals	use the Internet
ask your teacher a question	forget to turn off your cell phone

Note 4   *(Exercises 3–5)*
Put students in small groups. Give them a topic, such as personal grooming, housework, or the weather. Challenge them to make one sentence for each adverb of frequency and each time expression in the boxes at the top of page 259 in the Student Book. For example:
- I always drink coffee in the morning.
- I almost always make my bed.
- I frequently check my e-mail before school.
- In Bangkok it rains every day.
- My mother goes to the market twice a day.
- I buy gas three times a month.

Notes 5–6   *(Exercises 3–5)*
- Call on students to read the notes and the examples.
- On the board, write two kernel sentences:
  Franco is worried.
  Franco reads books in English.
- Also write the following frequency expressions on the board: *sometimes, usually, often, never, always, once in a while, every day.*
- Put students in pairs. Instruct them to insert each frequency adverb into the two kernel sentences in every possible position, as follows:
  —Franco is sometimes / usually / often / never / always worried.
  —Every day / Once in a while Franco is worried. / Franco is worried once in a while / every day.
  —Franco sometimes / usually / often / never / always reads books in English.
  —Sometimes / usually / often Franco reads books in English.
  —Once in a while Franco reads books in English. / Franco reads books in English once in a while.

- Check the students' sentences. Then have them change partners and form similar, true sentences about themselves. For example:
  —I am never late.
  —I always go to sleep after midnight.
  —Once in a while I forget to do my homework.

Focused Practice (pages 260–263)

Exercise 2
candlelit dinner: a romantic meal with light provided only by candles

wasting: the act of using more of something than you should

Exercise 3
thoughtful: helpful and considerate

curious: wanting to know or learn about something

taste: the particular type of music, food, clothes, or art that someone prefers

Exercise 5
free minutes: the number of free minutes included in a person's monthly cell phone fee

go over one's limit: to exceed the amount of time or money one is allowed

Walkman: TRADEMARK a portable music player

Communication Practice (pages 264–265)

Exercise 7
Before students listen, read the questions and answers and clarify vocabulary as needed.

Exercise 8
- Before students speak, clarify vocabulary as needed.
- Have students compose their questions and write them in the chart.
- As a follow-up, encourage students to add items to the box and to ask their classmates about them.

Exercise 9
This activity can also be done with pictures. Student A looks at a picture for one minute. Student B then asks questions about it, and Student A uses the present and present progressive to answer (without looking at the picture).

Exercise 10
Questions to generate ideas and elicit vocabulary:
- When do you leave your house every day?
- Where do you go?
- How do you get there?
- What do you do all day?
- When and where do you eat lunch?
- When and where do you shop?
- When and how do you go home?
- What do you normally do in the evening?
- When do you go to bed?
- What unusual event happened recently?

Further Practice
Have students fill out the following television survey questionnaire alone. Put them in pairs or small groups to compare and discuss their answers. They should ask each other complete questions and answer in full sentences:

A: How often do you watch television on weekends?

B: I always watch television on weekends.

Frequency Survey

How Often Do You Watch Television?

	Always	Very Often	Often	Sometimes	Rarely	Never
1. on weekdays						
2. on weekends						
3. while doing homework						
4. while eating						
5. instead of doing work I'm supposed to do						
6. before school or work						
7. because there's nothing else to do						
8. in bed						

GRAMMAR OUT OF THE BOX ......

Television survey. Use the same survey as in the Further Practice activity. Instruct students to interview one or more people outside of their class, such as a relative, neighbor, or coworker. Back in class, put students in small groups and have them report the results of their interview to their classmates. Students should report:
• whom they spoke to
• how this person answered each question
    For example: "I spoke to my neighbor. His name is Paul Levine. He said he never watches television on weekdays, but he always watches television on weekends." Monitor students for the proper pronunciation of the *-s* endings. (See Unit 8, Note 5, page 32.)

UNIT 27 Non-Action Verbs

Unit Overview

Students will learn:
• stative verbs in seven categories: state of being, emotion, sense or appearance, needs and preferences, mental states, possession, and measurement
• verb tenses to use with non-action verbs
• verbs that have both action and non-action meanings

Grammar in Context (page 266)

Background Notes

The tiny island of Bora Bora is part of the chain in the South Pacific islands known as French Polynesia. The island consists of an extinct volcano surrounded by a lagoon and a fringing reef. As of *2000*, the population was about 4,500 people. The name *Bora Bora* in the Tahitian language means "first born." The island's economy is based mainly on tourism.

Vocabulary

paradise: a place or situation that is extremely pleasant, beautiful, or enjoyable

invention: a useful machine, tool, instrument, or idea, made or produced for the first time

Comprehension Questions

• Who are the speakers? *(Heather and Rick)*
• Who is in Bora Bora? *(Aunt Janet and Uncle Fred)*
• What does it look like? *(It looks like paradise.)*
• What is Rick's profession? *(He is an inventor.)*
• Is he successful? *(It doesn't sound like it.)*

Discussion Topics

• Ask if any students have visited Bora Bora or any other tropical island. What did they see and do there?
• Ask students if they would like to take a vacation in Bora Bora. What would they enjoy doing there?

Grammar Presentation (pages 267–268)

Identify the Grammar

Is Bora Bora in the Pacific?
It looks like paradise.
(Aunt Janet and Uncle Fred) like everything there.
I agree.
Rick, remember . . .

Grammar Charts

• Copy the seven-column chart from page 267 in the Student Book onto the board or an OHT. Include the column heads and one example for each that is not found in the reading.
• Have students read the examples from Identify the Grammar and identify the verbs. Ask them which tense the verbs are in. *(present)*
• Explain that these verbs belong to a group called non-action, or stative, verbs because they do not describe actions. Many non-action verbs fall into the categories.
• Ask students to identify the category of each verb. Write, or have a student write, the verbs in the appropriate columns. (is—*state of being*; looks—*appearance*; like—*emotion*; agree—*mental state*; remember—*mental state*)
• Elicit additional verbs in each category and write them on the chart.
• Have the students study the chart on page 267 in the Student Book and compare the list on the board or OHT with the one in the book.

78 | *FOCUS ON GRAMMAR 2 TEACHER'S MANUAL*

Grammar Notes

Notes 1–2 *(Exercises 2–4)*
- Have students read the notes and the examples. As they read each sentence, have the reader identify the category of each verb.
- See the Further Practice section on the next page for a variety of activities you can do to practice the categories in Note 2.

Note 3 *(Exercises 3–4)*
- Have students read the note and the examples.
- Help students understand that non-action verbs can be used in the present tense with time expressions such as *now, at this moment,* and *today* to mean an action in progress at the moment of speaking. For example, both of the following sentences are correct:
  —I want something to eat now.
  —He's taking a shower now.
- However, as the book indicates, the following sentence is incorrect: *I'm wanting something to eat now.*

→ For additional practice, see the Supplementary Activities on page 131.

Note 4 *(Exercise 4)*
- Have students read the note and the examples.
- Demonstrate the action meaning of the verbs by using pantomime or body language. (This will work for all the verbs except *have*. For *have*, explain that *having trouble*—as well as *having a problem, having a party,* and a few others—are idioms.) For example, demonstrate *is looking* by putting your hand over your eyes and moving your head as if searching for something.
- Put students in pairs. Instruct them to create a pair of sentences for each verb in the note. One sentence should use the verb with an action meaning, and the other should use the verb with a non-action meaning. As an extra challenge, ask students to try to use the verb with both meanings in the same sentence. For example:
  —Ross is having a party tonight, but I can't go because I don't have a car.
  —Jorge is looking for his keys. He looks worried. Maybe he lost them.

Focused Practice *(pages 268–271)*

Exercise 1
foggy: describing weather that is not clear because of fog (cloudy air near the ground)

Exercise 2
tropical climate: weather that is hot and wet all year-round, found mainly near the equator

mosquitos: small flying insects that bite and suck the blood of people and animals, leaving red, itchy spots on the skin

lagoon: a shallow area of ocean bordering on land and separated from deep water by rocks, sand, or coral

Exercise 3
terrace: a flat outdoor area next to a hotel room or building where you can sit outside to eat and relax

Exercise 4
inviting: attractive

Exercise 5
double bed: a bed for two people

twin bed: a bed for one person

shuttle bus: a bus that makes regular short trips between two places, such as a hotel and the airport

sunscreen: cream that prevents sunburn

beach towel: a large towel suitable for use at the beach

pearl: a valuable, small, usually white, round object that forms inside an oyster and is used in jewelry

Communication Practice *(pages 271–273)*

Exercise 7
Before students get in pairs to begin working, go over the expressions in the box. Be aware that students who speak Latin languages tend to make the mistake "I am agree." Furthermore, students from many countries mispronounce "It depends" as "It's depend." As students work in pairs, walk around and note the errors you hear. Write them on the board for students to copy and correct for homework.

Exercise 8
- Before students begin Part A, go over the items in the box and clarify vocabulary as needed.
- Another way to do Part B is to go around the room and have each student make one sentence about his or her partner.

Exercise 9
- Before doing Part A, model the questions by filling in the blanks yourself and asking various students the questions.
- Part B can be done in groups of five, and the students in each group can choose one person to report the results to the class.

Exercise 10

Questions to generate ideas and elicit vocabulary:
• How does the object taste?
• What can you eat it with?
• What does the object look like or sound like?
• How does it feel?
• How does it smell?
• What can you do with it?

Further Practice

• Have students practice describing a place. Review the verbs of sense/appearance on page 267 in the Student Book. If possible, take your class outdoors. Put students in small groups. Have them stand close together. Have students take turns making true sentences about things they see, feel, and hear. For example:
—I feel the wind on my face.
—I see some birds.
—I hear a police siren.
If you cannot take your class outside, put students in small groups in the classroom. Tell them to imagine they are at a favorite outdoor place, tell their classmates where they are, and make sentences as described above.

• Tell students to imagine they will be going to a remote location (such as a desert island, an isolated mountain, or a very small town far away) for a period of two months. Have students make one list of the five most important items they *need* to take to this place, and another list of five items they *want* to take. Put students in groups to share their lists and explain why they chose the items they chose.

• Make a handout with sets of three related items like the ones listed below. Have students sit in groups. Their task is to state which item they prefer in each group and explain why. For example, "I prefer cats because I'm afraid of dogs and horses."
—cat, dog, horse
—swimming, jogging, playing tennis
—ocean, mountain, lake
—big city, small town, countryside
—morning, afternoon, evening
—green, orange, gray
—apple, banana, grape
—literature, mathematics, history

GRAMMAR OUT OF THE BOX . . . . . .

The price is right. This game is based on an American television game show by the same name. Contestants guess the price of a desirable item. The contestant who comes closest to guessing the real price without going over wins the item. Collect 10 or 12 small items that students might like to have, such as a candy bar, a pack of cards, a book, a pen, a comb, or a bottle of nail polish. (If your class meets before lunch, you might want to include several edible items!) Write the price of each item on a card. Keep each card and item together. Select three students at a time to be contestants in the game. Have them come up to the front of the room. Give a blank index card to each student. Select an item from your collection. Lay the price card face-down on your desk. Show the item to the contestants and the class. The contestants should guess the price and write their guesses on their index cards. After the contestants have written their guesses, have each person hold up his or her card and show it to the class. At the same time, the person should say "I think it costs _____." Have the class vote on which guess they think is correct. Point to each contestant and ask, "How many people agree with [Franco]? Who thinks Franco's guess is correct? Who believes this [comb] costs [59 cents]?" Finally, reveal the card with the item's actual price. Award the item to the contestant whose guess is closest to that price without going over it. Call up three new contestants and start again. You may select students to play the role of "Master of Ceremonies" instead of you.

UNIT 28 **Gerunds and Infinitives**

Unit Overview

Students will learn:
• the structure and use of gerunds and infinitives
• common verbs that are followed by gerunds, infinitives, or both

Grammar in Context (pages 274–275)

Vocabulary

software developer: a person who designs programs that tell a computer what to do

diplomat: someone who officially represents his or her government in a foreign country

carpenter: someone whose job is making and repairing wooden objects

auto mechanic: someone whose job is to repair cars

unpredictable: changing so much that you don't know what to expect

(advertising) executive: a manager in an advertising company who helps make important decisions

competitive: determined to be more successful than others

type A personality: relating to the type of people who are often determined, organized, and impatient

attorney: a lawyer

investment banker: a bank officer whose job is to manage clients' investments

stockbroker: a person or company whose job is to buy or sell stocks and bonds for other people

anthropologist: a professional whose job is the scientific study of people and their societies, cultures, and beliefs

guidance counselor: a person whose job is advising young people about their careers and education

social worker: someone who is trained to help people with family or social problems

physical therapist: a person whose job is to treat injuries and muscle problems with special exercises, massage, and heat

Comprehension Questions

- What is a good job for a person who likes to learn? *(scientist, anthropologist, writer, teacher)*
- Do chefs enjoy working with their hands? *(Yes, they do.)*
- Do musicians have unpredictable lives? *(Yes, they do.)*
- How is an attorney similar to a professional athlete? *(They are both competitive.)*
- Which jobs require casual clothes? *(carpenter, auto mechanic, farmer, child care worker)*
- Which jobs are good if you enjoy working with people? *(doctor, police officer, attorney, politician, child care worker, teacher, guidance counselor, psychologist or social worker, physical therapist, hotel manager)*

Discussion Topics

- Ask students which thought bubble best describes them and which job they would most enjoy having.

- Ask what career students are actually planning. Ask whether they think it is the right career for them, and why or why not.

Grammar Presentation (pages 275–276)

> ## Identify the Grammar
>
> *I like to learn.*
> *I hope to continue learning.*
> *I enjoy working with my hands.*
> *I expect to do something different.*
> *I hate losing.*
> *I can't stand wearing a suit.*
> *I avoid wearing formal clothes.*

Grammar Charts

- Write the example sentences from the reading on the board. Underline the verb in each example.
- Call on students to read each example sentence. In each case, ask, "What comes after the underlined verbs?" *(verb + -ing or to + verb)* Use two different colors to underline the gerund or infinitive in each example. Introduce the terms *infinitive* and *gerund*.
- Ask, "What part of the sentence are the gerunds and infinitives?" *(direct object)* Help students understand that in these examples, the gerunds and infinitives are nouns even though they look like verbs.
- Tell students to divide the verbs in the examples into two groups: those followed by gerunds and those followed by infinitives. *(gerund:* enjoy, hate, can't stand, avoid; *infinitive:* like, hope, expect)

Grammar Notes

Note 1 *(Exercises 2–3)*
- Call on students to read the note and the examples. Answer questions.
- Direct students to the left-hand column on the chart of verbs. Provide an example sentence for each verb in order to clarify the meanings of the verbs.
- Give the class a context, such as housework. Then go down the list of verbs and elicit a sentence about each. For example:

TEACHER: Avoid.

STUDENT: I avoid washing dishes.

Note 2 *(Exercises 2–3)*
- Repeat the procedure for Note 1.
- Put students in pairs. Have them write a short dialogue about a vacation using as many of

the verbs as possible. You may want to write the first line or two on the board. For example:

FLORA: *Do you intend to go on vacation this year, Avi?*

AVI: *Yes, I hope to go to Spain.*

Note 3   *(Exercise 2)*
• Have students read the note and the examples. Then tell them to look at the right-hand column on the verb chart on page 275 of the Student Book.
• Have students do a rapid transformation drill. Cue them with verbs and have them form sentences with gerunds and infinitives as follows:

TEACHER: Hate.

A: I hate to run.

B: I hate running.

TEACHER: Like.

C: I like to eat.

D: I like eating.

• Have students sit in pairs or small groups. Instruct them to form sentences with contrasting ideas, using a gerund in one part and an infinitive in the other. For example:
  • I hate washing dishes, but I love to cook.
  • I like to go to movies, but I don't like watching TV.
• Go around the room and have each student say one sentence.

→ For additional practice, see the Supplementary Activities on page 131.

Focused Practice (pages 276–278)

Exercise 1
avoid: to deliberately stay away from something or somebody; to deliberately not do something

Exercise 2
patience: the ability to wait calmly for a long time or to deal with difficulties without becoming annoyed or anxious

regret: to feel sorry about something you have done and wish you had not done it

try out: to show one's skills before a judge or judges in an attempt to be chosen for something, such as an acting role or sports team

Exercise 3
advanced degree: a certificate showing that a person has finished a program of study beyond the high-school level

courtroom dramas: television programs showing legal cases being tried in a court of law

previous: happening or existing before a particular event, time, or thing

Exercise 4
library science: the field of study in which one learns how to organize and manage a library

Communication Practice (pages 278–279)

Exercise 5
• Before students listen, read the questions and make sure they understand the directions.
• Point out that some statements may be true.

Exercise 6
After students speak about the six items in the exercise, encourage them to add items of their own.

Exercise 7
Expand this activity by teaching a few new verbs for students to use. For example:
• verbs + gerund: *discuss, quit*
• verbs + infinitive: *promise, offer*
• verbs + infinitive or gerund: *begin, continue*

Exercise 8
This activity can be done as a role play. One student plays the role of a career counselor, and the other is a job seeker. The counselor interviews the job seeker and recommends a job based on the job seeker's answers to the questions.

Exercise 9
Questions to generate ideas and elicit vocabulary:
• Who are you?
• What job are you applying for?
• What are your plans for the future?
• What are your qualifications for the job?
• Are you enclosing your résumé?

Further Practice
Make a handout of the following twelve statements for each student. Have students walk around the classroom and ask questions to find people who like doing these activities. When the answer is yes, write that person's name in the blank. Then speak to a different student. (Note: An alternative version of this activity is to have students write the items.)

Find someone who . . .

1. _____ likes watching horror movies.
2. _____ avoids eating meat.
3. _____ expects to be rich someday.
4. _____ loves to dance.
5. _____ can't stand waiting in line.
6. _____ keeps forgetting to use -s on third-person singular present tense verbs.
7. _____ hates to speak English.
8. _____ needs to go to the bank soon.
9. _____ hopes to become a teacher.
10. _____ is thinking about changing his or her hairstyle.
11. _____ hates speaking English in class in front of everyone.
12. _____ keeps on eating until late at night.

GRAMMAR OUT OF THE BOX ......

Questionnaires. Put students in groups of four and give each group a number. Tell students their group is going to write a questionnaire about a topic you will give them, using gerunds and infinitives. Make a blank template like the one below and give a copy to each student.

Questionnaire _____

	Yes	No
1.		
2.		
3.		
4.		
5.		

Tell students to write their group number in the blank following the word *Questionnaire*.

Assign each group a topic. For example:

food	drinks	animals
music	books	cars and driving
sports	computers	fashion

Group members must write five questions using gerunds and infinitives from this chapter. A few examples:

- Do you prefer to own a dog or a cat?
- Do you enjoy reading?
- Do you avoid drinking coffee in the evening?

Make new groups of four so that each student in the new group has a different questionnaire. For example, the new group might consist of members holding questionnaires 1, 2, 3, and 5. Now each student should use his or her questionnaire to interview the other members of the group. As group members answer yes or no, the student asking the questions should put a check in the corresponding column. Have students go back to their original groups and compare the answers they collected to the group's questions. They should tally all the yes and no responses to each question. Finally, students should make posters with graphs illustrating the information they collected. For example:

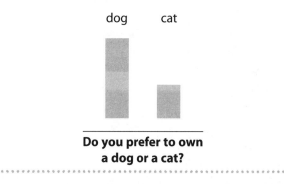

Do you prefer to own a dog or a cat?

UNIT 29

Review of the Simple Past

Unit Overview

Students will review regular and irregular past tense verbs in all forms:
- affirmative and negative statements
- *yes/no* questions
- *wh-* questions

Grammar in Context (pages 280–281)

Vocabulary

land: to fall or come down onto something after moving through the air

VCR: video cassette recorder; a machine used for recording television shows or watching videotapes

episode: a television or radio program that is one of a series of similar programs

pattern: a regularly repeated arrangement of shapes, events, words, or other things

game of chance: a game in which the results depend on luck, not skill

kept winning: continued to win over a period of time

producers: people whose job is to control the preparation of a play, movie, TV show, or event

admit: to accept unwillingly that something is true or that someone is right

business deal: a business agreement or arrangement involving money

he was robbed: someone stole his money

Comprehension Questions

• What was Michael Larsen's job? *(He drove an ice cream truck.)*
• What did he do after he lost his job? *(He began to watch quiz shows.)*
• What kind of show was *Press Your Luck? (It was a game of luck.)*
• What happened if you landed on a whammy? *(You lost everything.)*
• What "secret" did Larsen discover about *Press Your Luck? (It wasn't really a game of luck. There were different patterns.)*
• How much money did he win? *(over $100,000)*
• Did he cheat? *(no)*
• How did Larsen lose his money? *(He lost some in bad business deals, and he was robbed.)*

Discussion Topics

• Ask students to describe game shows from their countries.
• Ask students if they think game shows are fair, or if the producers "fix" the games so that only a few people can win.
• Ask if students would like to be contestants on a game show and why or why not.

Grammar Presentation (pages 281–283)

Identify the Grammar

Michael Larsen <u>was</u> an ice cream truck driver. In 1983, he <u>lost</u> his job.
You <u>pushed</u> a button and it <u>landed</u> on one of several squares.
The game <u>wasn't</u> really a game of chance.
How <u>did</u> he <u>do</u> it?
<u>Was</u> it a trick?
How much <u>did</u> he <u>win</u>?
What <u>happened</u> to Larsen?
<u>Did</u> he <u>enjoy</u> it?
His life <u>did not get</u> better.

Grammar Charts

• The grammar pertaining to the past tense was taught in Units 20–22. If a detailed review of the Grammar Charts is needed, see Student Book pages 190, 200–201, and 208.
• For a quick review number the sentences in Identify the Grammar 1–10. Make a handout or an OHT of the following table, but leave the Example number column blank. Instruct students to fill in the sentence numbers. Tell them to leave a space blank if there is no example of a structure.

Past-tense verb structure	Example number [answers provided for teacher]
Affirmative sentence (all verbs except *be*)	2, 3
Affirmative sentence with *be*	1
Negative sentence (all verbs except *be*)	10
Negative sentence with *be*	4
Yes/no question (all verbs except *be*)	9
Yes/no question with *be*	6
Wh- question	5, 7, 8
Wh- question with *be*	—
Wh- question about the subject (all verbs except *be*)	8
Wh- question about the subject with *be*	—

Grammar Notes

Notes 1–7 *(Exercises 1–4)*

• Put students into 10 pairs or teams, corresponding to the 10 charts on pages 281–282 in the Student Book. Students can also work alone if your class is small.
• Write the titles of the 10 charts on slips of paper and put the slips in a hat. Have each pair (team) of students pull one slip out of the hat.
• Instruct students to study their chart and write two sentences or questions like the ones in the chart. For example, if the slip says "*Wh-* Questions with *Be*," the students should

write two questions similar to the ones in the chart on page 282.

- In addition, have students find the note from pages 281–282 that matches their chart. For example, Note 6 matches the chart *Wh-Questions about the Subject*.

- Finally, have students stand and present their sentences, chart, and the matching note to the class. Have them write their sentences on the board or on an OHT, then point out the chart and the note(s) that match the sentences.

Focused Practice (pages 284–288)

Exercise 2

recluse: someone who likes to live alone and avoids other people

studio apartment: a small apartment with only one main room

outfit: a set of clothes worn together

auditor: a person whose job is to check a company's financial records to make sure they are correct

invest: to give money to a company or bank, or to buy something, in order to get a profit later

Exercise 3

degree: the qualification given to someone who has successfully completed a course of study at a university

YMCA: Young Men's Christian Association; an organization that provides places to stay, sports, activities, and training for young people

contribution: something that is done or given to help something or someone else be successful

Exercise 4

physician: a medical doctor

outstanding: better than anyone or anything else; excellent

admission: permission to enter a place or become a member of a school or organization

Communication Practice (pages 288–290)

Exercise 5

Before students listen, have them predict what some of the questions will be.

Exercise 6

If students are having difficulty thinking of questions, you can help by suggesting areas of knowledge for them to write about. Some examples are art, literature, science, history, movies, animals, and geography. You can also encourage students to think of subsections of these topics. For example, art can be divided into many subcategories such as painting, sculpture, architecture, and photography.

To make this activity a bit more exciting, you may wish to make it into a game with rounds consisting of eight to ten questions. Contestants can get points for each correct answer, and the winners of each round can then play against each other in a playoff. If you have time, you can keep going until you have a class winner.

Exercise 7

Make it clear that students are not limited to the language in columns A and B. Encourage them to make use of other adjectives they know in part A and to provide as much detail as possible in part B.

Exercise 8

After students have written their questions, have pairs of A students and pairs of B students respectively check each other's questions for errors. Then they can go on to do the activity in A-B pairs as described.

Exercise 9

Questions to generate ideas and elicit vocabulary:

- What is the musician's name?
- Where is he or she from?
- What was his or her childhood like?
- When and how did he or she become interested in music?
- What kind of music does he or she play or write?
- What is his or her most famous song or composition?
- Why do you like this musician?

Further Practice

Have students pick an incident from their past to write or talk about. Find a way to limit the time frame so that students are not overwhelmed by the task. For example, you can instruct students to write about: a scary/funny/dangerous experience, a moment/day that changed my life, five unforgettable minutes, or an important decision.

If you do this activity orally, follow these steps: Have students pick their topics and prepare their talks at home. Instruct them to make notes and look up words they will need, but not to write out the whole talk as a paragraph. Inform students ahead of time whether you will or will not allow them to use their notes as they speak. In class, have students speak to the whole group or in small groups, depending on the size of your class. Encourage listeners to ask questions.

GRAMMAR OUT OF THE BOX . . . . . .

Book report. Have students do a book report. Arrange for them to read short books suitable to their level. You may get these from your school library, an ESL publisher, or the children's section of a public library. Find a book report form online (search for "book report" + form), or create your own. Some typical topics to include are:
• title of book
• author
• genre
• number of pages
• setting
• time period
• main characters
• plot summary (beginning, middle, end)
  Additional questions:
• Did any of the characters in this book remind you of yourself? How?
• How did this book make you feel?
• Who was your favorite character, and why?
• What did you learn from this book?
• Would you recommend this book to a friend? Why or why not?

 UNIT 30 *Be Going to* for the Future

Unit Overview

Students will learn:
• *be going to* + base form in future sentences and questions
• short answers to questions with *be going to*
• future time markers
• the use of the present progressive tense with future meaning

Grammar in Context (pages 300–301)

Vocabulary

fitness: the condition of being healthy and strong

track: a course with a special surface for running

court: an area made for playing games such as basketball and tennis

tuition: money paid for attending a school

fancy: expensive and fashionable

state-of-the-art: newest and most modern

Comprehension Questions

• Where did these letters appear? *(in a college newspaper)*
• What are they about? *(a new fitness center)*
• Which writer is against it? *(the first one)*
• Why is this person against it? *(It's going to cost a lot of money, so tuition is probably going to increase.)*
• How does the other writer feel? *(She loves the idea.)*
• Why is she in favor of it? *(The gym will help students relax. Also, if they use the gym, they will not gain weight.)*

Discussion Topics

• If your school has a fitness center, ask students if they use it.
• Ask when, why, and how students attend a fitness center.
• Ask students which writer they agree with.

Grammar Presentation (pages 301–302)

Identify the Grammar

It's going to have a beautiful gym.
Where is the money going to come from?
We're not going to have time to study.
I'm going to go there every day.
We're going to pay for it.

Grammar Charts

• Write the examples of the target grammar point on the board. Call on students to read them, and ask them to identify the subject and the verb in each sentence.
• Ask the following questions to focus students' attention on the form:
  —Which form of *be* is used with *going to*? *(If the subject is singular, use* is. *If the subject is plural, use* are.)
  —Does the phrase *going to* change? *(no)*
  —What comes after *going to*? *(the base form of the verb)*
• Teach the reduced pronunciation of *going to,* /gonna/. Have students listen and repeat a complete conjugation after you:
  —I'm going to study for a test tonight.
  —You're going to study . . .
  —He's going to study . . .

- On the board or on an overhead transparency, prepare a chart like the one below. Give students cues and elicit the forms. Have students fill in the chart. For example:

TEACHER: Buy a new car. Affirmative.

A: I'm going to buy a new car.

TEACHER: Negative.

A: I'm not going to buy a new car.

		Short answers
Affirmative		
Negative		
Yes/no question		
Wh- question		

- When all the correct forms have been filled in, use the chart as a model for a transformation drill. Provide cues and indicate what you want students to say. You can drill each pattern separately. For example:

TEACHER: Eat dinner. I.

A: I'm going to eat dinner.

TEACHER: You.

B: You're going to eat dinner.

TEACHER: We.

C: We're going to eat dinner.

- To make the drill more challenging, mix patterns and persons, but change only one element each time. For example:

TEACHER: We're going to be late. *Yes/no.*

A: Are we going to be late?

TEACHER: Short answer, affirmative.

B: Yes, we are.

TEACHER: Negative statement.

C: We're not going to be late.

TEACHER: She.

D: She's not going to be late.

TEACHER: Study tonight.

E: She's not going to study tonight.

Grammar Notes

Note 1 *(Exercises 2–4)*
- Call on students to read the explanation and the notes.
- Inform students that they will learn about *will* in the next unit.

Note 2 *(Exercises 2–4)*
- Model the examples of uncontracted and contracted forms for the students.
- To make sure students can hear the difference, alternate saying sentences with contracted and uncontracted forms. Tell students to hold up one finger if they hear an uncontracted form and two fingers if they hear a contracted one.
- Do a transformation drill. Say sentences with uncontracted forms and have students produce the contracted form. For example:

TEACHER: It is going to ["gonna"] rain.

CLASS: It's going to ["gonna"] rain.

- Put students in pairs. Have them make sentences with contracted and uncontracted forms. Their partners should hold up fingers to indicate what they heard.
- Write a mix of correct and incorrect sentences on the board. Have students identify and correct the errors. (You can use the wrong sentences from the book.)
- Call on students to read the note and the examples.

Note 3 *(Exercises 2–4)*
- Have students read the explanation and the examples, matching each example with its meaning.
- Put students in pairs or small groups. Have them write two sentences for each meaning (facts, predictions, plans).
- Have pairs or groups share sentences.

Note 4 *(Exercise 4)*
- Have students read the explanation and the example. Then model a few sentences about your plans for the evening or the weekend.
- Go around the room and have each student make one sentence about what he or she will probably do this evening / this weekend.

Note 5 *(Exercise 5)*
- Have students read the note and the examples.
- Copy the time markers from the chart on the board.
- Put students in pairs for a role play. One student is a fortune-teller. The other student

is a client. The fortune-teller pretends to look into a crystal ball and makes predictions about the other student's future, using the time markers on the board. For example: "Tomorrow you're going to make a new friend. Next week you're going to have a small accident."
• Students switch roles.

Note 6
• Read the explanation and the examples. Reinforce the conditions where the present progressive is possible: with *go* and with words of movement and transportation. You may wish to list common pairs of verbs that are often coupled with the present progressive with future meaning:
—arrive/depart
—come/go
—take off/land (for planes)
—leave/arrive
• Write sentences with *be going to* on the board or an OHT. Instruct students to change the verb tense to present progressive if possible. Include a mix of action and non-action verbs. For example:
It's going to rain later tonight. (not possible)
My brother's train is going to leave at 8 P.M. (possible)
They're going to buy a new TV. (not possible)
I'm going to go to the supermarket. (possible)
The secretary is going to leave early today. (possible)
The new furniture is going to arrive next Wednesday. (possible)

Focused Practice (pages 303–307)

Exercise 1
mayor: someone who leads the government of a town or city

destroy: to damage something so badly that it no longer exists

Exercise 2
humid: warm and wet, as in moist air

taxes: money that workers must pay the government, often based on their income

Exercise 3
tower over: to be much taller than the people or things around you

construction: the process or method of building something large such as a house, road, or skyscraper

Exercise 4
nephew: the son of your brother or sister, or the son of your husband or wife's brother or sister

horror movie: a movie that is supposed to make you feel scared

Exercise 5
senior: an old person, especially over the age of 65

Exercise 6
newsletter: a short written report of news about a club, organization, or particular subject that is sent regularly to people

residents: people who live in a place

Communication Practice (pages 308–309)

Exercise 7
Before students listen, have them predict the reasons for and against building the new building.

Exercise 8
This activity can also be done in small groups.

Exercise 9
This activity can also be done in groups. In addition, students can decide what portion of the $200,000 they will devote to each thing they decide to do.

Exercise 10
Questions to generate ideas and elicit vocabulary:
• What are the advantages of the change you picked?
• What are the disadvantages?
• Who benefits from this change? Who loses?
• How much will this change cost?
• Will this change hurt the environment?

Further Practice
• Have students write you a letter (serious or funny) about a change they'd like you to make in the class and discuss how this change is going to affect them. For example, if your class begins early in the morning, students might ask you to start class an hour later. This will enable them to sleep longer, and they're going to be more active in your class.
• Put students in small groups. Assign each group one of the topics below, or have students pick their own. The group should make predictions with *be going to* and share them with the whole class. For example:
Transportation: In 50 years, cars are going to

use hydrogen fuel. They're not going to use gasoline.

transportation	government	food
computers	sports	music
health	schools	fashion

 **OUT OF THE BOX . . . . . .**

What's going to happen next? Bring in pictures that tell some kind of story. Put students in pairs or small groups and have them tell what has just happened and what is going to happen next. Have groups switch pictures every five minutes so that each group goes through several rounds of storytelling. This activity can also be done in writing. Collect several stories for each picture and post them on the wall or bulletin board with the picture. Leave them up for a few days so that students can read the various stories. A third possibility is to collect the pictures and stories and make a book out of them. Students can check out the book and take it home overnight.

 UNIT 31 *Will* **for the Future; Future Time Markers**

Unit Overview

Students will learn:
- the use of *will* + base form to express future predictions, promises, requests, offers, and refusals
- future time markers and contractions

Grammar in Context (pages 310–311)

Background Notes

Letters to the Editor are sent to the newspaper by readers who want to express their opinions about issues that are important to them.

Vocabulary

common: ordinary; easily found or seen

cold: an illness caused by a virus with symptoms of sneezing, runny nose, coughing, and weakness

solar energy: energy that comes from the sun

coin: a round piece of money made of metal

Comprehension Questions

In the year 2050,
- What won't people eat? *(meat or fish)*
- How will people look? *(bigger and taller)*
- How will we travel? *(solar cars and private planes)*
- Where will we go? *(to the moon and the past and future)*
- How long will we live? *(100 years on average)*

Discussion Topics

- Take a class vote on each of the predictions in the reading. See how many people think these things will happen by 2050.
- Ask students to make additional predictions about the future.

Grammar Presentation (pages 311–313)

Identify the Grammar

More people <u>will be</u> vegetarians.
There <u>will be</u> a cure for the common cold.
Travel to the moon <u>will be</u> common.

Grammar Charts

- Write the example sentences above on the board and have students read them.
- Ask students the following:
  —What form comes after *will*? *(base form)*
  —Does *will* change if the subject is singular or plural? *(no)*
- Elicit the negative statement, *yes/no* question, and short answer for the examples. Have students write these forms on the board as well.
  More people won't be vegetarians.
  Will more people be vegetarians? (Yes, they will. / No, they won't.)
  There won't be a cure for the common cold.
  Will there be a cure for the common cold? (Yes, there will. / No, there won't.)
  Travel to the moon won't be common.
  Will travel to the moon be common? (Yes, it will. / No, it won't.)
- Drill the affirmative and negative statements in the charts. Say the first-person singular form, then cue students with the other pronouns. For example:
  TEACHER: I will leave tomorrow. You.
  CLASS: You will leave tomorrow.
- For *yes/no* questions, model the first question. Indicate with your head whether the answer should be yes or no, and have the class

provide the short answer. After that, cue students with the remaining pronouns and have them form the questions. For example:

TEACHER: Will I arrive tomorrow?

CLASS: Yes, you will.

TEACHER: You.

CLASS: Will you arrive tomorrow?

(Indicate No)

CLASS: No, I won't.

TEACHER: He.

CLASS: Will he arrive tomorrow?

(Indicate Yes)

CLASS: Yes, he will.

• Drill the pronunciation of the contractions. First, say the contractions and have students repeat them. Second, say the uncontracted forms, and have students provide the contracted ones.
• Read the chart of future time markers and have the class repeat the expressions after you.

Grammar Notes

Notes 1–3 *(Exercises 2–5)*
• Have students read the explanations and the examples.
• Put students in groups of four or five. Instruct them to take turns reading the predictions in the reading, transforming them into the negative and question forms, and answering the questions according to their real opinion of what will happen. For example:

A [reading]: Robots will cook our meals.

B: Robots won't cook our meals.

C: Will robots cook our meals?

D: Yes, they will / No, they won't.

[If D says yes, continue as follows]

C: When?

D: In 20 years.

Note 4 *(Exercises 2–5)*
• Have students read the note and the examples.
• Pretend to be angry about things students have done. They should respond by promising to do or not to do those things in the future. For example:

TEACHER: You forgot to write your name on your paper.

STUDENT: Next time I'll write my name on my paper. / I won't forget next time.

Other student "misdeeds":
—You forgot your textbook.
—You didn't turn in your homework.
—You spilled coffee on the table.
—You didn't say good morning.
—You fell asleep in class.
—You forgot the teacher's birthday.

Note 5 *(Exercises 2–4)*
• Have students read the explanation and the examples.
• Write the situations below on slips of paper:
—You are carrying a load of books and cannot open the door.
—You dropped your pencil on the floor.
—You spilled coffee on your shirt.
—You want to open the window, but it's stuck.
—You're the teacher. You dropped all the students' papers on the floor.
—You can't open your bottle of correction fluid because it's glued shut.
• Put students in pairs. Give a slip to one of them. The student with the slip should pantomime the situation and ask for help, and the other should respond.
Example: You don't have an eraser.

A: Will you please lend me your eraser?

B: Sure I will. Here it is.

Note 6 *(Exercises 2–5)*
• Have students read the explanation and the examples.
• Elicit negative statements about tomorrow's weather in a variety of cities. For example:

TEACHER: Bangkok.

A: It won't snow tomorrow.

B: It won't be cold.

TEACHER: Amsterdam.

• Go around the room and have each student name a food or drink he or she will not eat or drink. For example:

A: I won't eat liver. I hate it.

B: I won't eat cheese. It's fattening.

C: I won't eat seaweed. It's too salty.

Note 7 *(Exercises 2–5)*
• Have students read the explanation and the example.
• Ask students to say what they will probably do next weekend.

Note 8 *(Exercises 2–5)*
• Read the examples first. Ask students to explain the difference between the first two

sentences (future) and the third one (past). Explain that time expressions with *this* can have two meanings, depending on the time of speaking. For example, at 7 P.M., *this morning* is in the past. At 8 A.M., *this morning* is in the present or future.

- Practice by giving students the following cues:
  —the time *now*
  —time marker with *this*
  —an action

For example:

TEACHER: 2 P.M., this morning, go to the doctor.

A: This morning I went to the doctor.

TEACHER: 11 A.M., this afternoon, go to the doctor.

B: This afternoon I'm going to the doctor. (Or: I'm going to go / will go).

Focused Practice (pages 314–316)

Exercise 2

forecast: description of what is likely to happen in the future, based on information you have now

shoot some hoops: play basketball

spoil one's appetite: take away a person's desire to eat a meal by eating snacks too soon before the meal

Exercise 3

shortly: in a short time

marriage proposal: an occasion when someone asks you to marry him or her

a shot: the act of putting medicine in someone's body by using a needle

Exercise 4

housing: the buildings that people live in

taxes: money that you must pay the government from the money you earn

crime: an action that is wrong and punishable by law

Exercise 5

fascinating: very interesting

Communication Practice (pages 317–318)

Exercise 7

Before students listen, explain the terms "TV news anchor," "lottery," and "winnings."

Exercise 8

To make this into a true survey, have students vote on each prediction. For example, ask,

"Who thinks more people will be vegetarians?" Record the results on the board. You can also write the students' own predictions on the board and have the class vote on them.

Exercise 9

Suggest categories of popular items, such as fashion, cars, hi-tech devices, styles of music, body decoration, dances, or slang words.

Exercise 10

This activity can also be done in pairs. Each student writes the other student's fortune on a piece of paper. Then, on a different paper, each student writes the fortune he or she would like to have. Each student then compares the fortune he or she wants with the fortune he or she got.

Further Practice

Put students in pairs and have them role-play one or more of the following situations, showing the different meanings of *will*.

- Student 1 is upset because Student 2 (spouse, roommate, relative) hasn't done his or her share of the housework. For example, he or she was supposed to wash the dinner dishes and hasn't done it. Student 1 confronts Student 2 and complains. Student 2 promises to do the work later.
- Student 1 asks Student 2 for help with something (homework, moving into a new apartment, getting to a doctor's appointment, buying a gift for someone). Student 2 agrees to help.
- Student 1 (a parent) agrees to lend the family car to Student 2 (the teenage son or daughter). As the child is leaving, the parent reminds the teenager of many things. For example, "Don't forget to lock the car." Each time the teenager patiently responds, "I won't."
- Student 1 (a pet-owner) is telling Student 2 (a veterinarian) why he or she is worried that his or her pet (dog, cat, bird, horse) is sick. For example, "He won't eat." The vet gives advice.

Fun with a song. Print out the lyrics for "All My Loving" by the Beatles, but leave blank spaces in place of *will* + base form of verb. Have students listen one time through and read along. Then, have students listen and try to fill in the verbs. Next, have students listen and check their work. Finally, play the song for students to sing along.

UNIT 32 *May* or *Might* for Possibility

Unit Overview

Students will learn the form and use of *may* and *might* to express possibility.

Grammar in Context (pages 319–320)

Vocabulary

meteorologist: a weather scientist

unseasonably: in a way that is warmer or colder than usual for a particular time of year

commute: the trip made to work every day

flooding: a situation in which an area that is usually dry becomes covered with water

mild: not too severe or serious

shower: a short period of rain

Comprehension Questions

• How will the weather be tomorrow? *(cold and windy)*
• Is it going to rain? *(yes)*
• Why should people use public transportation to go to work? *(There will be flooding on the highways.)*
• How will the weather be on Wednesday and Thursday? *(rainy on Wednesday and milder on Thursday)*
• Will it be sunny on Thursday? *(maybe)*
• Is Alex going to play soccer tomorrow? *(maybe)*
• How was the weather last Friday? *(awful)*
• Does Alex enjoy playing in the mud? *(yes)*

Discussion Topics

• Have students describe the typical weather for each season in their native region or country.
• Talk about how the weather in their country or region affects the types of sports that are played.
• Ask students how their routine changes when there is heavy rain.

Grammar Presentation (pages 320–321)

Identify the Grammar

There <u>may be</u> flooding on the highways.
The weather <u>may become</u> milder.
We <u>might see</u> some sun.

Grammar Charts

• Write the examples of target grammar on the board. Ask students to read them. Underline the words *may* and *might.* Ask:
—Are we sure there will be flooding? *(no)*
—Are we sure the weather will become milder? *(no)*
—Are we sure we will see sun? *(no)*
—What do *may* and *might* mean? *("maybe")*
—What word comes after *may* and *might*? *(base form of the verb)*
—Do we add *-s* to these words? *(no)*
• Do a substitution drill with affirmative statements and *may* or *might*. Give a base sentence, such as "I may go to a movie tonight." Then cue students with different pronouns, as follows:

TEACHER: You.

CLASS: You may go to a movie tonight.

TEACHER: We.

CLASS: We may go to a movie tonight.

• Follow the same procedure with a negative sentence and use *might*. For example, "They might not come."
• Repeat, cueing students with pronouns, sentence type (affirmative or negative), and *may* or *might*. For example:

TEACHER: I might go out later. Negative.

A: I might not go out later.

TEACHER: She may.

B: She may not go out later.

TEACHER: Affirmative.

C: She may go out later.

Grammar Notes

Notes 1–2 *(Exercises 2–3)*
• Ask a pair of students to read the first two examples. Ask a different student to read the explanations in both notes.
• In a chain, go around the room and ask students what they're going to do this weekend. Students should answer with *may/might*.

Notes 3–4   *(Exercise 3)*

- Ask a student to read the explanation in Note 3. You may wish to simplify it with the following simple rule: "Don't use *may* or *might* in questions about the future."
- Ask pairs of students to read the examples.
- Have students read Note 4 and the examples.
- Do an error correction exercise based on all the wrong sentences in Notes 2, 3, and 4. Write the following sentences on the board and have students correct them:

  Sana may to get married next year.

  Hector mightn't come to the class party.

  May Kang graduate this year?

  Marta is sure she might go to San Francisco next weekend.

  Might you return to your country after the end of this course?

  Peter might works for his father next year.

→ For additional practice, see the Supplementary Activities on page 132.

Note 5   *(Exercise 4)*

- Have students read the examples and transform them from *maybe* to *may/might* and vice versa.
- Drill the transformation. For example:

  TEACHER: Maybe the president will go to Japan.

  CLASS: The president might go to Japan.

  TEACHER: Maybe the class will go to Japan.

  CLASS: The class might go to Japan.

  TEACHER: Maybe it won't rain.

  CLASS: It might not rain.

- Reverse the order. Cue students with *may/might* and have them rephrase the sentences with *maybe*.
- Put students in pairs and have them ask each other about their plans for the weekend or the coming vacation, following the model in Note 1.

Focused Practice (pages 322–324)

Exercise 1

definitely: certainly and without any doubt

Exercise 2

forecast: a description of what is likely to happen in the future, based on information you have now

operation: the process of cutting into someone's body to fix or remove a part that is damaged

Exercise 3

pale: more white than usual

engine: the part of a machine that produces power to make it move

Communication Practice (pages 324–325)

Exercise 6

Before students listen, have them look at the list of items the man is taking and try to guess where he might be going.

Exercise 7

- Instruct students to answer truthfully.
- Model one or two exchanges with a student before the class divides into pairs.

Exercise 8

Questions to generate ideas and elicit vocabulary:

- How will the weather be tomorrow?
- What sport or activity can people do in this weather?
- What do they need to prepare for the weather?

Further Practice

Have students talk about plans for the future. Write the following on the board:

Five years from now . . .

100%	*will*
80%	*will probably*
50%	*may, might, may not, might not*
10%	*probably won't*
0%	*won't*

Put students in small groups to have a conversation about their plans for the future. Instruct students to ask each other questions with *will/be going to.* Their goal should be to use each of the structures above in their answers.

GRAMMAR OUT OF THE BOX . . . . . .

News reports. Bring newspapers to class. Assign stories to pairs of students, or let them choose their own. Students should read the article and prepare a short summary of what happened or is happening. Then they should use the expressions from Further Practice above to say three things that will or might happen next. Put pairs of students together and have each pair present their report to the other pair. Alternately, have the pairs of students present their reports to the whole class.

Questions with *Any/ Some/How Much/ How Many*; Quantity Expressions

UNIT 33

Unit Overview

This unit presents quantifiers with count and non-count nouns. Students will learn:
• how to form statements and questions with *some, any, how much, how many, a little,* and *a few*
• expressions with measure words and containers, such as *a quart of yogurt* and *a can of Coke*

Grammar in Context (pages 334–335)

Background Notes

Questionnaires are very popular in American magazines, especially questionnaires about health, money, and people's love lives. Questionnaires are entertaining and often informative, but readers should not consider the results to be scientific or authoritative.

Vocabulary

questionnaire: a written set of questions about a particular subject that is given to people in order to collect information

calculate: to find out something or to measure something using numbers

complete: to write the information that is needed on a form

serving: an amount of food that is enough for one person

Comprehension Questions

• What do you receive for filling out the questionnaire and sending your answers to *Health and Fitness* magazine? *(a free newsletter)*
• What does it mean if you have a high score? *(You are healthy.)*
• What does it mean if you have a low score? *(You are less healthy.)*

Discussion Topics

• Is your score high, average, or low?
• Do you have any bad habits that you could change in order to improve your health?

Grammar Presentation (pages 335–337)

Identify the Grammar

All the questions and answers in the reading provide examples of the target grammar for this unit. Rather than writing the entire reading on the board, have students refer to their books as you go over the Grammar Charts.

Grammar Charts

• Follow this general procedure:
  —Call on students to read each chart, or read the items and have students repeat after you.
  —Have students find an example from the reading that illustrates the information in each chart.
  —Ask questions to help students notice the grammar.
• Read the first chart and review the pronunciation of *a/an.* Elicit the rule from the students. Have them find examples from the reading. *(an hour, a day, a week)*
• Read the two charts dealing with *some/any.* Ask students:
  —What kind of noun comes after *some*? *(plural count or non-count noun)*
  —What kind of noun comes after *any*? *(plural count or non-count noun)*
  —Which word do we use in affirmative statements? *(some)*
  —Which word do we use in negative statements? *(any)*
  —Can we use both words in *yes/no* questions? *(yes)*
  —Can you find an example of these words in the reading? *(question 4—some candy)*
• Read the charts showing questions and answers with *how much.* Ask students:
  —What kind of noun comes after *how much*? *(non-count)*
  —What examples can you find in the reading? *(how much time, how much coffee, how much candy)*
  —How do we answer questions with *how much*? *(a lot of, two quarts of, etc.)*
  —Which answer doesn't use *of*? *(a little)*
  —What kind of noun do we use after *a little*? *(non-count)*
  —Which question shows examples of answers to *how much* questions? *(question 4)*
• Read the charts showing questions and answers with *how many.* Ask:
  —What kind of noun comes after *how many*? *(plural count)*

—What examples can you find in the reading? *(how many vegetables, how many vacations)*

—How do we answer questions with *how many*? Find examples in the reading. *(numbers 3 and 5—three vacations, six servings)*

—What kind of noun do we use after *a few*? *(plural count)*

Grammar Notes

Note 1 *(Exercise 2)*

It is probably enough to read the explanation and the examples in the Student Book. However, if you find it necessary to review *a/an*, have students list items in their pockets, purses, or lunch bags. This will elicit items such as *a wallet, some lipstick, an orange, a sandwich.*

Note 2 *(Exercises 3–4)*

• Since this note is long, present the uses of *some/any* first and have the class read the items and examples as a follow-up. First, to practice statements with *some/any*, prepare a chart like the one below and write it on the board or on an overhead transparency. Include both non-count and plural count nouns. To introduce the activity, provide a context for the items—for example, say that the items in the "yes" column, are in your refrigerator and you have run out of the items in the "no" column. Point to each item and have students make sentences. For example: "Ms. Estes has some milk in her refrigerator. She doesn't have any beer."

Yes	No
milk	*beer*
apples	*yogurt*
hot dogs	*carrots*
margarine	*eggs*

• Put students in pairs. Each student should make a similar chart with three or four items in each column.

• Students exchange papers and make sentences about their partner's refrigerator. *(I see that you have some cheese, but you don't have any chicken.)*

• To practice *yes/no* questions, keep students in pairs and have them ask questions about the contents of their partner's refrigerator, bathroom, book bag, lunchbox, or car. You can provide lists for students to ask about, or they can think of their own items. Provide the following model:

TEACHER: Do you have any potatoes in your refrigerator?

A: Yes, I do / No, I don't.

→ For additional practice, see the Supplementary Activities on page 132.

Note 3 *(Exercise 2)*

• Select students to read the explanation and the examples.

• Drill the contrast between *a little* and *a few*. Cue students with plural count and non-count nouns and have them put the nouns in phrases. For example:

TEACHER: Pictures.

CLASS: A few pictures.

TEACHER: Time.

CLASS: A little time.

Note 4 *(Exercise 5)*

• Select students to read the explanation and the examples.

• To practice, put students in pairs or small groups. Provide the following context: Each of them received a $100 gift certificate for their birthdays. They should make a list of five items they bought.

• Next, students should practice conversations like the one below:

A: I bought some CDs.

B: How many did you buy?

A: Three.

B: Well, I bought some wine.

A: How much did you buy?

B: Three bottles.

• Encourage students to add comments and questions to the conversation. For example, A might want to ask B which CDs he or she bought.

Note 5 *(Exercise 2)*

• If possible, bring in real objects illustrating the measurements and containers in the note, such as a quart of apple juice or a cup of coffee.

• Write the measure words and containers on the board. Elicit from the students other items that come in these quantities and list those on the board as well.

• Put students in pairs. Have them say which of the items on the board they have used or bought recently. For example:

—Yesterday I bought a quart of milk.

—This morning I had a cup of coffee.

Note 6

- Have students read the explanation and the examples.
- Tell them they're going on a trip to _____. What will they pack? Have them make a list.
- Ask one student to read his or her list to the class. The class should respond with *"That's enough"* or *"That's not enough."*
- Have students continue the activity in pairs.

Focused Practice (pages 338–341)

Exercise 2

soda: carbonated beverages such as Coca-Cola

shelf: a long, flat board attached to a wall or in a frame that you can put things on

pie: a kind of pastry, usually filled with fruit

Exercise 3

rate: to express your opinion about the value or worth of something

report to: to tell someone, especially your manager, about what has been happening or what you are doing as part of your job

Exercise 4

out of shape: in a bad state of health or physical fitness

Exercise 6

treadmill: a piece of exercise equipment on which you can run or walk while staying in the same place

Communication Practice (pages 341–343)

Exercise 7

Before listening, have students fill in the blanks orally with suitable items, such as *six cans of Coke, five tomatoes, a head of lettuce, a few oranges, a can of tomato sauce, a bunch of carrots.*

Exercise 8

To keep students' energy high, have them do this exercise orally first. Then ask groups to come to an agreement on answers, tally how many questions they formed correctly, and tally how many questions they answered correctly.

Exercise 9

Instead of buying food for a week, students could buy food for a dinner party, birthday party, or other special occasion.

Exercise 10

Have students get up and move around while they are doing their survey.

Exercise 11

Questions to generate ideas and elicit vocabulary:
- Which questions did you ask?
- How many people did you survey?
- What results did you expect to get for the first question?
- What results did you expect to get for the second question?

Further Practice

Make a list of items that tourists must pay for when they travel. For example: a (first-class) hotel room, a cup of coffee, a theater ticket, a taxi, parking, meals, and tips. Put students in small groups. Give them the list. Have them talk about the cost of the items on the list in their home cities. Remind them to use *how much, how many, some, any, a little,* and *a few.* For example, "How much does a theater ticket cost in your city?" Have students determine which city would be the most and least expensive to visit.

 **GRAMMAR OUT OF THE BOX** ......

Packing a virtual suitcase. In this activity, students will pack a virtual suitcase for a classmate who is going to visit their city. Students must make decisions about where their classmate will stay (if the classmate stays with the student's family, there is no need to pack any towels), what they will eat, what they will see, and so on. Put students' names into a hat. Draw pairs of names to create partners. Explain the activity to the class. Tell students, "Your partner is going to visit your city for [one week] during the month of _____. Pack a suitcase with everything your partner will need." Have students write a list. You may wish to create a drawing of an open suitcase, and students can put the list inside. Have partners sit together and present their lists to each other. Have them ask and answer questions about the items their partner chose to pack. For example:

A: I packed some insect repellent for you.

B: Why? Are insects a problem?

A: Yes. There are lots of mosquitoes in Tel Aviv in June.

UNIT 34 *Too Much / Too Many / Too + Adjective*

Grammar in Context (pages 344–346)

Vocabulary

pizza place: in casual speech, *place* is sometimes used instead of *restaurant*

Comprehension Questions

- (Climate) Which of the following cities could the woman live in?
  a. Caracas, Venezuela
  b. Montreal, Canada
  c. San Diego, California
  d. Rome, Italy
  (Montreal)
- (Employment) What is good about the place where the man lives? *(His family and friends are there.)*
- (Culture & Leisure) Does the man probably live in the countryside, a small town, or a city? *(small town)*
- (Health) Why isn't the woman worried about the number of doctors? *(She's young.)*
- (Environment) Is the man planning to stay in the place where he lives? *(yes)*
- (Education) Does the woman have children? *(yes)*

Discussion Topics

- Which city in your country has the best climate, employment, and culture?
- Can you think of any city that has a high quality of life in all six areas in the survey?

Grammar Presentation (page 346)

Identify the Grammar

There's too much air pollution.
There are too few doctors.
The winters are too long.

Grammar Charts

- Have students read the examples. Underline the phrases with *too*. Then elicit the rules from the class:
  —What kind of noun comes after *too much*? *(non-count)*
  —What kind of noun comes after *too few*? *(plural count)*
  —What kind of word comes after *too* by itself? *(an adjective)*
  —Are these examples of good things or bad things? *(bad things)*
- Go over each chart. Have students read the examples. Elicit the following:
  —What kind of noun comes after *too many*? *(plural count)*
  —What comes after *too little*? *(non-count noun)*

Grammar Notes

Notes 1–2 *(Exercises 2–7)*
- Have students read the explanations and the examples.
- Make a handout with the following chart, or write it on the board and have students copy:

too much	
too many	
too few	
too little	
too + adjective	

- Put students in pairs or small groups. Give them a context and have them make sentences using the structures in the chart. They should write the nouns or adjectives in the right-hand column. For example, if your classroom is uncomfortable, students can make sentences like the following:
  —There's too much noise.
  —There are too many students, and the room is too small.
  —There are too few windows.
  —There's too little air.
  —The room is too cold.
- Other contexts to talk about:
  —students' dorm rooms
  —their cars
  —the bus or train they take to come to school
  —a restaurant
  —a gym or sports facility
- Have pairs or groups compare sentences.

Focused Practice (pages 347–351)

Exercise 1

expressway: a wide road in a city on which cars can travel fast

rush hour: the time of day when there are a lot of vehicles on the road because people are going to and from work

bugs: insects

Exercise 2

highway: similar to an expressway or a freeway

Exercise 4

violent: likely to attack, kill, or hurt people

Exercise 6

neither: not one or the other

Exercise 7

boss: the person who employs you or who is in charge of your work

Communication Practice (pages 351–352)

Exercise 8

Before students listen, ask students for ideas of things people might like and dislike about apartments.

Exercise 9

Have two students read the examples in front of the class. Once students are in pairs, they can do all five scenarios, or you can assign each couple one scenario and then ask them to perform it in front of the class.

Exercise 10

Write all the quantifiers on the board. Elicit one sentence for each quantifier. Try using a different context to avoid modeling sentences that students might want to make in groups.

Exercise 11

Questions to generate ideas and elicit vocabulary:
• What is the name of a book, movie, or TV show that you didn't like?
• Why didn't you like it?

Further Practice

On the board, list all the quantifiers practiced in Units 33 and 34. They include *one, a few, some, many, much, a lot of, any, a little, too*

many, too much, and *not enough.* Have students role-play a short phone conversation about the situation they practiced in Grammar Notes, using the quantifiers on the board. Put students in pairs. One student is the complainer. The other student is a friend or family member who listens sympathetically and gives advice (See Unit 19). For example:

A: I hate my dorm room.

B: Why? What's wrong?

A: The air conditioner doesn't work, so it's always too hot. Also, there's too little light.

B: Why don't you buy another lamp?

Movie talk. Bring in a movie and watch it together. Afterward, have students discuss what they liked and didn't like about it. Elements to consider:
• the story line
• the characters: their looks, personality, or behavior
• technical aspects of the film, such as the sound, special effects, and cinematography
• the music
• the length of the movie
• the quality of the acting

 UNIT 35 **Possessives**

Unit Overview

Students will:
• learn possessive adjectives (*my* bike) and possessive pronouns (The bike is *mine.*)
• review subject and object pronouns

Grammar in Context (pages 353–354)

Vocabulary

tell (them) apart: to recognize differences between one or more things

license (plate): a sign with numbers and letters on it at the front and back of a car

horn: the thing in a car that you push to make a sound as a warning

Before students answer the questions, have students look at the pictures and try to find the differences among the four bikes. Help students with bicycle vocabulary such as seat, license, basket, and horn.

Comprehension Questions

• Where did Jasmine's family buy the bikes? *(at a huge sale)*
• What is special about Jasmine's bike? *(It has a basket in the front.)*
• What does Johnny's bike have? *(a license in the back)*
• Which bike has a higher seat? *(Johnny's)*
• What does Amy's bike have? *(a bag in the back)*
• Whose bike has a horn? *(Roger and Ted's)*

Discussion Topics

• Do you have a bike? What does it look like?
• Who rides bicycles in your family or culture—men, women, young people, old people, teenagers, rich people, poor people, or all of these?

Grammar Presentation (pages 354–355)

Identify the Grammar

POSSESSIVE ADJECTIVES
1. *Your family's bikes are all the same.*
2. *That one is my brother Johnny's bike.*

POSSESSIVE PRONOUNS
3. *Mine has a basket in the front.*
4. *His has a higher seat.*
5. *Hers has a bag in the back.*
6. *The rest of ours don't.*
7. *Theirs has a horn.*

Grammar Charts

• Write the examples from Identify the Grammar on the board. Call on students to read them. As students read, underline the target structures *(Your, my, Mine, His, Hers, ours, Theirs)*. Point to and identify each example as a possessive adjective or a possessive pronoun.
• To demonstrate the difference, ask students to identify the nouns in sentences 1 and 2 *(bikes, one, bike)*. Explain that the "belonging" words before the nouns are adjectives.

• Ask students to identify the part of speech of the underlined words in sentences 3–7. *(All are subjects except* ours, *which is the object of a preposition.)* Point out that these words are possessive pronouns. If necessary, remind students that pronouns replace nouns.
• Read the sentences in the top chart. Have students repeat after you.
• Make a handout like the chart on the bottom of Student Book page 354, but leave in only one example of each type of pronoun. Have students sit in pairs or small groups and fill in the missing pronouns.
• Optional drill: Make an overhead transparency of the handout you created. Project the transparency. Point to boxes on the chart and have students orally provide the missing pronoun.

Grammar Notes

Note 1 *(Exercises 2–4)*
• Have students read the explanation and the examples.
• Demonstrate the possessive adjectives using objects belonging to different people in the class. For example, hold up your purse and say, "This is my purse." Have students repeat.
• Drill: Hold up objects, point to people, and have students form phrases such as *your book, his pencil,* and *our desks.*
• Call up one or more students to take the role of teacher, holding up objects and pointing to people.

Note 2 *(Exercises 3–4)*
Continue demonstrating with objects belonging to people in the room. Form pairs of sentences. Say, "This is my wallet. It's mine." Hold up a book, point to a student, and look straight at him or her. Say, "This is your book. It's yours." Hold up a book and point at a male student a few feet away. Say, "This is Robert's book. It's his book. It's his."

Note 3 *(Exercise 5)*
• Have students read the explanation and the examples.
• Drill: Say sentences and have students transform them, as follows:

TEACHER: My eyes are blue.

A: Mine are blue.

TEACHER: His car is red.

B: His is red.

Focused Practice (pages 355–358)

Exercise 5

missing: not in the place where something or someone is normally expected to be

mountain bike: a strong bicycle with wide, thick tires that you can ride on rough ground

Communication Practice (pages 358–359)

Exercise 7

Before students listen, ask them to look at the picture and imagine what the young man is dreaming.

Exercise 8

- For a variation, if most students have a cell phone, collect all of the phones and put them in a bag.
- Pull the phones out of the bag one by one. As students see each phone, they should guess who the owner is by pointing at the person and saying "It's his" or "It's hers."
- If they are unable to guess, the owner of the phone should say "It's mine."

Exercise 9

Questions to generate ideas and elicit vocabulary:
- What place do/did you share with someone?
- Whom do/did you share it with? What is your relationship to this person?
- Which part of the place is/was yours? Which part is/was the other person's?
- How are the parts different?
- Is/was it difficult for you to share this space?

Further Practice

Have students bring in photos of themselves with their family and/or friends. Have them sit in small groups and tell their classmates about the people in the photos. For example, "This is my oldest brother. His name is Stefan. He's a university student at the Sorbonne in Paris. His major is economics."

 **GRAMMAR OUT OF THE BOX** ......

Photo matching. The purpose of this activity is for students to match pictures of people with their pets, homes, and cars. Collect four or five photos of each of the following:

- people (include at least one photo showing a couple or family as opposed to individuals)
- animals
- houses
- cars

Mount each set of pictures on a sheet of paper and number the pictures. Divide the class into groups ahead of time. Copy a set of pictures for each group. Put students in groups and give them a set of pictures. Instruct students to match each person with his/her/their pet, house, and car. This will take some negotiating. Put the following model exchange on the board:

A: I think the dog is the little girl's pet.

B: I disagree. I think the bird is her pet.

C: No, the snake is hers. The dog is the old man's.

There are no correct answers. At the end, one student from each group should present the group's choices to the whole class.

 UNIT 36 *Can* or *May* **for Permission**

Unit Overview

Students will learn to ask for permission and respond to requests for permission using the words *can, can't, may,* and *may not.*

Grammar in Context (pages 368–369)

Vocabulary

gain (10 pounds): to become fatter

on her own: alone

nutritionist: a medical professional who gives people advice on healthy foods to eat

calorie: a unit for measuring the amount of energy a food can produce (and, therefore, for indicating how fattening a food is)

reduction: a decrease in something, such as size, amount, or price

dieters: people trying to lose weight by controlling what they eat

eat out: to eat meals in restaurants

strict: having rules that must be obeyed

grains: foods such as corn, wheat, or rice

thrilled: very happy

keep off (weight): to stay at one's desired weight after losing weight on a diet

Comprehension Questions

- How much weight did Marita gain in college? *(She gained ten pounds.)*
- How did she try to lose weight at first? *(She tried on her own.)*
- How do people lose weight on Weight Watchers? *(They use a point system. They can't eat more than a certain number of points in a day.)*
- On Weight Watchers, where can dieters meet other dieters? *(in a weekly class)*
- How much weight did Marita lose? *(five pounds)*
- Why is Bill overweight? *(He works long hours and eats many meals out.)*
- What diet is he following? *(Atkins)*
- What can Bill eat on his diet? *(foods high in protein and fat)*
- How much weight did Bill lose? *(ten pounds)*

Discussion Topics

- Which diet is easier for you—Weight Watchers or Atkins?
- Many Americans are fat. Why do you think this is?
- Are there many fat people in your country?

Grammar Presentation (pages 370–371)

Identify the Grammar

You <u>can</u> eat any food, but you <u>may not</u> eat more than a certain number of points each day.
In this diet you <u>may</u> eat foods high in protein and fat, but you <u>can't</u> eat carbohydrates.

Grammar Charts

- Write the examples from Identify the Grammar on the board. Call on students to read them. Underline *can, may not, may, can't.*
- Ask students:
  —Which words do we use to give permission? *(can/may + verb)*
  —Which words do we use to deny permission? *(can't / may not + verb)*
- Have students look at the chart of *yes/no* questions. Ask, "What is the subject in each example?" *(I)* Explain that when we ask for permission, the subject has to be *I* or *we.*
- Ask two students to read the second question in the chart *(Can / May I help you?)* and the responses. Ask:

—If I say this, am I asking for permission? *(no)*
—What am I doing? *(offering to help someone)*
—If someone says "No thanks, I'm just looking," where is the person? *(in a shop)*
- Call on students to read the questions in the last chart. Elicit answers to the questions. *(tomorrow / this evening; behind the building / on the other side of the street)*

Grammar Notes

Note 1 *(Exercise 2)*
- Have students read the explanation and the examples.
- Elicit examples of things students can (may) and can't (may not) do in your classroom. Have them write these rules on the board. For example, *Students can drink coffee. They can't sit on the desks.* Call on different students to read the sentences and correct any errors.
- Change *can't* to *mayn't* in the sentences on the board. Ask students if this is correct. *(no)*

Note 2 *(Exercise 3)*
- Call on students to read the explanation and the examples.
- Point out that we often ask for permission when we want to borrow something. Do a chain drill in which students ask to borrow items from each other. For example:

TEACHER: May I please borrow your dictionary?

A: Sure. [To B] Can I borrow your pencil?

B: I'm sorry. I'm using it. [To C] May I borrow your car?

Note 3
- Have a student read the explanation. Have two students role play the examples.
- Ask students where people might ask "May I help you?" *(any place where people do services for clients, such as restaurants, shops, or a dry cleaner)*
- Make sure students learn the phrase *I'm just looking.*

→ For additional practice, see the Supplementary Activities on page 132.

Focused Practice (pages 371–373)

Exercise 1
patient: someone who is getting medical treatment

liquids: substances such as water, juice, or milk that are not solid or gas

registration: an official piece of paper containing details about a vehicle and the name of the owner

Exercise 2

dressing: a mixture of oil and other ingredients that you pour over a salad

(dressing) on the side: served in a small dish beside a salad instead of on it

wonton: a Chinese dish consisting of filled pockets of noodle dough served boiled (in soup) or fried

ceremony: a formal or traditional set of actions used at an important social or religious event

operation: surgery

Exercise 4

installment: one of a series of regular payments you make until you have paid all the money you owe

Communication Practice (pages 374–375)

Exercise 5

Before students listen, define the word *swelling.* Ask students what the problem could be if the woman has swelling and pain.

Exercise 6

Put students in pairs. Assign or let students choose roles A and B. The directions for Information Gap activities can be confusing. Therefore, give students time to read their directions (A or B) before they begin talking. Circulate and answer questions about vocabulary.

Exercise 7

Questions to generate ideas and elicit vocabulary:
• What sport or game do you know well?
• Are there teams? How many players are there?
• What equipment do players need?
• What is the goal of the game?
• What can players do?
• What can't players do?

Further Practice

Make a handout with the following instructions and questions. Have students sit in small groups and discuss the questions.

Instructions: Imagine that you are the people on the list. Tell what you are / are not permitted to do. Use *can / can't* and *may / may not.*

Example: a 14-year-old girl
I can't drive yet.
I can walk to school by myself.

What can you do if you are ...

a woman in your country
a man in your country
a soldier
the president of your country
a five-year-old child
a citizen of your country
a visitor in your country
a teacher at your school
a student at your school
a married person
a passenger on an airplane
a pedestrian
a _____ (add your own)

Silly laws. Below are examples of real laws that are still on the books even though they are not relevant to modern life. It is fun to read the laws and to imagine how they came about. Copy the list of laws onto a handout or an OHT. Put students in groups and have them discuss:
• What could be the origin (history) of this law?
• What will happen if someone breaks this law today?
• Do you know of any silly laws in your country?

• California: In Los Angeles, you cannot bathe two babies in the same tub at the same time.
• Canada: In Quebec, margarine cannot be the same color as butter.
• Colorado: In Denver, you may not lend your vacuum cleaner to your next-door neighbor.
• England: You cannot sell most goods on a Sunday, but you may sell a carrot.
• France: You may not land a flying saucer in a vineyard.
• Illinois: In Kirkland, bees cannot fly over the village or through any of its streets.

- **Indiana:** In Gary, people may not attend a theater or ride a public streetcar within four hours of eating garlic.
- **Kentucky:** In Lexington, you may not carry an ice cream cone in your pocket.
- **Michigan:** A woman may not cut her own hair without her husband's permission.
- **New York:** In Carmel, a man can't go outside while wearing a jacket and pants that do not match.
- **Pennsylvania:** You may not sing in the bathtub.
- **Tennessee:** In Memphis, a woman cannot drive a car unless there is a man either running or walking in front of it waving a red flag to warn approaching motorists and pedestrians.
- **Washington:** In Wilbur, people may not ride an ugly horse.
- **West Virginia:** In Nicholas County, members of the clergy cannot tell jokes during a church service.

UNIT 37 Requests, Desires, and Offers: *Would You Please . . . ?, I'd Like . . . , Would You Like . . . ?*

Unit Overview

Students will learn how to:
- make and respond to polite requests with *would you / could you / can you*
- talk about desires with *would like* and the contracted form *I'd, you'd*, etc.
- make, accept, and turn down offers with *would you like*

Grammar in Context (pages 376–377)

Vocabulary

favor: something you do for someone to help him/her

hurt: to make someone feel very upset or unhappy

Comprehension Questions

- What is an advice columnist? *(a person who works for a newspaper or magazine and publishes the answers to letters for advice from readers)*
- What favors did Monique do for Gina? *(drove her to the airport, watered her plants, and walked her dog)*

- What did Monique ask Gina to do? *(help her paint her bedroom)*
- Why did Gina say she couldn't help? *(She said she was going shopping.)*
- How did Monique feel? *(angry and hurt)*
- What did the columnist advise Monique to do? *(tell Gina how she feels)*

Discussion Topics

- If your friend asks you for a favor, will you change your plans in order to help your friend?
- What are some favors that you have done for your friends?
- What are some favors that friends have done for you?

Grammar Presentation (pages 377–378)

Identify the Grammar

QUESTIONS
Can you drive me to the airport?
Would you like me to pick you up?
Could you help me out?
Would you help me?

RESPONSES
I'd be glad to.
Of course.
Sure.
I'd like to, but I'm going shopping.

Grammar Charts

- Write the examples from Identify the Grammar on the board.
- Ask the following questions to draw students' attention to the target structures:
  —Which questions can you use to ask for a favor? *(Can you drive . . . , Could you help . . . , Would you help me?)*
  —Which question can you use to offer to help someone? *(Would you like me to . . . ?)*
  —What are some ways of agreeing to do someone a favor? *(I'd be glad to, sure, of course)*
  —How can you say that you refuse to do someone a favor? *(I'd like to, but . . .)*
- Call on students to read the Polite Requests chart. Instruct them to write three requests using *would you, could you*, and *can you*. To make it more lively, instruct them to write silly or unusual requests, such as *Could you give me a hundred dollars?* Then pair the

students up. Have them read their requests to a partner. Partners should respond with short answers from the chart.

• Have students read the Desires and Contractions charts silently. Then model the contracted forms and have students repeat after you. For example: "I'd like to help. You'd like to help." Go around the room and ask students if they're hungry or thirsty. If they say yes, ask what they'd like to eat or drink. *(I'd like a bagel. I'd like some coffee.)*

• Call on students to read the last two charts. To practice, tell students to pretend some friends have come to their home for dinner. Set up a drill like this:

TEACHER: Blueberries.

A: Would you like some blueberries?

B: Yes, thank you.

TEACHER: Coffee.

B: Would you like some coffee?

C: No, thanks.

TEACHER: Tea.

C: Would you like some tea?

D: Yes, I would.

Grammar Notes

Note 1 *(Exercises 2–5)*

• Read the first line of the Examples column, *Please help me carry these books.* Ask pairs of students to read the next three examples.

• Ask the class, "What are the three new ways of making requests? How can you agree to a request? How can you say no politely?"

• To practice, make a diagram of an empty bedroom similar to the following:

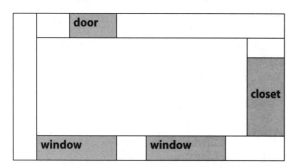

• Then give students a list of items like the following:

bed	television	2 large framed
desk	nightstand	posters
computer	dresser	bicycle
	floor lamp	shoes

• Put students in groups of three.

• Tell students to imagine they're moving into a new apartment with the help of classmates. Right now the bedroom is empty. They should use polite requests and short answers to tell their friends where to put their belongings. For example:

A: Would you please put my shoes in the closet?

B: Sure.

Note 2 *(Exercises 2–5)*

• Call on students to read the note and the examples.

• Put students in groups. Tell them to imagine they are at an ice-cream shop and have them describe the ice-cream cone they'd like to order. They should say what kind of cone they want (plain, sugar, waffle), the kind of ice cream, how many scoops, and what kind of topping. For example, "I'd like a sugar cone with one scoop of mint chip and one scoop of vanilla, and I'd like a cherry topping."

Notes 3–4 *(Exercises 2–5)*

• Call on students to read the notes and the examples.

• To practice, do mini–role plays. Give students a list of the contexts like the ones below. Have them take turns offering services or help and accepting or rejecting the offers. For example:

—a flight attendant and a passenger on an airplane:

ATTENDANT: Would you like a pillow?

PASSENGER: Yes, thank you.

—a barrista (server) taking an order from a customer at a coffee bar

—two neighbors; one has an orange tree full of ripe oranges

—two female friends; one has some beautiful clothes that don't fit her anymore, but they fit her friend

—Two people are on a bus. One is seated, and the other is standing. The seated one offers his or her seat to the other.

—A person is standing outside a supermarket with a box of kittens. The person offers to give away the kittens to shoppers as they exit the market.

Focused Practice (pages 379–381)

Exercise 1
give someone a ride: to offer to take someone somewhere in your car

lemonade: a drink made of water, lemon juice, and sugar

dumpling: a small round mass of dough, sometimes filled with meat or vegetables, cooked in boiling liquid or steamed

Exercise 3
a lift: a ride in a car

counter: a flat surface in the kitchen where you prepare food

Exercise 5
scrambled eggs: eggs that have been cooked after mixing the white and yellow parts together

rye: a type of grain that is used for making bread

Communication Practice (pages 382–384)

Exercise 7
Before students listen, have them read the directions and imagine some things that a business manager might ask his assistant to do.

Exercise 8
You may need to clarify that this is a discussion activity, not a role play. Students may think they are supposed to ask their classmates the questions.

Exercise 9
Call on two students to read the example. Ask the class for various ways that Maki could respond to the request.

Exercise 10
Call on two students to read the example. After the students finish, call on pairs to perform the various situations in front of the whole class.

Exercise 11
Questions to generate ideas and elicit vocabulary:
• Have you ever asked a classmate for a favor? What was it?
• What is something you need right now? What company sells it? Can you order it by mail?
• What are some reasons why people might ask a company to return their money?

• What are some ways that people who live together help each other?
• What favors have you done for the people you live with? What have they done for you?

Further Practice
Have students make lists of special places like the following:
• places they would like to visit before they finish this English course and return to their countries
• places they would like to visit on their next vacation
• the place they would like to visit on their honeymoon
Put students in small groups. Tell them to compare and discuss their lists and to use the language from this unit to extend the conversation. Remind students to use contractions. Example:

A: On my honeymoon, I'd like to go to Tahiti.

B: Why?

A: I saw pictures, and I think it's the most beautiful place in the world.

C: What would you like to do there?

A: Just relax, walk on the beach, swim, and eat wonderful food.

B: Could you take me with you?

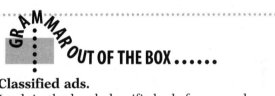
GRAMMAR OUT OF THE BOX . . . . . .

Classified ads.
Look in the local classified ads for several items for sale. Cut each one out and paste them on individual index cards. For each ad, write a brief description of a "wanted to buy" item similar to the one in the ad. Include a price limit that the person will pay for the item. Hand out the cards to the whole class, or give sets of cards to small groups. Instruct the students to walk around and talk to each other, beginning with either "Would you like to buy a . . . ?" or "I'd like to buy a . . ." Once the students find their match, they should ask questions about the item. Give them the phrase, *Could you tell me more about the (car)?* Next, they need to talk about price. Give them phrases to use, such as *How much would you like to pay?* or *I'd like to pay . . .* After everyone has agreed on a price for their items, they have to determine how the item will be delivered.

They should use phrases such as *Can you pick it up?* or *Could you deliver it to my house?* Finally, have the students report to the class on what they are buying or selling, for how much, and how the item will be delivered.

Advice: *Should, Shouldn't, Ought to, Had Better,* and *Had Better Not*

UNIT 38

Unit Overview

Students will learn modals for giving advice and talking about the right action to take in a particular situation.

Grammar in Context (pages 385–387)

Vocabulary

reception: a large formal party to celebrate something or to welcome someone

lap: the upper part of your legs when you are sitting down

palm: the inside surface of your hand between the base of your fingers and your wrist

slapping: hitting quickly with the flat part of your hand

insult: to say or do something that offends someone by showing that you do not respect him or her

sole: the bottom of your foot or shoe

deliveries: the act of bringing things somewhere or to someone

address: to use a particular name or title when speaking directly to a person or group

country of origin: the place where a person or that person's ancestors were born

Comprehension Questions

- When do people take vacations in Chile? *(in January and February)*
- In Chile, who shakes hands? Who hugs? Who kisses? *(Everyone shakes hands. Men sometimes hug. Women hug and touch cheeks while kissing the air.)*
- Which gesture means "stupid" in Chile? *(an open palm with the fingers separated)*
- Which gesture is impolite? *(slapping your right fist into your left open palm)*
- When are offices closed in Egypt? *(on Fridays)*
- Which hand should you eat with in Egypt? Why? *(The right hand. The left hand is considered unclean.)*

- In Egypt, what will happen if you put salt on your food? *(You might insult the cook.)*
- What should you do with your legs in Egypt? *(keep them on the floor)*
- Is it OK to be late in Hungary? *(no)*
- What is the normal order of names in Hungary? *(last name, first name)*

Discussion Topics

- When do people take vacations in your culture? When is your day of rest?
- In your culture, which kind of touching is normal between people who know each other well and between those who don't know each other well?
- Which gestures or behaviors are insulting in your culture?
- In your culture, what are some rules for polite behavior when people are eating?
- In your culture, what is the proper way to address people in business situations?

Grammar Presentation (pages 387–389)

Identify the Grammar

When you eat, you should keep your hands on the table.	You should not plan a business trip during (January and February) in Chile. You shouldn't eat everything on your plate.
You ought to greet and shake hands with everyone.	?
?	You'd better not make that gesture.

Grammar Charts

- Write the chart above on the board, but don't underline the target grammar. Affirmative forms are on the left, and negatives are on the right. The question marks indicate forms to elicit from the students. Ask students to read the examples. Underline the target forms as they read. Then ask questions such as the following:
  —What is the general meaning of the underlined forms? *(advice, or the right thing to do)*

—What are the affirmative forms? *(should, ought to, had better)*

—What are the negative forms? *(should not or shouldn't, had better not)* [*Ought not* is not used in modern American English.]

- Have students transform the first affirmative forms into questions as follows:

  —Should you keep your hands on the table in Chile?

  —Where should you keep your hands? Point out that we do not generally ask questions with *ought to*.

- Elicit the answer to the question "Should you keep your hands on the table in Chile?" *(Yes, you should.)* Ask a similar question to elicit a negative response: "Should you eat all the food on your plate in Egypt?" *(No, you shouldn't.)*

- Call on students to read the statements with *had better*. Ask, "What does this expression mean?" *(Something bad might happen if you don't follow the advice.)*

- Say a sentence with each of the contracted forms and have students repeat. For example, "I'd better leave now. You'd better leave now. He'd better leave now."

Grammar Notes

Notes 1–2   *(Exercise 2)*

- Call on students to read the explanation and the examples.

- Have students give more examples of cultural customs related to flowers. For example, ask them to make sentences about the types, colors, and numbers of flowers that are appropriate for different occasions in their culture. Tell them to use *should* and *shouldn't*. For example:

  —In Iran, you shouldn't give people yellow flowers as a gift.

  —In China, you shouldn't give people white flowers.

  —In Armenia, you should give people uneven numbers of flowers on happy occasions.

Note 3   *(Exercise 3)*

- Have students read the explanation and the examples. Make sure students understand that we use *ought to* only in affirmative statements. In questions and negatives, we use *should*.

- Put students in small groups. Give them the list of problems (or write your own). Instruct them to talk about what people ought to do or shouldn't do in these situations.

---

1. An American family has invited you to come to their house for Christmas dinner. You don't know what kind of gift to bring.

2. Your American teacher often touches your shoulder or arm when he or she is talking to you. This makes you uncomfortable.

3. Your neighbor has a big dog that barks late at night and early in the morning. This wakes you up.

4. You are renting a room in a house that belongs to an American man. You are sure that he is listening to your phone conversations and going into your room when you are not home.

5. You always bring your lunch to work and put it in the office refrigerator. Your lunch has disappeared from the refrigerator three times in the past two weeks. This has also happened to one of your coworkers.

Notes 4–5   *(Exercise 4)*

- Call on students to read the explanation and the examples.

- Put students in pairs and instruct each student to look at a different box (below). Students should take turns reading the items in their boxes. Partners should respond with "had better" or "had better not," using the correct subject pronoun.

Example:

A: They just washed the floor, and it's still wet.

B: I'd better not walk on it. / I'd better not go in.

STUDENT 1

---

1. You have a bad cold.
2. My midterm exam in grammar is tomorrow. I haven't started studying.
3. Coffee makes Mary nervous.
4. John has very white, sensitive skin.
5. The chicken in your refrigerator smells bad.

STUDENT 2

---

1. It is raining very hard, and you need to go to work.
2. Juan smokes, and he knows that smoking is very bad for his health.
3. You're late for an important appointment.
4. Blanca's car is almost out of gas.
5. You forgot to pay your cell phone bill.

Focused Practice (pages 389–392)

Exercise 1
present: to give something to someone, especially at an official or public occasion

Exercise 2
blow one's nose: to clear your nose by forcing air through it into a cloth or tissue

silence: complete quiet

Exercise 3
congratulate: to tell someone that you are happy because she or he has achieved something, or because something good has happened to him or her

Exercise 4
open-ended ticket: a ticket without a definite return date

postmarked: having an official mark that shows the date and time something was sent

to be lost: to feel unconfident or unable to take care of yourself

Exercise 5
stone: rock, or a hard mineral substance

officer: the title used when speaking to a policeman or policewoman

Communication Practice (pages 393–394)

Exercise 6
Before students listen, have them think of four questions they would ask before taking a trip to Japan. If students are Japanese, ask them to repeat questions foreigners have asked them about their country.

Exercise 7
Explain that the responses are not in the same order as the statements. When responding, students need to listen carefully and choose the proper response.

Exercise 8
Questions to generate ideas and elicit vocabulary:
• What culture do you know well?
• What are some common mistakes that people from other cultures make when they are doing business in that culture?
• What tips can you give a person who wants to do business in that culture?

Further Practice
A blooper is an inadvertent mistake, a faux pas. Tell students that they're going to discuss cultural bloopers—mistakes they have made in this culture because they were not aware of the local customs or traditions. Give an example of a mistake you made while traveling or living abroad. Use the target structures from this unit. For example: "When I went to France, I wanted to mail a letter to my family, so I went to the post office. When I got there, I was very confused because there weren't any lines. I saw a big crowd of people and I couldn't understand how to get to the window to buy some stamps. I was there for 15 minutes, and finally I just left. Later, somebody explained to me that in France, people don't stand in lines at the post office. If you want to buy stamps, you shouldn't stand there patiently. You should just push your way to the front like everybody else."

Have students from different countries sit together in small groups and tell their stories. Finally, have students share stories about cultural bloopers with the class.

GRAMMAR OUT OF THE BOX ......

Culture fair. Students will work together to gather information about customs and traditions. They will write their findings on posters, which are displayed in the classroom. Students work alone or in teams. Each student or team is given (or selects) one topic to research. (See the list below or choose your own.) They should survey students from different countries, collect the responses, and write them on a poster. For example:

Using Names	
United States	You shouldn't call old people by their first names without permission.
Korea	You should use a person's title with his or her name.
China	You shouldn't call a woman by her husband's name.

An excellent reference is the book *Multicultural Manners* by Norine Dresser (John Wiley & Sons, 1996 and 2005).

Topics:

- greetings
- smiling
- eye contact
- good luck / bad luck colors
- wedding customs
- baby customs
- food taboos
- New Year's customs
- good luck / bad luck numbers
- money customs
- being on time
- naming traditions
- giving compliments
- saying no
- eating customs
- gestures
- gifts for different occasions
- death and funerals

UNIT 39 Necessity: *Have to, Don't Have to, Must, Mustn't*

Unit Overview

Students will learn present and past forms of the modals of necessity or obligation, including *have to, don't have to, must,* and *must not* in:
- statements and questions
- short answers to *yes/no* questions with *have to*
- statements with *had to*

Grammar in Context (pages 395–396)

Vocabulary

requirements: things that must be done because of a rule or law

period: a length of time

midterm: an examination given in the middle of a school term

term paper: an extended piece of writing that students must submit as one of the requirements of a course

bibliography: a list of all the books and articles used in the preparation of a piece of writing, or a list of books and articles on a particular subject

hand in: to give (to a professor)

outline: a plan for a piece of writing in which each new idea is written on a separate line

hard copy: information from a computer that is printed onto paper, or the printed papers themselves

semester: one of two periods into which a year at school or college is divided

Comprehension Questions

- What period of American history does the course cover? *(Civil War to the present)*
- Which exams will students have? *(a midterm and a final exam)*
- What score must students get to pass the course? *(65)*
- What are the requirements for the term paper? *(It must be at least 10 pages. It must include a bibliography.)*
- When is the term paper due? *(by December 15)*
- Do the students have to buy a textbook? *(yes)*
- Who wrote the textbook? *(Professor Anderson)*

Discussion Topics

- Have you taken a history course? What period was covered?
- What were the course requirements?
- Have you ever written a term paper?
- Is it unusual for the professor to write a textbook and require his or her students to buy it?

Grammar Presentation (pages 396–398)

Identify the Grammar

NECESSARY
The term paper must be at least 10 pages.
You have to include a bibliography.
It must not be late.

NOT NECESSARY
You don't have to give me a hard copy.

Grammar Charts

- Write the examples of the target grammar points on the board, categorized as you see above. This division makes it clear from the outset that *must* and *must not* are not opposites, a common misconception among English learners. Have students read the examples. As they read, underline the modals and the verbs that follow. Then ask students the following questions:
—What do we mean when we say something is necessary? *(It is required. We have no choice in deciding whether to do it or not.)*
—Which affirmative structures do we use to say that something is necessary? (Must / have to + *verb*)
—What is the meaning of *must not*? *(Something is forbidden.)*
—If we must not do something, do we have a choice? *(no)*

—What is the meaning of *don't have to*? (*You can do it if you choose, but it is not required or necessary.*)

• Have students read the charts with the affirmative and negative forms of *have to*. Drill the forms by cueing students with the pronouns. For the affirmative forms, you may want to bring back the large letter *-s* you made earlier in the course, when students were learning the present tense. Hold it up to cue students that an *-s* ending is needed. For example:

TEACHER: I have to pay my phone bill today. You.

CLASS: You have to pay your phone bill today.

TEACHER: He.

CLASS: He has to pay . . .

• To build fluency, do a transformation drill. Provide the affirmative form. Students should change it to the negative, or vice-versa.

• Have students read the charts of *yes/no* questions. Drill by having them transform statements into questions. (Use your *-s* cue card as needed.) Example:

TEACHER: I have to go to the dentist.

CLASS: Do I have to go to the dentist?

TEACHER: You.

CLASS: Do you have to go to the dentist?

• Next, do a chain drill using *yes/no* questions with short answers. Have students read the chart of short answers. Choose a context and provide cues to form questions. Instruct students to answer truthfully. For example:

TEACHER: In the place where you live, do you have to make your bed?

A: No, I don't.

TEACHER: Cook dinner.

A: Do you have to cook dinner?

B: Yes, I do.

TEACHER: Vacuum the living room.

B: Do you have to vacuum the living room?

C: Yes, I do.

• Have students read the chart with examples of *must* and *mustn't*. (Note: Do not do a transformation drill with these two forms, as that would wrongly reinforce the notion that these forms are opposite in meaning.) To practice *must*, put students in pairs. Give them a list of chores. Instruct them to make sentences with *must*. For example:

Dotan lives with an American family. He does not pay rent, but he has to do work around the house. These are his responsibilities:

babysit the children on Saturday nights
mow the lawn every Sunday
cook dinner three times a week
take out the trash
wash the family car
clean the kitchen after dinner

To observe good manners while eating, do not:

talk with food in your mouth
put your elbows on the table
reach across another person's plate
throw objects across the table
blow your nose at the table
criticize the food
make noise while eating
blow on hot food to cool it down
use your napkin as a handkerchief
put your fingers into the serving bowls

Grammar Notes

Notes 1–2 *(Exercises 2–4)*

• Call on students to read the explanation and the examples. Clarify the difference between *must* and *have to* as follows: *Have to* is used in both speaking and writing. *Must* is used in writing but rarely in speaking. Encourage students to use *have to* in conversation.

• Put students in groups of four or five for a discussion on one of the topics below (or choose your own). Instruct students to use *have to* and *don't have to* as well as other structures needed in order to answer classmates' questions.

Topics

1. Graduation requirements in a student's major. Example:
My major is French. To graduate, I have to take eight courses . . . I have to pass a reading exam . . . I have to write . . . but I don't have to speak fluently.

2. Requirements to get a certain job in your country. Example:
To be a doctor in the United States, first you have to get a B.A. You don't have to major in science, but it helps. After that you have to go to medical school . . .

Note 3 *(Exercise 4)*

- Call on students to read the note and the examples.
- Since *mustn't* is seldom used except when talking to children, have students work in small groups and write a list of five things that a kindergarten teacher might say to young students. For example:
  —You mustn't push.
  —You mustn't take another child's toys.
  —You mustn't shout indoors.
- Put two groups together. Ask the students in one group to share their sentences with the other group, speaking in the manner of a kindergarten teacher.

Focused Practice (pages 398–401)

Exercise 1

tire: a thick, round piece of rubber that fits around the wheel of a car or bicycle

vote: to show which person you want to elect by marking a paper with a pen or using a machine

interpreter: someone who changes the spoken words of one language into another

Exercise 3

check: a printed piece of paper that you can sign and use to pay for things

casual: comfortable and informal

Exercise 4

I.D.: abbreviation of *identification,* used for a card that shows a photo of the owner along with the person's name, address, and birth date

bare: not covered by clothes or shoes

poison: a substance that can kill you or make you sick if it enters your body

Exercise 5

exceed: to go beyond an official or legal limit

Communication Practice (pages 401–402)

Exercise 6

- Before students listen, explain that an MBA is a master's degree in business administration. In the United States, a master's degree usually requires two additional years of university study beyond the bachelor's degree.
- Ask if any of the students in the class plan to get an MBA and what they have to do in order to get accepted into a program.

Exercise 7

Before students begin working in pairs, provide one or two examples from your own life for each category. For example, "I have to pay taxes this month. I don't have to start Christmas shopping yet, but I should in order to avoid the crowds next month." If students are still confused about the difference between *have to* and *don't have to,* clarify by asking, "Do I have a choice?"

Exercise 8

This activity could be an interesting cross-cultural discussion. For example, schools and companies differ in what they require students and employees to wear. Students in American public schools, for example, don't usually have to wear uniforms. In many companies there has been a trend toward more casual dress. Employees at high-tech companies rarely have to wear suits or formal clothes.

Exercise 9

Questions to generate ideas and elicit vocabulary:

- What do children at your elementary school say when the teacher enters the room?
- How must students address the teacher?
- What must they wear?
- How must they behave in class?
- When can they talk? When do they have to be quiet?
- Do they have to clean their classroom?

Further Practice

Put students in small groups and encourage discussion of the following topics to elicit the use of *have to, don't have to,* and *must not.*
In your country,

- What are the obligations of children (in school and at home)?
- What are the obligations of citizens (for voting and military service)?
- What do people have to do to get a driver's license?
- How do people lose weight? How do they reduce their blood pressure or become physically fit?
- What are some dos and don'ts with respect to body language and gestures?
- What are some gift-giving customs?

OUT OF THE BOX ......

Classified ads. In this activity, students read newspaper ads for job vacancies. They describe the requirements for the jobs, and they choose the job they would like to have. Bring in a selection of help-wanted ads from an English-language newspaper. If your class is small, bring in one ad per student. If the class is large, plan on groups of four or five students, find four or five ads, and make one set of copies per group.

Choose ads with information that students can use to make sentences with *have to, must,* and *don't have to.* The following is an example of a useful ad:

Drivers * Taxi
Make good money! We provide car.
25 or older. Clean driving record.
Will train. Drug testing. 310-555-1857

This ad lends itself to sentences such as the following:
• You don't have to have your own car.
• You must be older than 25.
• You must have a clean driving record.
• You don't have to have experience. They will train you.
• You have to take a drug test.

If the class will be working as a whole, distribute one ad per student. Otherwise, put students into groups, and within each group, give each student a different ad. Give students time to read their ads and ask questions. Circulate and clarify abbreviations and vocabulary. Instruct students to write as many sentences as they can using the target grammar. Have students present their ads to the class or to their groups. They should say what kind of job it is and what the job requirements are. For example, "This is an ad for a taxi driver. If you want this job, you have to be older than 25. You don't have to have a car, but you must have a clean driving record."

As an optional last step, have students choose the job they would like to have based on what they learned.

UNIT 40 The Comparative

Unit Overview

Students will learn:
• the comparative form of adjectives with one, two, and more than two syllables
• irregular comparatives, such as *far* and *farther*
• questions with *which: Which is bigger?*

Grammar in Context (pages 412–413)

Vocabulary

port: a place where ships are loaded and unloaded
elevation: height above the level of the sea
mild: not too cold or wet and not too hot
temperate: mild; never very hot or very cold
sunbathe: to sit or lie outside in the sun in order to get a tan
diverse: very different from each other
founders: people who establish an organization

Comprehension Questions

• Where is Maine? Where is Oregon? *(east coast; west coast)*
• Why are the two cities named Portland? *(They have ports.)*
• Which Portland is bigger? *(Portland, Oregon)*
• Where is Portland, Maine located? *(on the coast, 45 minutes from mountains)*
• Where is Portland, Oregon located? *(on a river)*
• Which city is older? *(Portland, Maine)*
• Why do they have the same name? *(Portland, Oregon is named after Portland, Maine.)*

Discussion Topics

• Which city is better for you: Portland, Oregon or Portland, Maine? Why?
• Is there a port close to your home? Is it on a river or on the sea?
• How do cities get their names?

Grammar Presentation (pages 413–415)

Identify the Grammar

Portland, Oregon is <u>higher than</u> Portland, Maine.
Portland, Oregon is <u>farther from</u> the ocean.
Portland, Oregon is <u>more diverse than</u> the other Portland.

Grammar Charts

- Write the sentences from Identify the Grammar on the board and ask students to read them. Ask students:
  —Which two things are we comparing? *(Portland, Maine, and Portland, Oregon)*
  —Which words form the comparison? *(be + comparative + than)*
  —For each comparative form, what is the base form of the adjective? *(high, far, diverse)*
  —Which comparative is irregular? *(farther)*
  —Which adjectives have one syllable? *(high, far)*
  —How do we form the comparative? *(We add -er.)*
  —Which adjective has two syllables? *(diverse)*
  —How do we form the comparative? *(more + adjective)*
- Have students look at the first chart. Ask:
  —For each comparative form, what is the base form of the adjective? *(big, busy, crowded)*
  —How do you spell *busy*? How do we form the comparative of an adjective that ends in *-y*? *(The y changes to i. Then add -er.)*
- Repeat the same procedure for the second chart. Elicit the base forms of the comparatives *better (good), worse (bad),* and *farther (far).*
- Make a handout or an overhead projector transparency of the list of adjectives below. Put students in pairs or small groups and instruct them to write the comparative forms of the adjectives.

good	bad	far
interesting	pretty	long
mild	temperate	funny
formal	sweet	dangerous
famous	old	friendly

- Have students read the chart of questions with *which*. Model questions using the adjectives in the chart above. Have students answer with their opinions. For example:

TEACHER: Which is better: coffee or tea?

A: I think coffee is better.

TEACHER: Which is worse: hot weather or cold weather?

B: I think hot weather is worse.

- Put students in small groups and have them continue asking and answering questions in the same way. Walk around and monitor for errors.

- Write incorrect sentences you hear on the board. When students finish talking in groups, have them correct the errors.

Grammar Notes

Notes 2–4, 9 *(Exercises 2–4)*
- Have students read all the explanations and examples.
- Have them sit in pairs or small groups. Tell them to make true sentences about themselves and their partners using the adjectives in these notes.
- Walk around and monitor students' sentences. Note errors.
- Write the errors on the board and have students correct them.

Note 5 *(Exercise 2)*
Using the adjectives in Note 4, have students transform their earlier sentences into sentences with *less.* Go around the room and have each student form a pair of sentences. For example:
Sheila is quieter than Jonathan.
Jonathan is less quiet than Sheila.

Notes 6–7 *(Exercises 3–4)*
- Have students read the explanations and the examples.
- To practice *good–better* and *bad–worse,* ask students to name the last movie they saw. Write the names of the films on the board. Call a student to the board and have him or her point to two films. Ask who has seen both of them. Call on a student who raises his or her hand, and ask which film was better and why. Encourage other students who saw the same films to agree or disagree using the words *better* and *worse.*
- To practice *farther,* ask several students how far they live from the school. Call on other students to form comparative sentences, such as *Kim lives farther from school than Yoshi.*

Note 8 *(Exercises 2–4)*
- Have students read the first two (correct) examples. Ask, "What are we comparing here?" *(John's home and William's home)* Then have someone read the wrong sentence and ask the same question. Help students see the error. Then read the explanation.
- Write pairs of phrases like the following on the board. Then have students form incorrect sentences on purpose and write them on the board.

Carla's hair	*Jin's hair*	*(Carla's hair is longer than Jin.)*
Richard's car	*Sato's car*	*(Richard's car is newer than Sato.)*
American food	*Chinese food*	*(American food is worse than China.)*

- Call other students to the board to correct the errors.
- Choose two people for the class to compare. Write several adjectives on the board. Have students make formal and informal comparisons between the two people. For example:
  —Domingo is taller than he [Diego] is.
  —Domingo is taller than he.
  —Domingo is taller than him.

→ For additional practice, see the Supplementary Activities on page 133.

Focused Practice (pages 416–419)

Exercise 1

recommend: to advise someone to do something

suburbs: areas away from the center of the city, where a lot of people live

drama: a serious play for the theater, television, or radio

documentary: a movie or television program that gives facts and information on something

Exercise 2

income: the money that you earn from working or from investments

Exercise 5

convenient: useful because it makes something easier or saves time

Communication Practice (pages 420–421)

Exercise 6

- Before students listen, define the terms *advantages* and *disadvantages*.
- Talk about some advantages and disadvantages of your home. Then have a few students do the same.

Exercise 7

- Call on a pair of students to read the example.
- Choose two other ways to travel, such as a train and a car, and role play the examples

with another student. Then have students work in pairs.
- Afterwards, call on pairs of students to role play items 2–4.

Exercise 8

It is also possible to start this activity at step 2. Elicit the adjectives and write them on the board. Then put students in pairs and have them ask questions comparing their partner's hometown to the city where they are living now.

Exercise 9

Questions to generate ideas and elicit vocabulary:
- What are two movies you have seen that have the same theme?
- What was the theme?
- Who were the actors in both movies?
- How were the movies similar?
- How were they different?
- Which one did you like better?
- What are two movies you have seen in the same series?
- Did both movies have the same actors?
- Did the sequel have any new characters?
- How were the first and second movies different?
- Which one did you enjoy more? Why?

Further Practice

Play a comparison game. In this game, students try to find differences between items that are very similar. Prepare a handout of items like the one below. Put students in pairs or groups. Instruct them to make as many sentences as they can about the differences between the items using comparative forms of adjectives. For example, *Coke is sweeter than Pepsi. Pepsi is fizzier than Coke.*

Coca-Cola and Pepsi cola
a horse and a pony
a car and a van
a tree and a bush
an adjective and an adverb
a shoe and a sandal
a lemon and a lime
a square and a rectangle
a Honda Accord and a Toyota Camry

Have students read their sentences out loud. They get one point for each sentence that no other group has. The team with the most points is the winner.

GRAMMAR OUT OF THE BOX ......

Comparing songs. The purpose of this activity is for students to compare two songs that are similar in theme. An example using two old songs is "Leader of the Band" by Dan Fogelberg and "Father and Son" by Cat Stevens. Both songs are about the singers' fathers. Fogelberg's is a loving tribute. Stevens's song, on the other hand, is angry.

Print out the lyrics to the two songs and, if possible, find recordings of both.

Explain the activity to the students. Then write the titles of the songs and the singers' names on the board. Find out what the students already know about the songs and the singers. Prepare a handout of a two-column chart like the one below. Leave room for students to write notes as they listen. Write the names of the songs in place of **Song 1** and **Song 2.** Define the elements in the left-hand column before listening.

	Song 1	Song 2
Tempo (speed)		
Volume		
Rhythm		
Melody		
Instruments used		
Singer (male/female)		
Voice		

Play both songs in class. Have students take notes on the musical elements above. Afterwards, have them make sentences with comparatives. For example, *Song 1 is faster than Song 2.* Finally, ask them which song they like better. Hand out copies of the words, including definitions of unfamiliar words and phrases, and a list of comprehension questions for students to answer. This can be done in groups. After having students work in groups, bring the class together and ask students to summarize the story or the message of the songs. Ask questions with comparatives: "Which song is happier/sadder? Which song is more meaningful to you?" As an optional step, read the lyrics line by line and have the

students repeat after you. Play the songs again and have students sing along. This activity can be followed by a compare-and-contrast writing assignment.

UNIT 41 — Adverbs of Manner

Unit Overview

Students will learn:
• the form and use of adverbs of manner such as *slowly, hard,* and *carefully*
• the difference between adjectives and adverbs ending in *-ly*
• the use of adjectives after linking verbs

Grammar in Context (pages 422–423)

Vocabulary

audience: the people watching or listening to a performance

applause: the sound of people hitting their hands together in order to show that they approve of something

Comprehension Questions

• When was the speaker's first speech in front of a large audience? *(15 years ago)*
• What did the speaker include in the speech? *(a lot of facts; big words; long sentences)*
• How did he speak? *(seriously and fast)*
• What was the response of the audience? *(polite applause)*
• What did he do the next time he had to give a speech? *(asked a friend for help)*
• How many ideas did his second speech have? *(three)*
• How did he speak? *(slowly, clearly, and honestly)*
• How did the audience respond this time? *(The applause was long and loud.)*

Discussion Topics

• Ask students to tell about a memorable speech they heard. What did the speaker say or do that made the speech memorable?
• In students' cultures, is it customary to tell jokes in a speech?
• What advice would students give to someone giving a speech in English for the first time?

Grammar Presentation (pages 423–424)

Identify the Grammar

I spoke <u>seriously</u> and <u>fast</u>.
I worked <u>hard</u>.

Grammar Charts

- Write the example sentences on the board. Ask students to read the sentences and identify the adverbs. Ask the following questions to help students focus on the target grammar:
  —How did the person speak in the first sentence? *(seriously and fast)*
  —How did the person work in the second sentence? *(hard)*
  —What part of speech are the words *spoke* and *worked*? *(verbs)*
  —What part of speech do adverbs modify? *(verbs)*
  —What information do adverbs give? *(the manner in which something happens)*
  —Do all adverbs end in *-ly*? *(no)*
  —Where do adverbs of manner appear in the sentence? *(after the verb)*
- Write the following template on the board: *Subject + Verb + Adverb.*
- Divide the class into pairs or small groups. Assign a few adverbs from the chart to each group. Their task is to form sentences that use the adverbs and follow the template. Make sure they have dictionaries in order to look up words they don't know.
- Go around the room and have students recite their sentences.

Grammar Notes

Notes 1–2   *(Exercises 2–3)*
- Call on students to read the notes and the examples.
- Do a paired transformation drill. Students hear sentences with adjectives and change them to sentences with adverbs. Make two handouts with the sentences from the following chart and model the drill. For example:

TEACHER: He's a fast talker.

CLASS: He talks fast.

Student 1	Student 2
He's an accurate singer.	He's a quiet eater.
She's a bad speller.	He's a sarcastic speaker.
He's a careful worker.	She's a serious reader.
She's a clear writer.	He's a slow writer.
He's a fluent French speaker.	The cat is a soft walker.
He's a free spender of money.	The teacher is an early riser.
She is a loud talker.	The salesman is a fast talker.
She's a neat typist.	The athlete had a hard workout.
He's a nervous speaker.	On weekends they are late sleepers.
He's a quick walker.	

- Circulate and note errors. Write them on the board. When students finish talking, call on students to correct the errors.

Note 3   *(Exercises 2–3)*
- Have students read the explanation and the example.
- Write the following words on the board: *hard, early, fast, late.*
- Put students in pairs and tell them to make sentences about themselves like the example. *(I'm not an early riser. I don't get up early.)*
- Ask several students to write their sentences on the board. Call on others to read them and correct any errors.

Note 4   *(Exercises 2–3)*
- Write the following exchange on the board:

A: How do you feel?

B: I feel well.

- Ask students if they have ever heard this exchange. Chances are they will say no. It's more likely that they have heard "I feel fine" or "I feel good," which is now an established phrase in American conversational English. Tell students that in formal situations, they should use *well* or *fine,* but in casual situations, *good* is acceptable.
- Have students read the explanation and the examples.
- Put students in pairs and instruct them to compose three sentences:
  —a sentence with *good* used as an adjective *(This is good cake.)*
  —a sentence with *well* used as an adverb *(She speaks English well.)*

—a sentence with *well* used as an adjective *(I don't feel well today.)*

- Go around the room and have students share their sentences with the class.

Note 5   *(Exercise 3)*

- Write the linking verbs on the board.
- Bring in some photos or magazine pictures showing people in a place where they are eating, such as a restaurant or a picnic. Pictures of you and your friends or family are ideal.
- Tell a story (true or false) to fit the picture(s) and use as many linking verbs as possible. For example: "Here is a picture of me and my friends at my 30th birthday party. I remember it was a warm day. The air smelled fresh, and I felt great. My parents were there, and they looked happy."
- When you finish telling the story, ask the class questions and have them retell the story using the linking verbs. For example, "How did the air feel?" *(It felt warm.)* "How did my parents look?" *(They looked happy.)*
- Explain the grammar. Ask students if they noticed the use of the adjective form after the linking verbs. Have them read the explanation and examples. Focus their attention on the incorrect sentence *The eggs taste well.*
- If possible, show another, similar picture to the whole class and have them make sentences using linking verbs.
- Put students in small groups. Instruct them to talk about their last birthday party. They should give the facts—who was there, where the party was held, etc.—and describe the people, the food, and the ambiance using the linking verbs on the board.

Focused Practice (pages 424–426)

Exercise 1

entertain: to do something that interests and amuses people

inspire: to encourage someone to do or to produce something good

move: to make someone feel a strong emotion, especially sadness or sympathy

emotion: a strong human feeling such as love or hate

Exercise 3

debate: a discussion or argument on a subject in which people express different opinions

Communication Practice (pages 426–427)

Exercise 5

Before students listen, prepare them in the following way:

- Look up the words in a dictionary and put the definitions on the board.
- Explain that sometimes meaning comes not from the words we say but from the way in which we say them.
- As an example, model the phrase *I love you* convincingly, questioningly, sarcastically, sadly, and angrily. Say the phrase and have students tell you which emotion is conveyed by the tone. (Note: To convey sarcasm, pronounce the word *love* with strong stress and a long, drawn-out rising and falling intonation.)

Exercise 6

After students work in pairs, call on individuals to say the sentence in the ways listed. Help with intonation when needed.

Exercise 7

Questions to generate ideas and elicit vocabulary:

- Where and when did the speech take place?
- Who was the speaker?
- What was the topic of the speech?
- What was the purpose of the speech: to entertain, to inform, or to inspire?
- What details did the speaker give?
- How did he or she speak?
- How did the audience respond to the speech?

Further Practice

Play the "mime" game. Prepare two sets of cards, one set with adverbs of manner and the other with short actions that can be mimed. For example:

1. slowly	a. type on a computer keyboard
2. fast	b. drink a cup of tea
3. happily	c. brush someone's hair
4. nervously	d. scrub a pot
5. angrily	e. look at a photograph
6. lovingly	f. read a letter
7. gently	g. pull off a bandage

8. violently	h. hang a picture on the wall
9. carefully	i. paint your fingernails
10. sadly	j. take a shower

Cut up the adverbs and the actions and put them in separate piles or bags. Have a student choose one adverb and one action and mime the combination. The other students have to guess what they're seeing and form a grammatical sentence. For example, "You are typing angrily."

 **OUT OF THE BOX ......**

Famous speeches. Many great historical speeches can be heard on the Internet. A search will yield a number of sites with audio. One of the best is the History Channel website, where students can listen to short segments of historical speeches. If you have access to a listening lab, take your students and allow them to choose the speeches they want to listen to. Have them fill out a listening report like the one below. It is also useful to ask students to print out the web page on which they find the speech so that you can go back and find it if necessary.

> **Listening Report**
>
> 1. Website title:
> 2. Address:
> 3. Speaker:
> 4. Date of speech:
> 5. Audience:
> 6. Topic:
> 7. Main idea:
> 8. Length:
> 9. Two facts I learned:
> 10. Two new words I learned:
> 11. How did the speaker sound or speak? (Use adverbs of manner.)

UNIT 42 *Enough; Too/Very; As + Adjective + As; Same/Different*

Unit Overview

Students will learn the form and meaning of the following structures:
• adjective + *enough*: *It's warm enough to go swimming.*

• adjective + *too*: *It was too cold to go swimming.*
• *very* + adjective: *It was a very warm day.*
• *as* + adjective + *as*: *Today is as warm as yesterday.*
• *the same as*: *Today's weather is the same as yesterday's.*
• *different from*: *Seattle's weather is different from Atlanta's.*

Grammar in Context (pages 428–429)

Vocabulary

overripe: not good to eat because something is too old and therefore too soft

fussy: concerned or worried about things that are not very important

Comprehension Questions

• Why is Penny in a hurry? *(It's getting late.)*
• What is Sally looking for? *(the perfect melon)*
• What is wrong with the melons Penny suggests? *(too small, too big, too soft, too hard)*
• What does *fussy* mean? *(Sally is a perfectionist; she's difficult to please.)*

Discussion Topics

• When you shop for fruit, are you more like Penny or more like Sally?
• Which fruits are common in your home culture or country? What do they cost? Are there special occasions when you eat special fruits?

Grammar Presentation (pages 429–431)

> **Identify the Grammar**
>
> 1. *That one's way <u>too small</u>.*
> 2. *It's about the <u>same size as</u> the other one.*
> 3. *Is it <u>big enough</u>?*
> 4. *It's <u>very soft</u>.*
> 5. *I think it's <u>too soft</u>.*
> 6. *You're <u>much too fussy</u>.*

Grammar Charts

• Write the example sentences on the board.
• Instruct students to number the charts from 1 to 7. Put them in small groups. Have them read the charts together and match the example sentences on the board to the information in the charts. Point out to students that some charts do not have an example on the board. *(Chart 1: example 3. Chart 2: examples 1, 5, 6. Chart 3: example 4.*

Chart 4: no example. Chart 5: no example.
Chart 6: no example. Chart 7: example 2.)
- Go over the answers with the whole class.
- To reinforce the patterns in the charts, bring in three pieces of fruit. If possible, bring in three melons: one perfect, one overripe, and one underripe. Bananas will work well too.
- Allow students to examine the fruit. (If your class is large, call up a few representative students to do this.)
- Once again, go through all the charts and have students form sentences about the fruit. For example:
  —This melon is ripe enough to eat.
  —This one isn't ripe enough.
  —This one is too soft.
  —This banana is the same color as that one.

Grammar Notes

Note 1 *(Exercise 2)*
- Call on students to read the explanation and the examples. Clarify the word *sufficient* if necessary. Explain that it's a good thing if you have *enough.*
- Write the following on the board:
  ride a train by myself
  drive a car
  vote
  drink alcohol
  live alone
  get married
  retire
- Put students in pairs and tell them to make true sentences (affirmative or negative) with *enough.* For example:
  —I'm old enough to drive, but I'm not old enough to vote.
  —I'm old enough to drive, and I'm also old enough to vote.
- This can also be done as a circle drill. Go around the room and have each student make one sentence.

Notes 2–3 *(Exercises 2–4)*
- Call on students to read the explanations and the examples.
- Draw a chart like the following on the board or on an OHT. (Select topics to match the interests of your students.)

Movies	*Singers*	*Restaurants*	*Cities*

- Ask students to come up to the board and, in the appropriate columns, write the names of items that they did not like or enjoy.
- Point to the items. Have students who didn't like them raise their hands. When you call on them, they should make sentences with *too* or *not* + adjective + *enough* to explain why they didn't like the items. For example:
  —I didn't like *Million Dollar Baby* because it was too violent and too sad.
  —I don't like Gary's Grill because the service isn't fast enough.

Note 4 *(Exercise 4)*
- Illustrate this grammar point by drawing cartoon figures on the board or on an OHT. (If you cannot draw well, ask a student to do it for you.) Draw the following:
  —a very tall, thin person (male or female)
  —the same tall person squeezed into an airplane seat
  —a very short person with a basketball hoop way above the person's head
- Point to the tall person and say, "He's (She's) very tall." Point to the picture of the tall person in the plane and say, "He's too tall to fit in an airplane seat." Point to the short person and say, "She's very short." Point to the basketball hoop and say, "She's too short to dunk a basketball."
- Point to the pictures in turn and have the class repeat the sentences.
- Call on students to read the explanation and the examples.
- Write the following nouns and adjectives on the board. Put students in pairs. Tell them to make one sentence with *very* and another with *too* and an infinitive. For example:
  soup—hot   (*This soup is very hot.*)
                 (*This soup is too hot to eat.*)
  book—long
  weather—cold
  weather—hot
  sofa—heavy
  tea—sweet
  I—tired
  child—big
  homework—difficult

Notes 5–6 *(Exercises 3–5)*
- To illustrate the grammar in these notes, have several or all the students line up according to their height.
- Pull people out of the line and make model sentences like the ones in the book:
  —Sally is as tall as Paula.
  —They're the same height.

—Sally is the same height as Paula.

—Paru isn't as tall as Fanny.

—Fanny is taller.

- Pull other students out of the line and elicit similar sentences from the group. Write one example of each of the structures on the board.
- Have the class sit down. Call on students to read the explanations and the examples.
- Put students in pairs. Tell them to make sentences about themselves following the five patterns on the board using these adjectives and nouns:

Adjectives	Nouns
tall	height
short	weight
thin	hair color
heavy	hair length
long	eye color

- Circulate and make notes about errors. Write sentences with mistakes on the board and call on students to correct them.

→ For additional practice, see the Supplementary Activities on page 133.

Focused Practice (pages 431–435)

Exercise 1

medium: of middle size or amount

complain: to say that you are annoyed, not satisfied, or unhappy about something or someone

to have something in common: to have the same interests or attitudes as someone else

opposites attract: an expression meaning that people who are very different from one another tend to be interested in or drawn to one another

puzzle: a game or toy with a lot of pieces that you have to fit together

initials: the first letters of each part of a person's name

Exercise 2

tough: difficult to cut or eat

sofa bed: a piece of furniture that serves as a couch when folded up and as a bed when opened

Exercise 3

height: how tall something or someone is

expiration date: the end of a period of time during which an official document is allowed to be used

weight: how much something or someone weighs

Exercise 4

interview: a formal meeting in which someone is asked questions, usually to find out if she or he is good enough for a job

applicant: someone who has formally asked for a job, place at a college, or visa, especially by writing a letter

tight: fitting part of your body very closely

Exercise 5

promotion: a move to a more important job or rank in a company or organization

graphic artist: a professional who draws, paints, or makes prints, especially with the use of a computer

dependable: always doing what is expected or needed

talented: having a very advanced ability or skill

switch: a complete change from one thing to another

Communication Practice (pages 435–437)

Exercise 7

Before students listen, have them re-read Exercise 5 and predict some reasons why Lou didn't get the job. After students listen and do the exercise, discuss whether their predictions were correct.

Exercise 8

Before students do the exercise, go over the vocabulary items in the box. Model a few statements with sentences about yourself or a family member.

Exercise 9

- To begin, explain to students that English has many colorful expressions formed with *as . . . as.* Ask students if they know any. If not, provide a few examples: *The chair was as hard as a rock. Her handshake was as cold as ice.*
- Have students look at the pictures and the words underneath. Ask, "What are the typical qualities of each one?" *(A mouse is fast/quiet/hungry.)*

Exercise 10

Have students look at the chart and use the information to form questions they will ask their classmates. For example:
- In what month were you born?
- What color are your eyes?
- What kind of movies do you like?
- How many brothers and sisters do you have?

Exercise 11

Questions to generate ideas and elicit vocabulary:

- What is the item used for?
- How big is it?
- What color is it?
- How old is it?
- What is it made of?
- Is it valuable?
- Does everybody have one?

Further Practice

Have students do a ranking activity. In this activity, students use the target structures from this unit to rank items on a scale.

Prepare a grid like the one below. This example uses cars, but you can make a grid out of any related items, such as foods, hobbies, animals, vacation spots, and jobs. (Note: It is important for some of the items to be similar so that students can form sentences with *as . . . as.*)

	Expensive	Fast	Beautiful	Economical
Ferrari				
Corvette				
Honda Accord				
Toyota Camry				
Mini Cooper				

Put students in groups of four. Make copies of the grid and distribute them. The objective of the activity is for students to rank order the five items from 1 to 5 under each adjective. For example, if they agree that a Ferrari is the most expensive car, they would rank it number 1. To encourage discussion and to elicit the target structures, students must agree on the rankings. This activity can be repeated with different grids.

Personal shopper. In this activity, students alternate roles between a personal shopper and a customer. Personal shoppers work in high-quality department stores. Their job is to help individual customers find items that meet their needs and their budgets. Bring in a large variety of catalogues, including clothing, furniture, electronics, cars, shoes, and gifts. Large catalogues (such as the Sears or J.C. Penney catalogues) can be divided into sections. Put students in pairs and explain the task. Distribute the catalogues or let students pick one they want. Model the language you want students to use. For example, if the customer likes an item that the personal shopper picked, he or she can say, "I like it. It's very nice/colorful/elegant." If a customer doesn't like an item, he or she can say, "It's too large/expensive." As students continue talking and the personal shopper shows the customer additional items, the customer might say, "This shirt is as ugly as the other one you picked" or, "I like this shirt. It isn't as tight as the other one." Tell the personal shoppers they need to pick at least eight items they think their customer will like. To make the activity livelier, the personal shopper can intentionally choose items he or she knows the customer will hate!

UNIT 43 The Superlative

Unit Overview

Students will learn:
- the superlative forms of regular and irregular adjectives
- how to use the superlative with *one of the*

Grammar in Context (pages 438–439)

Vocabulary

upright: standing, sitting, or pointing straight up

waddle: to walk with short steps, moving from one side to another like a duck

equator: an imaginary circle around the earth that divides it equally into its northern and southern halves

indigo: a dark purplish blue color

emperor: the ruler of an empire—a group of countries that are all controlled by one ruler or government

tuxedo: a man's suit that is usually black, worn on formal occasions

Comprehension Questions

- What do penguins look like? (*They have black backs and white bellies. They look fat. They stand upright and waddle.*)

- Where and when did explorers first see penguins? *(South America, 1519)*
- What language does the word *penguin* come from? *(Spanish)*
- How many kinds of penguins are there? *(17)*
- Where do they all live? *(below the equator)*
- What color are fairy penguins? *(blue)*
- Where do fairy penguins live? *(warm waters off southern Australia and New Zealand)*
- How tall is the largest penguin? *(4 feet)*
- Where does it live? *(Antarctica)*

Discussion Topics

- Have you ever seen a penguin? Where?
- Which birds are the largest, smallest, most colorful, most common, most intelligent, and rarest?

Grammar Presentation (pages 439–441)

Identify the Grammar

They thought this type of bird was <u>one of the strangest</u> birds in the world.
Little blue penguins are <u>the smallest</u> of all.
<u>The largest</u> penguin is the emperor penguin.
People say penguins are <u>the cutest, the funniest,</u> and <u>the most loved</u> birds.
They're also <u>the most formal</u>.

Grammar Charts

- Write the examples from Identify the Grammar on the board, but don't underline the superlatives. Call one student up to the board. Tell this student to underline the superlatives as other students read the sentences.
- Sentence by sentence, ask students what the adjective is. Ask students if it is one syllable or more than one syllable. Then elicit the rules for forming the superlative. *Adjectives: funny, easy, strange, small, large, cute, loved, formal.* (See notes for the rules.)
- Elicit the meaning of *one of the strangest birds.* Ask students, "Is the penguin the strangest bird, or are there other birds that are very strange?" *(There are other birds that are strange.)* If further clarification is needed, ask three tall students to stand up. Then say, "[Student 1] is one of the tallest students in the class. [Student 2] is also one of the tallest. [Student 3] is one of the tallest, too."
- Using a different color marker, underline the phrases *in the world* and *of all.* Ask students to identify the type of phrases these are. *(prepositional)*

- Go through the charts. Have students read the sentences. For each sentence, ask students what the adjective is, ask how many syllables it has and elicit the rules for forming the superlative. Then have students recall the comparative form of each adjective. Have them recite the three forms of each adjective: *big, bigger, the biggest.*
- Repeat the last step for the irregular superlatives.

Grammar Notes

Notes 1–5   (Exercises 2–4)
- Have students read the explanations and the examples.
- Give students a list of adjectives like the one below and have them say or write the superlative of each word. Monitor carefully for the use of *the.*

cute	large	far
small	fat	cold
funny	busy	easy
good	strange	exciting
interesting	formal	beautiful

- Do a quick drill. Say an adjective and point to a student. The student gives the three forms of the adjective: *fat, fatter, the fattest.*

Notes 6–8   *(Exercises 3–4)*
- Have students read the explanations and the examples.
- Put students in groups. Give them a list of categories like the one below. Their task is to form sentences containing a superlative and the category. They choose their own adjectives. For example:

cities   *New York is one of the noisiest cities in the world.*

animals	singers	movies
restaurants	sports	students
amusement parks	books	cars
desserts	climates	inventions

- Appoint a panel of students to be monitors. Go around the room and have each student recite one sentence from above. The job of the monitors is to correct any errors like the ones in Notes 7 and 8. (If you feel like it, you could "plant" some errors by arranging with a few students ahead of time to make mistakes on purpose.)

Focused Practice (pages 441–444)

Exercise 1

venomous: poisonous

Exercise 2

explorer: someone who travels to places that few or no people have visited before

flashy: very big, bright, or expensive

Exercise 4

tusk: one of the two very long teeth that stick out of an animal's mouth, such as an elephant's

surroundings: the area around the place where something or someone is

aggressive: behaving in an angry or violent way

Communication Practice (pages 445–446)

Exercise 6

Before students listen, write the names of the planets on the board: *Mercury, Venus, Earth, Mars, Jupiter, Saturn, Uranus, Neptune, Pluto.* Have students try to answer the quiz questions. Define the word *volcano* if necessary.

Exercise 7

Have students peer-correct their Part A questions. For Part B, have students get up and walk around to do their surveys. To report on the results, go around the room and have each student form one sentence. For example: "Selim thinks Bill Gates is the most powerful person in the world. Five students said Mario's is the best restaurant near our school."

Exercise 8

- After you have read the directions and examples for this activity, you can provide further models by saying something nice about each of your students.
- A way to vary the activity is to put all the students' names into a hat. Have each student draw a name and make up a compliment about that person. Go around the room and have each student say his or her compliment out loud. For example: "Patricia, I think you are the most fashionable person in our class. Every day you wear a different outfit. You always look good."

Exercise 9

Begin by having students ask you questions about a city you know well. Model sentences using the superlative.

Exercise 10

Questions to generate ideas and elicit vocabulary:
- When was your unforgettable day?
- Where were you?
- What were you doing?
- Why were you there?
- How was the weather?
- Who was with you?
- What was unusual about that day?
- What happened to make it unforgettable?
- How did you feel?

Further Practice

- Have students prepare one-minute speeches about an unforgettable person. Encourage students to use superlatives wherever possible. Write the following on the board to help students prepare:
What is the person's name?
How do you know this person?
Use adjectives to describe this person's character.
What is something special that this person did?
How do you feel about this person?
- If you have time, put students in pairs. Let them practice their speeches with a partner before doing them in front of the class. Have students speak in front of the class. To increase participation and involvement, do one of the following: Provide a chart in which students take notes on each speech. They can write the name of the person and the adjectives/superlatives used to describe the person. For each speaker, appoint a questioner whose job is to ask at least one question after the end of the speech. (Other students can be encouraged to ask questions as well.)

GRAMMAR OUT OF THE BOX ......

Jeopardy. "Jeopardy" is a well-known game show in the United States. Contestants are given the answers to questions in a category of their choice. They provide the questions. For example, in the category of geography, a contestant would read, "the lowest place in the world." The correct answer would be, "Where/What is the Dead Sea?" Prepare a "Jeopardy" game to play with the class. For categories and questions, a good source is the *Guinness Book of World Records.* (There is also a Guinness website.) The number of categories and questions you prepare will depend on the size of your class; seven categories with five questions in each is usually enough for 20 students. Decide in advance how you will score the game. One option is simply to give one point for each correct question. (Remember: You provide the answers. Contestants provide the questions.) You may also wish to include bonus answers worth two points each. Write each answer on one side of an index card. Write the questions on the other side. Organize the questions into categories. Write the categories on the board. Lay the groups of index cards on a desk or table. Divide the class into two teams. Two students at a time will play the game. Toss a coin to decide which team goes first. The person whose turn it is chooses a category. The host then reads an answer. The student responds with a question. If the question is correct, the team scores a point. If the question is incorrect, the other team gets a chance to form the correct question. A student who has had a turn goes to the end of the line. The game ends when all the answers have been used or when time is up.

Supplementary Activities

Unit 4   Grammar Notes

- Use this exercise to review all the notes. Put students in groups. Have students divide a piece of paper into six parts and label as follows:

Singular with *a*	Regular plural
Singular with *an*	Irregular plural
Proper	Always plural

- Instruct students to think of at least three items to write in each category. Remind them to write the singular articles.
- Follow up by having students read the Grammar Notes for Unit 4 in small groups. Circulate and answer questions. You may also have students read the notes for homework.

Unit 5   Note 5

- Put students in groups. Hand out a list of scrambled sentences. You can use the sentences from the notes on page 52 or write your own. Example: *place a beautiful It's*
- At your signal, students should work to unscramble the sentences. The first group to rewrite all the sentences correctly wins.

Unit 6   Grammar Charts

- This activity gets students out of their seats and reinforces the grammar. Have students line up in an order you select, such as by height, age, or alphabetically. Show students where the beginning and end of the line should be. Teach them to ask, "How do you spell your name?" so that they can position themselves correctly in line.
- Once they have lined up, ask questions to get students to use the prepositions. Example:

A: Where is Lila?

B: She's next to Pablo. / She's between Pablo and Monique. / She's at the front of the line. / She's not near Sun Hee.

Unit 7   Grammar Notes

- Use this exercise to review all the notes. Put students in pairs and give each pair a handout like the one below.
- Have students choose one of the topics in the left-hand column and write questions about it. They should use contractions if possible.
- Have pairs exchange papers and answer each other's questions.

Topic	Questions	Answers
Example: Food	*Who's* Wolfgang Puck? *What's* a burrito? *Where's* the Sundance Café? *Why* is the soup cold?	*Short:* A famous chef. *Long:* He's a famous chef. *Short:* A kind of Mexican food with beans. *Long:* A burrito is a kind of Mexican food with beans. *Short:* Near the university. *Long:* It's near the university. *Short:* It's fruit soup. *Long:* It's cold because it's fruit soup.
Sports		
Art		
Movies		

Unit 9   Grammar Notes

- The purpose of this exercise is for students, working in pairs, to practice asking each other questions with *do* or *be* until they find three things they have in common. Example questions:
  Are you married?
  Do you like cats?
  Do you live with your relatives?
  Do you drink coffee in the morning?
- When time is up, have each student report one thing that he or she has in common with his or her partner. Example: "We both like chocolate."

Unit 11   Note 3

- Model the pronunciation of ordinal numbers and have students repeat after you.
- Tell students to "count off" using cardinal numbers. Go row by row. In the end, each student will have a number.
- Once every student has a number, ask selected students to stand up. Use ordinal numbers in your request. For example: "Stand up if you are the 7th student. Stand up if you are the 23rd student."

- When everyone is standing, write a number on the board and have students call out the ordinal number. For example, write *14* on the board. Say, "Sit down if you are the _____ student." Students should respond, "14th."

Unit 12   Grammar Charts

- This exercise provides practice for using possessive adjectives and forming questions.
- Bring in a large sack, such as a pillowcase. Walk around the room and have each student put an item in the sack so that no one sees what the item is. Make sure there is at least one set of keys and a pair of sunglasses in the sack in order to elicit plurals.
- When the sack is full, walk around the room again and have each student withdraw an item from the sack. Make sure students do not choose their own items.
- Have students stand up and walk around. As they meet each other, the following conversations should take place:

A: Is this your _____? **B:** Yes, it's my _____. ↓	**A:** Is this your _____? **B:** No, it's not my _____. I think it's _____'s. ↓
In this case, student A should put the object on the teacher's desk.	In this case, student A should approach the person named and again ask him or her, "Is this your _____?" When student A finds the owner, he or she should put the object on the teacher's desk.

Notes 2–5

- Prepare a set of eight or ten sentences that include the spelling contrasts for apostrophes used to show possession versus third-person singular of the present of *be*. (See Unit 12, Notes 2–5, of this Teacher's Manual.)
- Put students in groups. Have a competition to see who can insert apostrophes where needed. The first group to finish without any mistakes is the winner.

Unit 13   Grammar Charts

- Bring in a bag of M&M candies to class. (Avoid peanut M&Ms in case of peanut allergies.) Put some of the candies near you, on your desk. Place others a little farther away, perhaps on a student's desk.
- Pick up the candies on your desk and use *this/these* to model sentences: "This one is green. These are red."
- Point to the candies farther away and repeat with *that/those*.
- Ask a student to make new sentences like the ones you modeled. Ask the student, "Do you want the red one or the green one?" *(I want the _____ one.)* Let the student eat the candy.
- Put students in groups of four. Distribute candy to them and ask everyone to do what the student modeled. Let them eat the candy afterwards.
- The same procedure can be adapted to colored buttons, beads, or other colored items.

Unit 14   Notes 1–3

- Choose two students to come up to the front of the class. Tell the class that these two students have a surprise announcement: They're getting married! Of course the class would like to buy some gifts for them.
- Have students ask the "couple" about items they might need. The "couple" should use *one* in their answers. Example:

STUDENT: Do you need a vacuum cleaner?

COUPLE: Yes, we do. We don't have one.

STUDENT: Do you have a can opener?

COUPLE: [Roman] has one, but it's old. We need a new one.

Unit 16   Grammar Charts

- On a piece of paper, write a set of present-progressive statements about actions that can be mimed. For example:

  —You are brushing your teeth.

  —You are opening a can.

  —You are unlocking a door.

  —You are putting a stamp on an envelope.

  —You are changing a baby's diaper.

  —You are sending a text message.

  —You are cooking a hamburger.

  —You are vacuuming a rug.

- Cut the paper up into individual sentences and put them into a box, bag, or hat.
- In class, have one student pull a sentence out of the container and mime the action described.
- While the student is miming, the class forms *yes/no* questions: "Are you opening something?" "Are you holding something?" "Are you cooking?"
- Tell students to begin asking questions immediately and to continue during the entire mime. Do not allow the mime to go on in silence.

Unit 17   Note 3

- Use the OHP or make a handout with signs and symbols, such as traffic signs or danger warnings.
- Have students look at the signs and say what they mean. Examples:
  —"Don't smoke."
  —"Don't stop."
  —"Don't walk."
  —"Don't park here."

Unit 19   Note 3

- Write a list of medical conditions or maladies on the board. For example:

can't sleep	*dizzy*
too fat	*headache*
too thin	*upset stomach*
feet hurt	*warts*
can't see	*depressed*
can't hear	

- Choose one of the maladies and pretend that you have this problem. Ask the students for advice. Reject their advice several times and give a reason. Accept the final suggestion. Example:

TEACHER: I can't sleep well. Every night I go to bed, and I stay awake for two or three hours. In the morning it's hard to get out of bed. I'm really worried about this. What should I do?

A: Why don't you have some wine before you go to bed?

TEACHER: Oh, no. Wine gives me a headache.

B: Then why don't you exercise more?

TEACHER: I can't. I don't have time.

C: Why don't you drink milk before you go to bed?

TEACHER: I hate milk!

D: Then why don't you go see a doctor?

TEACHER: That's a good idea.

- Put students in groups of four and have them follow the same procedure. If students feel comfortable, they can share a real problem they are having and ask for real advice.

Unit 20   Notes 3–5

- Prepare a chart like the following on the board or OHT:

Usually	Last week
visit mother on Tuesday evening	*visit mother on Wednesday*
exercise in the morning	*exercise in the evening*
start work at 8 A.M.	*start work at 8:30 A.M.*

- Tell a story about yourself, someone the students know, or someone famous or fictitious. Make sentences about what this person usually does and what the person did differently last week. Examples:
"Last week was a strange week for me. My wife was out of town, so my schedule was different. For example, I usually visit my mother on Tuesday evening, but last week I didn't visit her on Tuesday. I visited her on Wednesday."

"Normally I exercise in the morning, but last week I didn't exercise in the morning because I stayed out late the night before with my friends. I exercised in the evening."

- Put students in pairs. Give each student a different list of verbs. Instruct students to make up stories about their unusual week, following your example. Ask them to talk about things they did differently last week. Make sure each student's list includes verbs with all three past-tense pronunciations. For example:

Student A	Student B
call	start
finish	enjoy
help	relax
visit	change
worry	watch

Unit 23   Note 4

- Put students in pairs. Have each student make a general sketch of his or her bedroom.
- Ask students to use *there is / there are, there isn't / there aren't,* and *any* to talk about their rooms. As they speak about various objects, they should draw them in the appropriate location. Example:

A: Is there a computer in your room?

B: Yes, it's here, on my desk.

A: What else do you have on your desk?

B: Well, there are several textbooks here, and there's a box of pencils and pens here.

A: Do you have a trash can in your room?

B: Yes, there's a trash can on the floor by the door.

Unit 24   Grammar Charts

- Write sentences with the patterns from this lesson on an overhead transparency or a piece of construction paper. Choose verbs from the chart on Student Book page 233. Cut the sentences into strips. Then cut up each strip into phrases consisting of subject, verb, direct object, *[to],* indirect object.
- Put students in pairs and give one cut-up sentence to each pair. Tell students to put the phrases in order to form a sentence.
- Call students up to the OHP to share their sentences with the class.
- Here are some examples of cut-up sentences:

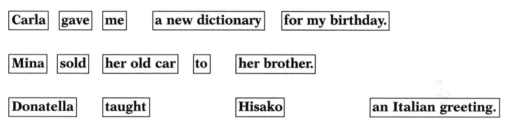

Note 5

- This is a chain drill using some of the verbs that take *to.* The sequence is as follows:

TEACHER: Car.

A: Kobe, I want to go to Santa Barbara. Would you lend me your car?

B: Sorry, I can't. I already lent it to Robert.

TEACHER: Cell phone.

B: Soon Mi, would you lend me your cell phone?

C: Sorry, I can't. I lent it to my brother.

TEACHER: Textbook.

C: Alma, would you lend me your textbook?

D: Sorry, I can't. I already lent it to Katja.

- Repeat the drill with the verbs *give* and *sell.*

Unit 25   Note 4

- Tell students that you want to redecorate the classroom.
- Prepare a list of items like the following. Write each one on a slip of paper and pass the slips out to different students.
  a potted palm
  plants
  a sofa
  a coffee machine
  travel posters
  wind chimes
- Students in turn should read the item on their slip, then say where they will place the item. Example: "Bowl of fruit. I'm going to put the bowl of fruit on the teacher's desk."

Unit 27   Note 3

- For this game you will need a ball or a beanbag. The goal is for students to practice making simple present statements with non-action verbs.
- Have students stand in a circle or at their desks.
- Toss the ball to a student and say an action or non-action verb. Choose non-action verbs from Student Book page 267.
- If you say a non-action verb, the student should respond with a sentence in the present tense. Example:

  TEACHER: Remember.

  A: I don't remember your name.

- If you say an action verb, the student should respond with a sentence in the present progressive. Example:

  TEACHER: Write.

  A: I'm writing a note to my teacher.

- After a student forms a sentence, he or she should toss the ball to another student.
- Try having the student holding the ball call out the next verb as he or she tosses the ball to the next student.

Unit 28   Note 3

Ball Toss
- Write all the verbs from the chart on Student Book page 275 on slips of paper. Put the slips in a hat.
- Have students stand in a circle. Toss the ball to the first student. Pull a slip out of the hat and read the verb to him or her.
- The student must make a correct sentence with an infinitive or a gerund. If the student makes a mistake, he or she sits down and the ball comes back to you.
- If the student's sentence is correct, he or she tosses the ball to another student, you pull out another slip from the hat, and the next round begins.

Game
- Use the same slips of paper used in preparation for the Ball Toss (above).
- Divide the class into two teams. Each team should form a line.
- Toss a coin to determine which team will get the first turn.
- Select a slip of paper. Read the verb. The student at the head of the line makes a sentence with a gerund or an infinitive. If the sentence is correct, the team gets a point. The student goes to the back of the line.
- If the sentence is incorrect, the first student from the other team gets a chance to make a sentence. Then that student also goes to the back of the line.

Unit 32   Note 3

• Put students in pairs. Each student should look at one of the boxes below and read the sentences to his or her partner. The partner responds with a statement using *may / might (not)* or *maybe*.

BOX 1

No one is answering the phone at your mother's house.
There are black clouds in the sky.
Tomás is absent.
Petra usually walks to school.

BOX 2

The dog refuses to eat his food.
Jorge always sits next to Carmen.
Lee never eats cake, candy, or ice cream.
Fabio is never home in the evenings.

Unit 33   Note 2

• To have students practice using the word *some* in offers and requests, select a student ahead of time and prepare him or her to do a restaurant role play with you. You will play the role of the server. The student will play the role of the customer. Teach the student to make a request with *some. (May I have some sugar, please?)*

• Do the role play in front of the class. Inform students that it is breakfast time in a restaurant. Have the "customer" sit in front of the class. If possible, wear an apron or some other prop to reinforce your role as the server. After greeting your customer, ask typical questions, such as the following:
"Would you like some coffee to start your meal?"
"What would you like to order?"

• Depending on the student's answer, you can then ask the following:
"Would you like some ketchup with your scrambled eggs?"
"Would you like some honey for your oatmeal?"

• As a follow-up, put students in pairs and have them repeat the role play. You can vary the activity by having them talk about lunch instead of breakfast, for example.

Unit 36   Note 3

• Copy the following list of situations onto a handout. Put students in pairs. Have them take turns asking *May/Can I help you?* and responding in a way that is appropriate to the situation. For example:
a coffee shop

A: May I help you?

B: Yes, I'd like a cappuccino, please.

---

a restaurant	a doctor's office
a dry cleaner	a flower shop
a computer store	a video store
a clothing store	a post office
a bank	

Unit 40   Note 8

- Have students form two concentric circles, one inside the other. The people on the inside should face the people on the outside.
- Tell the students you are going to play some music. Both circles should move in a clockwise direction. When you stop the music, they should stand still and face the person opposite them, forming a pair.
- Pairs of students should find five differences between them and form sentences using informal comparatives, such as "You're older than me."
- After students have had a few minutes to talk, stop them. Go around and have each student make one sentence like the example above.
- Tell students to sit down. Remind the class that in formal English, we use subject pronouns after *than*. Call several students to the board to write formal sentences about the differences between themselves and their partners.
- Call on other students to read the sentences on the board and correct any errors.

Unit 42   Notes 5–6

- Put students from different countries or regions into small groups.
- Instruct them to talk about the weather in their area season by season and compare it to the weather in the city where they are learning English. Provide examples using a region you know well. For example:
  "Los Angeles isn't as cold as Jerusalem in the winter."
  "Jerusalem is much colder."
  "Tel Aviv has the same amount of rain as Los Angeles."
  "Tel Aviv has the same summer weather as New York. It's very humid."
- Write the following weather-related nouns and adjectives on the board:

Nouns	Adjectives
rain snow humidity sunshine wind	rainy snowy sunny warm, cold, hot dry, wet windy humid

Scoring Rubric for Speaking

Tips for using the speaking rubric

- Give a copy of the speaking rubric to the class before you use it.
- Tell students that you will evaluate their speaking using the rubric.
- The speaking rubric can also be found in a printable format on the Power Point® presentations CD-ROM found in the back of this Teacher's Manual.
- Give feedback for the different areas identified in the rubric: vocabulary, grammar, pronunciation, fluidity, topic organization, and communication. Point out some strong points and weak points. Use language that a student can understand and give examples of what the student did or didn't say when possible. Example comments: *You used a lot of vocabulary and expressions from the unit.* OR *You need to work on verb forms. Review the verb forms needed for the present progressive.*
- It's recommended that you discuss the assigned rating and your feedback with each student in a timely manner in order to be most effective and helpful.

SPEAKING RUBRIC

Rating	Vocabulary	Grammar	Pronunciation	Fluidity	Topic	Communication
4	Uses variety, with few errors	Uses a variety of structures, with few errors	Almost always clear and accurate	Speaks smoothly, little hesitation	Successfully organizes and develops topic	Communicates information and opinions effectively
3	Uses variety, makes some errors in word choice	Uses a variety of structures, makes some errors	Usually clear and accurate, some problem areas	Speaks with some hesitation, does not usually interfere with communication	Topic is organized, needs more development	Most information and opinions are communicated clearly
2	Uses limited vocabulary and expressions, some errors	Uses basic structures, makes frequent errors	Errors sometimes make it difficult to understand student	Speaks with hesitation, frequently interferes with communication	Topic not organized, needs development	Information and opinions are not clear
1	Uses basic vocabulary and expressions, makes many errors	Uses basic structures, makes many errors	Very weak; student cannot be understood	Hesitates frequently when speaking, interferes with communication	Does not stay on the topic	Is not able to communicate information and opinions

Scoring Rubric for Writing

Tips for using the writing rubric

- Give a copy of the rubric to the class before you use it.
- Tell students that you will evaluate their writing using the rubric.
- The writing rubric can also be found in a printable format on the Power Point® presentations CD-ROM found in the back of this Teacher's Manual.
- Give feedback by writing comments for the different areas identified in the rubric: topic, sentence structure, vocabulary, grammar.
- Use language that a student can understand and, when possible, give examples of what the student did or didn't do. Example comments: *You addressed the topic and gave very clear examples to support your ideas.* OR *You tried to use a lot of vocabulary and expressions from the unit, but review the meanings of the items I marked in red.* OR *You need to work on verb forms. Review regular and irregular verb forms in the simple past.*
- It's recommended that you discuss the assigned rating and your feedback with each student in a timely manner in order to be most effective and helpful.

Rating	WRITING RUBRIC
5	• Topic is addressed and well organized; includes clear explanations or details • Includes mostly complex sentence types, with few errors • Uses a variety of vocabulary and idiomatic expressions; makes few errors in word choice • Uses complex grammar structures, with few errors
4	• Topic is addressed and generally well organized; includes some explanations or details • Includes some variety of sentence types, but with occasional errors • Varies vocabulary and expressions, but makes occasional errors in word choice • Uses some complex grammar structures, but with errors
3	• Topic is not addressed completely, but writing is organized; explanations or details need more development • Uses little variety in sentence type, but does not have many errors • Attempts to vary vocabulary and expressions, but makes some errors in word choice • Does not use complex grammar structures, but does not make many grammar errors
2	• Topic is somewhat addressed, but writing is not organized and lacks explanations or details • Uses only basic sentence types and makes frequent errors • Uses limited vocabulary and with frequent errors • Uses simple grammar structures, but with some errors
1	• Topic is not addressed; there are no explanations or details • Most sentences have errors • Has many errors in vocabulary usage, even at the basic level • Uses only simple grammar structures, and makes many errors

Audioscript

Unit 1

Exercise 3 (page 8)

Parminder Nagra is an actor. She is the star of the movie *Bend It Like Beckham*. It is a comedy. In the movie, Nagra is a young Indian girl in England. She is a good soccer player and she loves soccer. But her parents are traditional. They are not happy. They don't want her to play soccer. They say, "Soccer is not for girls. Marriage is for girls. Look at your sister." She says, "I am not my sister."

Exercise 7 (page 10)

Hideki Matsui and Mia Hamm are athletes. Matsui is a baseball player. He's from Japan. Hamm is a soccer player. She's from the United States.

Ang Lee and Steven Spielberg are movie directors. Ang Lee is from Taiwan. Steven Spielberg is from the United States.

Paulina Rubio and Beyoncé are singers. Rubio is from Mexico. Beyoncé is from the United States.

J. K. Rowling and Gabriel Garcia Marquez are writers. Rowling is from England. Garcia Marquez is from Colombia.

Unit 2

Exercise 6 (page 19)

A: Tell me about your class, Hugo. Is your teacher a man?

B: Yes, he is. He's about fifty years old. He's from Canada. I think he's good.

A: What about the students? Are they all from the same country?

B: No. They're from all over the world. They're from Mexico, Chile, Canada, Poland, Korea, and Japan.

A: That's interesting. How's their English?

B: It's hard to say. Some students are good at speaking but not good at writing. Some students are good at writing but not good at speaking.

A: What about you? How are you doing?

B: I don't know. I think I'm good at speaking, but writing and grammar are hard for me.

Unit 3

Exercise 2 (page 25)

1. A: Was Emily at the party?

  B: Yes, she was. Why?

  A: She's not in the photos.

  B: She was the photographer.

2. A: Were Ali and Mo in school on Monday?

  B: Yes, they were. Why?

  A: Their names are not on the attendance sheet.

  B: I think they were late.

3. A: How's the weather in Montreal?

  B: It's cold. It was cold yesterday too.

  A: Was it cold the day before?

  B: I think so.

Exercise 9 (page 29)

Message 1
Hey Jay. This is Dan. Thanks again for the tickets. The concert was great and the seats were super.

Message 2
Hello Jay. This is Emiko. I was out of town all last week. I'm back now. Please call me. My number is 917-865-4821.

Message 3
Jay. This is John. I'm sorry I wasn't at the meeting. Please call me at 876-421-0090. Thanks.

Unit 4

Exercise 7 (page 45)

1. The photos are ready.
2. Our classes are from 10:00 to 1:00.
3. Be careful. The scissors are sharp.
4. The boxes are full of old clothes.
5. My pants have two pockets.
6. I don't see well without glasses.
7. Our books are open to page 20.

Unit 5

Exercise 4 (page 51)

Russ: Hello?

Emiko: Hi, it's Emiko.

Russ: Emiko. Where are you?

Emiko: I'm in Colorado, in Mesa Verde National Park.

Russ: How is it?

Emiko: Mesa Verde is strange and awesome. There are very old cliff dwellings. Some are like cities.

Russ: It sounds great. Is your hotel nice?

Emiko: Not really, but it's clean and it's near the park.

Russ: How's the weather?

Emiko: It's cold, but there's one good thing about that—the park is not crowded.

Unit 6

Exercise 3 (page 57)

A: Where do you want to meet?

B: On Third Avenue between Fifth and Sixth Streets.

A: Okay. Let's meet in front of the restaurant.

B: There are two restaurants.

A: Oh? Well, I mean the restaurant between the card shop and the bakery.

B: What's the name of the restaurant?

A: Moon Palace Restaurant.

Exercise 6 (page 58)

1. This country is in Asia. It's between Japan and China. It's near Mongolia. What country is it?
2. This country is in South America. It's between Colombia and Peru. What country is it?
3. This country is in Africa. It's an island. It's near Mozambique. What country is it?
4. This country is in Europe. It's between Portugal and France. What country is it?

Unit 7

Exercise 5 (page 63)

Dana: Who's there?

John: It's John.

Dana: Come on in. What's that?

John: It's a gift for you. It's a painting.

Dana: Thanks. It's great. Who's the artist?

John: My brother.

Dana: He's excellent.

John: Thanks. I think so too.

Dana: What's the name of the painting?

John: It's called *Pears*.

Dana: I really like his work.

John: He has a lot more paintings in his gallery. Do you want to go there?

Dana: Sure. Where's his gallery?

John: It's on Second Avenue, but it's closed today.

Dana: Why is it closed?

John: It's always closed on Monday.

Unit 8

Exercise 6 (page 75)

1. He shops a lot.
2. She buys clothes at discount stores.
3. She uses that word a lot.
4. It costs a hundred dollars.
5. He knows his business.
6. She carries a cell phone.
7. He misses her.
8. She watches fashion shows on TV.
9. He thinks about his clothes.

Unit 9

Exercise 4 (page 82)

A: So tell me about your new roommate. Do you like him?

B: Yes, I do. He's a really nice guy.

A: I know he speaks English fluently, but he's not American. Does he come from England?

B: No, he doesn't. He comes from Australia.

A: Oh? Does he come from Sydney?

B: No, he doesn't. He comes from Melbourne.

A: What's he studying?

B: Music.

A: Do you like the same kind of music?

B: Yes, we do. We both like classical music. He has a good CD player and hundreds of CDs.

A: Does he have relatives here?

B: Yes, he does. His uncle and aunt live here. I was at their home last night.

A: Really? Do you see them often?

B: Yes, we do. They invite the two of us for a meal at least once a month. They're great cooks and interesting people. He's a conductor and she's an opera singer.

A: Do you bring them a small gift when you visit?

B: No, I don't. I'm a poor student.

A: Hey, you're not that poor.

Exercise 6 (page 84)

VALENTINA: So, Andrea, I have just a few more questions.

ANDREA: OK.

VALENTINA: Tell me Andrea . . . Do you like parties?

ANDREA: Not really. I like to see one or maybe two people at a time. I also like to be alone.

VALENTINA: OK. That's good to know. Do you listen to music?

ANDREA: Yes. I love jazz. I listen to it a lot.

VALENTINA: How about sports? Are you into sports?

ANDREA: No. Sometimes I go to the gym, but not often.

VALENTINA: Finally, what time do you study? And where?

ANDREA: I study at night in my room.

VALENTINA: Thank you. I'll get back to you soon.

Unit 10

Exercise 6 (page 93)

DR. FOX: So Diane. Tell me about your dream.

DIANE: OK, Dr. Fox. I'm in a forest. A tall man with a beard is behind me. He has a big stick in his hand. I think he wants to catch me. I start to walk fast. Then he walks fast. I run. Then he runs. Then I wake up. So, Dr. Fox. What does it mean?

DR. FOX: Hmm. Let me see . . . Diane, are you very busy?

DIANE: Yes. I have a full-time job and I'm in school.

DR. FOX: Well, that's it. You're too busy. You need a vacation.

Unit 11

Exercise 6 (page 109)

VICTOR: Their apartment is on Commercial Avenue, right?

LISA: No, it's not. Their apartment's on Seventy-fifth Street.

VICTOR: It's between First and Second Avenue.

LISA: No, it's between Second and Third Avenue.

VICTOR: It's on the fifth floor, right?

LISA: No, it's on the *third* floor.

VICTOR: Whose apartment are you talking about?

LISA: John and Alice's apartment.

VICTOR: The party isn't at John and Alice's apartment. It's at John and Maria's apartment.

Unit 12

Exercise 8 (page 120)

1. **A:** Is that Maria's?
   B: I think so.
2. **A:** Is that Maria?
   B: No, it's her sister Carmen. They look alike.
3. **A:** We have two Marias in our class.
   B: It's a popular name.
4. **A:** Is this your partner's composition?
   B: No, it's my composition.
5. **A:** Do you like to work with a partner?
   B: Sometimes.
6. **A:** Sometimes we work with partners and sometimes we work in small groups.
   B: We do too.

Unit 13

Exercise 4 (page 127)

1. These are interesting plants.
2. This tree is a pine tree.
3. Are these plants poisonous?
4. Is this the busy season?
5. Is this the gift shop?
6. These earrings are expensive.
7. These women are rangers.

Exercise 6 (page 127)

MARIA: My backpack is too full. I can't take everything. What do you think? Do I need these boots?

CARLOS: Those boots are heavy. Forget them.

MARIA: How about this sweatshirt?

CARLOS: Sweatshirts are always good. You don't need all those guidebooks. They're heavy. Just take one.

MARIA: OK. Do I need an umbrella?

CARLOS: Yes, you do.

MARIA: How about these batteries?

CARLOS: Yes. And you need some heavy pants.

MARIA: Are these OK?

CARLOS: They're fine.

Unit 14

Exercise 6 (page 134)

A: Do you need to buy a lot of gifts?

B: Yes. I have a long list. I want some cute and inexpensive ones for my cousins and my friends. I need a funny one for my brother. We always exchange funny gifts.

Then I need a beautiful gift for my grandma. I need one that's nice for an older woman. I want a practical one for my dad. He doesn't like gifts that have no use.

And I want a big gift for my mom. The price isn't important. So, do you have any good ideas?

Unit 15

Exercise 6 (page 148)

EMILY: Hello?

MOM: Emily?

EMILY: Mom? Where are you?

MOM: I'm on the train. Is Dad there?

EMILY: Sure. Hold on. Dad? It's Mom.

DAD: I'm making dinner. Tell Mom I can't talk now.

EMILY: Mom, Dad's cooking.

MOM: OK. So how are you doing? Are you doing your homework?

EMILY: Well, I was. I'm helping Dad now.

MOM: Oh. That's great. What are you and Dad making for dinner?

EMILY: Your favorite—spinach lasagna and a big salad.

MOM: Great. I'm hungry. I'm looking forward to it. Tell Dad the train arrives at 7:15.

EMILY: OK. Bye Mom. Love ya.

MOM: Bye Sweetheart.

Unit 16

Exercise 3 (page 155)

GREG: Hello.

ABBY: Hi Greg. How are you feeling? Are you feeling any better?

GREG: No, I'm not.

ABBY: Are you taking the medicine?

GREG: No.

ABBY: Well, take it. It's good for you.

GREG: Where are you calling from?

ABBY: I'm on Fifth Avenue, and listen to this. Renée Zellweger is walking ahead of me.

GREG: No kidding! What street are you walking on?

ABBY: I'm on Fifth Avenue between 55th and 56th Street.

GREG: What's she wearing?

ABBY: She's wearing a pink suit. She looks great.

GREG: Is she talking to anyone?

ABBY: She's talking to a man and three women. She's giving them her autograph. What are you doing? Are you watching TV?

GREG: I'm looking at Renée Zellweger too. I'm watching the movie *Chicago*.

ABBY: That was a good movie. What's happening?

GREG: Renée Zellweger and Catherine Zeta-Jones are dancing.

ABBY: Oh. I remember that part. Well, feel better! I'll be home after my class. Bye, hon.

GREG: Bye. Bye.

Exercise 6 (page 156)

ROBERTO: Hey Cesar. What're you listening to?

CESAR: The ball game.

ROBERTO: Who's playing?

CESAR: The Red Sox and the Astros.

ROBERTO: Where are they playing?

CESAR: In Fenway Park.

ROBERTO: Who's winning?

CESAR: It's a tie. It's the bottom of the ninth. Wait. . . . Something's happening. Everyone's shouting.

ROBERTO: What's happening?

CESAR: It's a home run.

ROBERTO: Yes! That's terrific. The Red Sox won!

Unit 17

Exercise 7 (page 166)

Hi Penny. This is Denise. Please call me when you get this message. My number is 224-3479. Thanks.

Hi Steve. It's Gary. I have free tickets to the basketball game. Call if you're interested. 420-9097.

Hi, Steve. It's me, Penny. Please don't eat the cheesecake. It's for Aunt Lyn.

Steve, hello. It's Mom. Listen, dear, I need your advice. Please call me this evening. But don't call before eight. And please don't forget to call. OK, bye. Oh . . . send my love to Penny and the kids.

Unit 18

Exercise 6 (page 171)

1. My friend can **sew,** but he can't **cook.**
2. My dog can **sit,** but it can't **beg.**
3. Kelly can **lift** 100 kilos, but Nitza **can't.**
4. José can **play** tennis. He can **play** basketball, too.
5. Elena can **read** English newspapers but she can't **understand** spoken English well.

Unit 19

Exercise 6 (page 179)

ARDA: So, what do you want to do today?

RODICA: I want to buy some baskets.

ARDA: Then let's go to the market. They make beautiful handmade baskets there.

RODICA: That's a great idea.

SHIRA: Why don't we do that in the morning? Then in the afternoon let's go whale watching.

RODICA: Whale watching? Where?

SHIRA: There's a boat. It takes people out to see whales. I read that over 1,500 whales swim from Alaska to Hawaii every winter.

ARDA: That sounds like fun. So in the morning we can go to the market and in the afternoon we can go whale watching.

Unit 20

Exercise 2 (page 192)

1. I'm sorry I'm late. I missed my train.
2. The plane arrived on time.
3. Last night she visited the Art Museum.
4. He cooked a delicious meal for us.
5. I'm tired. I walked up a lot of hills in San Francisco this morning.
6. We wanted to take a tour of Alcatraz in the afternoon but the tour was filled.
7. We borrowed a guidebook from our friends.
8. Two nights ago they watched a parade.
9. The comedian joked about the politicians.
10. Everyone hugged and kissed us when we left.

Exercise 8 (page 195)

A: Any mail?

B: Yes. A postcard from Marta.

A: Where was she?

B: In Japan. But she's back in Mexico now.

A: Did she stay with her Japanese friends?

B: Not this time. This time she stayed at a traditional ryokan. That's a traditional Japanese inn. She loved it.

A: What else did she write?

B: Well, she practiced her Japanese with tour guides and shopkeepers.

A: That's great. I'll bet her Japanese is good. Did she rent a car?

B: No, she used the trains to get around. She visited all the different areas of Tokyo. Ginza is her favorite.

A: Did she like the food?

B: Yes, and she learned to use chopsticks properly. Now she's an expert and promises to teach us.

A: It sounds like she had a great time.

Unit 21

Exercise 6 (page 204)

PAUL: As a young child I spent a lot of time with my grandparents. My grandfather loved to play with me. I was six when my grandfather died. A few months before he died, he gave me a beautiful blue blanket. I loved that blanket because it reminded me of my grandfather. But after a couple of years, the blanket didn't look good. I didn't want to throw it away so my mother made it into a book bag. I used it to carry my books to school for a couple of years. Then the book bag tore. I didn't want to throw it away so my mom made it into a pencil case. One day I lost the case. I felt terrible. My friends said, "Forget about it." I couldn't forget about it. I wrote about it instead. Last week my son found my story in the attic of our house. My son asked about the blanket and he asked about my grandfather. Grandpa and his blanket are not forgotten.

Unit 22

Exercise 6 (page 213)

ALI: That was a good story. Where did you first hear it?

BERRIN: My grandfather told it to me.

ALI: Did you live with him?

BERRIN: No, but I saw him often. He had a large farm and I went there every summer and many weekends.

ALI: What did your grandmother do?

BERRIN: She helped him on the farm. She also brought up my father and his five sisters and brothers. Later she wrote poetry.

ALI: Wow! Where did your grandparents meet?

BERRIN: Their parents arranged their marriage.

ALI: Did they have a happy marriage?

BERRIN: I think so. I never asked. They never complained.

Unit 23

Exercise 8 (page 228)

A: Excuse me, is there a mall around here?

B: Uh-huh. There's a big mall up ahead. Follow me. I'm going there.

A: Is there a pizza place at the mall?

B: I don't know, but I know there's a food court. It's on the third level. There are at least ten different places to eat.

A: Sounds good. Thanks.

Unit 24

Exercise 7 (page 237)

1. **A:** I bought a used car with lots of problems.

   B: Who sold it to you?

   A: My boss's son. I think he sold me a lemon.

   B: That's terrible.

2. **A:** Hector left a strange message.

   B: What did he say?

   A: He said, "I'm calling from jail." He nearly gave me a heart attack.

   B: What did he mean?

   A: He was visiting his brother at *Yale*. That's a university in Connecticut. He wasn't in *jail*.

3. **A:** Twice Anna disappointed me. She promised to meet me, and she never showed.

   B: That's awful.

   A: I know. I decided to teach her a lesson. I told her to meet me and I never showed.

   B: I guess that'll teach her.

4. **A:** Did Andrea eat the cookies?

   B: Yes, she did.

   A: Did she admit it?

   B: No. She told a tall tale. She said a monster came and ate them.

   A: She's a funny little girl.

5. **A:** John, please lend me a hand and help me put up these paintings.

   B: Sure, Carol. No problem.

Unit 25

Exercise 9 (page 247)

THERESA: Hi. You're early. The party isn't until 8:00.

BORIS: I know. I'm here to help. I have my car. Can I get you anything?

THERESA: Thanks. Yes. We need soda and chips. And a jar of hot salsa and three cans of tuna fish.

BORIS: How about ice?

THERESA: Good idea. Get some ice.

BORIS: OK. I'll be back soon.

BORIS: Here you are. Here's the soda, the chips, the salsa, the tuna, and the ice.

THERESA: There's a little problem.

BORIS: A problem? What's the matter?

THERESA: This is tuna for cats.

BORIS: Oh, no.

THERESA: It's OK. I can return it.

BORIS: I feel sick.

THERESA: Why? You didn't eat it.

BORIS: Not today, but this is the tuna I usually eat. Meow. Meow.

2ND WOMAN: What's going on?

THERESA: Boris is learning a new language.

Unit 26

Exercise 5 (page 263)

MIKE: Michelle, what are you doing?

MICHELLE: I'm calling Janet.

MIKE: But you're using my phone.

MICHELLE: That's because you always have a lot of free minutes left, and I don't. Dad said I can't go over my limit this month.

MIKE: I don't understand you. You and Janet talk on the phone at least five times a day.

MICHELLE: No, we don't.

MIKE: Yes, you do.

MICHELLE: Well, you e-mail people all the time.

MIKE: That's different.

MICHELLE: I just need to make one phone call. Please. It's really important. You can use my iPod.

MIKE: Can I borrow your jean jacket too?

MICHELLE: Oh, OK. Hi, Janet. This is Michelle. What are you doing?

Exercise 7 (page 264)

MAN: Something strange is going on.

WOMAN: Why do you say that?

MAN: Well, take a look at John. He's drinking water, not coffee. He's smiling and talking to Anne . . . He's not eating a donut. It looks like he's eating an apple.

WOMAN: You're right. Let's find out what's happening.

WOMAN: Hey John. What's going on?

JOHN: Not much. Why?

WOMAN: Well, you always drink coffee, not water. You never talk to anyone. You usually don't eat apples. And you look relaxed.

JOHN: Ah, you see a difference? That's great. I spoke to Tal, the psychologist. He says I need to change my habits or I'll get sick. So, do you like the new me?

MAN: So far so good.

Unit 27

Exercise 6 (page 271)

JANET: Fred, look. That's Gail and Jim Byrd. They belong to our gym back home.

FRED: Hey, you're right.

JANET: Let's say hello.

FRED: Why? Jim is such a pain.

JANET: But Gail is so nice. And how many people do we know here?

FRED: I guess you're right. Let's go over.

JANET: Gail, Jim. Hello.

GAIL: What a small world! Janet and Fred. When did you two arrive here?

JANET: A few hours ago. What a place! It's like a dream.

JIM: It's OK, but watch out. There are a lot of mosquitoes.

JANET: So . . . where are you staying?

JIM: We're at the Grand Hotel.

JANET: So are we. It looks beautiful.

JIM: It is nice, but it costs a fortune, and don't expect to sleep late. The birds start singing at five in the morning.

JANET: That's no problem for us. We like to get up early. How's the food?

GAIL: Delicious.

JIM: Too spicy.

JANET: The people here seem very friendly.

JIM: How do you know? They don't speak English.

GAIL: Jim! Stop complaining. Why should they speak English? You don't speak French or Tahitian.

JIM: I'm not complaining. I'm just telling it like it is.

Unit 28

Exercise 5 (page 278)

KEN: Cindy? Cindy Lee?

CINDY: That's me. And you're Ken Walters. It's great to see you again. I heard you became a physical therapist. Is it true?

KEN: Uh-huh.

CINDY: Do you like it?

KEN: I like it a lot. Actually, I intend to go back to school for more training in the fall. What about you? Did you become an accountant?

CINDY: Uh-huh, but I got tired of working for a big company.

KEN: So what are you doing?

CINDY: I decided to start my own business.

KEN: That takes guts. What kind of business?

CINDY: I'm a wedding planner. Here's my card.

KEN: How's it going?

CINDY: Great. I enjoy planning parties and I like to work with people.

KEN: Terrific.

CINDY: I plan to open a branch in Middletown next month.

KEN: Now I'm really impressed. Listen, I'd love to hear more about your life. Are you free for dinner this Saturday?

CINDY: I'm sorry. I have a wedding.

KEN: Friday?

CINDY: I have a dinner party for the out-of-town guests that night. I guess that's the downside of this business. Any chance we could meet on Monday night?

KEN: Monday? Why not?

Unit 29

Exercise 5 (page 288)

TOM: Let's watch *Win a Fortune.* It's on in two minutes.

CAROLINA: OK.

HOST: Good evening and welcome to *Win a Fortune.* With us tonight are Jim daSilva from Naples, Florida, and Amy O'Donnell from Racine, Wisconsin.

Jim, Amy, press the button as soon as you know the answer. Then give three more correct answers on that topic and you win $5,000. OK. Now. Our first question is in the field of art. Who painted *The Night Watch?*

HOST: OK, Amy?

AMY: Rembrandt.

HOST: Good. Next. In what century did Rembrandt live?

AMY: The seventeenth century.

HOST: Great. You're doing very well. Now where was Rembrandt born? In what country?

AMY: In Holland.

HOST: Good. Now, you have just one more question to answer . . . What is Rembrandt's full name?

AMY: Hmm . . . I . . . uh . . . I don't know.

TOM: It's Rembrandt van Rijn.

HOST: I'm sorry, Amy. It's Rembrandt van Rijn.

CAROLINA: Hey, you're good Tom.

HOST: Our next question is in the field of music. Who married Yoko Ono?

HOST: Jim?

JIM: John Lennon.

HOST: OK. Now. What was the name of John Lennon's group?

JIM: The Beatles.

HOST: Good. Now two more correct answers and you win. Where did the Beatles come from?

JIM: Liverpool, England.

HOST: Right again. Now for our final question. When did the Beatles make their last appearance together?

JIM: 1965?

TOM: He's wrong. It was 1966.

HOST: I'm sorry, Jim. It was 1966. Well, it's time for a new question.

CAROLINA: You're pretty smart, Tom. Why don't you go on the show?

TOM: Maybe I will.

Unit 30

Exercise 7 (page 308)

MAN: Let's get the paper. I wrote a letter to the editor. I want to see if it's in the paper.

WOMAN: What was your letter about?

MAN: That new twenty-story building on West Street.

WOMAN: Are you for or against it?

MAN: I'm for it.

WOMAN: Why?

MAN: Well, there aren't enough apartments in the area. Many young people are moving away because they can't find a place to live. The new building is going to have two hundred apartments.

WOMAN: Oh.

MAN: And it's going to have a pool.

WOMAN: That's great. Can anyone join it?

MAN: That's what they say. And there are going to be shops on the street level.

WOMAN: But there's going to be more noise and traffic.

MAN: It's not going to be so bad.

WOMAN: It's certainly going to spoil the view for people in nearby homes.

MAN: That's true, but I still think it's going to improve the area.

Unit 31

Exercise 7 (page 317)

TV NEWS ANCHOR: Good evening. Here with me now are our two lucky lottery winners, Susan Kerins and Jim Morris. So, Susan, now that you're so rich, what are you going to do?

SUSAN: Well . . . I'll probably leave my job. I'm a waitress. My customers are nice, but after fifteen years . . . I'm ready to see new places.

ANCHOR: Will you travel?

SUSAN: I think so. I'll probably go to Ireland. That's where my grandparents were born. And I'll buy a house with room for my friends and relatives.

ANCHOR: Sounds wonderful. How about you, Jim? What will you do with all your money?

JIM: I think I'll give it away.

ANCHOR: What was that? You'll give it away?

JIM: That's right. I want it to go to people who really need the money. I'll ask people to write to me and explain why they need the money. And I'll choose the people who need it most.

ANCHOR: Wow! That's very unusual . . . and generous. Uh . . . what about your wife and family? Do you have any idea what they'll say?

JIM: I'm sure my wife will want me to keep the money and my family will be angry. But that won't matter to me.

ANCHOR: Ladies and gentlemen, get out your pens and start writing those letters. A letter to Jim may get you a lot of money.

Unit 32

Exercise 6 (page 324)

ALISON: Jack, your suitcase is so heavy. Are you sure you need everything?

JACK: Oh yes. I'm pretty sure I need everything.

ALISON: Boots?

JACK: We may go mountain climbing. Crater Lake has some great trails.

ALISON: Well, in that case I'll take mine, too. What about this raincoat?

JACK: It might rain.

ALISON: Do you need two hats?

JACK: Yes. I have a sun hat because it might be very sunny, and a rain hat in case . . .

ALISON: I know. It might rain. Jack, you packed two thick books. When are you going to read them?

JACK: At night. Sometimes I wake up during the night. I like to have something to read.

ALISON: And why the sports jacket? We're not going to do anything formal.

JACK: Just in case we go to a fancy restaurant.

ALISON: Well, you know, these days the airlines are very strict. You may pay extra if your suitcase is too heavy.

JACK: Oh? Really? . . . You know, I may not need so much. I might not take the jacket. And maybe I'll forget about this book. And maybe . . .

ALISON: That's a good idea.

Unit 33

Exercise 7 (page 341)

A: Do you have a piece of paper? I want to make a shopping list.

B: Here you go. So what are you going to get?

A: Six cans of vegetable soup. I also want five containers of yogurt, a head of lettuce, and a few packages of frozen vegetables. Can I get you anything? Remember, we're trying to buy only healthy foods.

B: OK. How about a can of nuts and a bunch of grapes?

A: Right. I'll be back in an hour. Just thinking about these healthy foods makes me feel better.

B: Not me. Thinking about these foods makes me want a chocolate bar.

Unit 34

Exercise 8 (page 351)

AGENT: Well, what did you think of the three apartments?

MALE: Honestly, the first, the one on Maple Street, was too small.

FEMALE: And there were too few closets. It was on a beautiful street, but it really wasn't big enough for us.

AGENT: OK. How about the second one, the one across from the park?

FEMALE: That was the right size and had a great view, but it was too noisy. And there were too many people all around.

AGENT: Did you like the last apartment?

MALE: Yes. I liked it a lot. It was big enough and it wasn't too noisy. I'd like to go there again. How about you Sandy? What did you think of it?

FEMALE: I agree. The only problem was the kitchen. It had too few cabinets.

MALE: That's true, but I can build some cabinets. There was enough room.

AGENT: OK. I'll make an appointment to see the apartment again. Is Saturday morning OK?

MALE: Yes, that'd be great. Thank you.

Unit 35

Exercise 7 (page 358)

SON: What are these?

FATHER: The keys to your new red sports car.

SON: Mine?

FATHER: Yes, yours. It's a present for you for your eighteenth birthday.

SON: Wow. Are you sure?

FATHER: Of course. Every young man needs his own sports car.

SON: You're so right!

Unit 36

Exercise 5 (page 374)

JANE: Hello, this is Jane Merrin. May I please speak to Dr. Finkel? I'm calling for the results of an X-ray.

RECEPTIONIST: One moment please.

DR. FINKEL: Hello, this is Dr. Finkel.

JANE: Hi, Dr. Finkel, this is Jane Merrin.

DR. FINKEL: How's the ankle?

JANE: It really hurts.

DR. FINKEL: Well, the X-rays came in. Nothing is broken.

JANE: That's good. But it's still swollen and it really hurts.

DR. FINKEL: Keep your foot up whenever possible. You can also take two extra-strength Tylenol every four hours.

JANE: Can I go to work?

DR. FINKEL: Yes, you can. You can work. You can drive.

JANE: Can I play tennis?

DR. FINKEL: No, I'm afraid not. No sports for three weeks.

JANE: OK. Thanks, Dr. Finkel.

DR. FINKEL: Bye, Jane.

JANE: Bye.

Unit 37

Exercise 7 (page 382)

ROBERT: John, can you please call Bill and get me an appointment for next Tuesday at nine?

JOHN: Is that Bill Richards?

ROBERT: Yes.

JOHN: OK, Robert. Anything else?

ROBERT: Yes. John, would you please write thank-you notes to everyone at the meeting yesterday?

JOHN: Of course.

ROBERT: And John, can you look at my report? See if you find any way to shorten it.

JOHN: Sure.

ROBERT: By the way, John, did I tell you that I'm going to be in Lima, Peru, all next week? I'd like you to contact me if Dr. Rice calls. I'll send you my contact information when I get there.

Unit 38

Exercise 6 (page 393)

MAX: Kaori, Sho, I just got my plane ticket to Japan. Now I've got a lot of questions.

KAORI: Well, I hope we can help.

MAX: First of all, should I bring along cash or can I use a credit card everywhere?

KAORI: You can use credit cards in major stores, but if you shop at small stores, cash is better. So, I say, bring some cash. Sho, what do you think?

SHO: I agree. Definitely bring cash.

MAX: OK. That was easy. Now I know that people bow in Japan. I feel funny bowing, but do you think I should bow when I meet someone?

SHO: No, it's not necessary for you to bow. You're a foreigner and Japanese know that it's not your custom. And a lot of younger Japanese don't bow these days either.

MAX: What about when I enter a home? Should I remove my shoes?

KAORI: Yes, you should. You will find some slippers near the door. Put them on and leave your shoes by the door.

MAX: OK. Should I learn a few phrases in Japanese? I can't learn very much. Is it worth it?

SHO: I think so. You should learn some phrases because people will appreciate the effort.

MAX: Well, I'm sure I'll have more questions before I leave. Thanks so much.

SHO: Wait. There's one important thing you forgot.

MAX: What?

SHO: This is really important. Nobody goes to Japan without a translator. You'd better get a ticket for me.

MAX: And translators only travel first class, right?

SHO: How did you know?

Unit 39

Exercise 6 (page 401)

PROF. GRANT: Hi Bill, can I help you?

BILL: Yes, Professor Grant. I know it's a long way off, but I'm thinking about getting a masters in business administration. What do you advise?

PROF. GRANT: That is a long way off, but it's always good to know what you should do. First of all, you have to have a bachelor's degree. It's a good idea to take courses in economics. Then you have to take a test called the GMAT. It's a test of your ability in business. Then you have to check with the schools you're interested in. Each school has different requirements. These days many schools like students to get some work experience before they study for an MBA. You don't have to work, but it's a good idea. It makes your studies more meaningful.

BILL: Thanks a lot, Dr. Grant.

Unit 40

Exercise 6 (page 420)

A: So how do you like your new apartment?

B: Well, it's a lot farther from school than my old one and it's not as convenient to shopping, but I like it a lot more.

A: How come?

B: I have an extra bedroom, the building is newer, and the apartment is much larger. My old apartment was in an old building. There were always a lot of problems with the heating and the plumbing.

A: I know your old place faced another building. How's the view from this place?

B: Much better. I can see a park from my living room and my bedroom faces a garden.

A: That's really nice. How are the neighbors?

B: Well, the people in my old building were friendlier. They were mostly students or retired people. My neighbors here have jobs so they're always busy. They're quieter than my old neighbors, but I miss my old neighbors.

Unit 41

Exercise 5 (page 426)

1. That was a good speech.
2. That was a good speech.
3. That was a good speech.
4. That was a good speech.
5. That was a good speech.

Unit 42

Exercise 7 (page 435)

JAMES: Lou feels very bad.

VICKIE: I know. He really wanted that promotion, but we couldn't give it to him. He's just too critical of others. Nobody's work is good enough for him. It's too bad. But Lou never thinks he's wrong. He always thinks it's the other guy.

JAMES: Yeah. I feel good about Mary, though. She's bright and confident, and she'll bring out the best in others. Also, Mary is very fair. Her word is as good as gold. Lou is not as fair as Mary, and she's a real team player.

Unit 43

Exercise 6 (page 445)

JIM: Good evening and welcome to *How Much Do You Know?* where guests answer questions and win all sorts of wonderful prizes. Tonight, back for the third week, is Mariella Barilla. Mariella, you know the rules.

MARIELLA: Yes, Jim.

JIM: Five seconds to answer the question. Are you ready?

MARIELLA: I'm ready.

JIM: OK. Pick a card. . . . Well, I see you picked the category of planets. Our first question is: Which planet in our solar system is both the lightest and the second biggest?

MARIELLA: I think it's Saturn.

JIM: You're right. For that answer you win a beautiful 100% cashmere jacket.

MARIELLA: It's beautiful. Thank you.

JIM: You're very welcome. . . . Next. What is the brightest planet, the one you can see with the naked eye?

MARIELLA: That's Venus.

JIM: You're right again. Now for our third question. This planet is the largest in our solar system.

MARIELLA: Jupiter.

JIM: Excellent. And you've just won a trip for two to London for four days.

MARIELLA: That's fantastic.

JIM: And for our last question. This planet has the largest volcano in the solar system. The volcano is 27 kilometers high.

MARIELLA: Is it Mars?

JIM: Yes, it is. Fantastic. And for that you win a brand-new bright red sports car. Congratulations, Mariella.

Student Book Answer Key

UNIT 1 The Present of *Be*: Statements
(pages 4–11)

Before You Read 1. T   2. F   3. F   4. F   5. F

After You Read A. 1. F   2. T   3. T
                    B. 1. 're   2. 's   3. is not

1

4. √ Circle **They're**   7. √
5. √   8. √ Circle **He's**
6. Circle **It's**

2

1. is   3. am, am
2. is, is   4. are

3

2. is   7. are not
3. is   8. is not
4. is   9. is
5. is   10. am not
6. are

4

Answers will vary.
1. I'm a student. OR I'm not a student.
2. I'm from London. OR I'm not from London.
3. He's famous in this country. OR He's not famous in this country. (He isn't famous in this country.)
4. It's popular in my country. OR It's not popular in my country. (It isn't popular in my country.)
5. He's Brazilian.
6. They're great soccer players.
7. My friend and I are big soccer fans. OR My friend and I are not big soccer fans. OR My friend and I aren't big soccer fans.

5

2. He's   5. They're
3. We're   6. She's
4. It's   7. They're

6

My parents ~~they~~ *are* teachers. Alessandra is my sister. She *is* ^ an engineer. Marco ~~be~~ *is* my brother. ~~Is~~ *He is* a businessman. They *are* ^ far away, but thanks to e-mail, ~~we~~ *we're* close.

7

Hideki Matsui, baseball player, Japan
Mia Hamm, soccer player, the United States
Ang Lee, movie director, Taiwan
Steven Spielberg, movie director, the United States
Paulina Rubio, singer, Mexico
Beyoncé, singer, the United States
J. K. Rowling, writer, England
Gabriel Garcia Marquez, writer, Colombia

8

Corrections after 'That's wrong' will vary.
1. That's wrong.   5. That's wrong.
2. That's right.   6. That's wrong.
3. That's wrong.   7. That's right.
4. That's wrong.   8. That's wrong.

UNIT 2 The Present of *Be*: *Yes/No* Questions
(pages 12–21)

After You Read
1. No.
2. Yes.
3. Yes.
4. No. (She is, but he isn't.)
5. I don't know.

1

2. c   4. b   6. g
3. a   5. e   7. d

2. Is today Tuesday?
3. Are we in the right room?
4. Are you a new student?
5. Is she the teacher?
6. Is it ten o'clock?
7. Are they in our class?
8. is this your pen?
9. Are Kaori and Marco here?
10. Am I in the right room?

3

2. **A:** Is your watch from Switzerland?
   B: Yes, it is. OR No, it isn't.
3. **A:** Are your shoes comfortable?
   B: Yes, they are. OR No, they aren't. (No, they're not.)
4. **A:** Are camera phones expensive in your country?
   B: Yes, they are. OR No, they aren't. (No, they're not.)
5. **A:** Is your name easy to pronounce?
   B: Yes, it is. OR No, it isn't. (No, it's not.)
6. **A:** Is Tasmania in Australia?
   B: Yes, it is.
7. **A:** Are you and your classmates from different cities?
   B: Yes, we are. OR No, we aren't. (No, we're not.)
8. **A:** Are your classmates busy now?
   B: Yes, they are. OR No, they aren't. (No, they're not.)

4

A. 2. **A:** Are her friends interesting and fun?
      B: Yes, they are.
   3. **A:** Are her friends on time?
      B: No, they're not. OR No, they aren't.
   4. **A:** Is Dr. Brown a psychologist?
      B: Yes, she is.

B. *Answers will vary.*
   2. **A:** Are her friends unhappy?
   3. **A:** Are her friends important?
   4. **A:** Are her friends good at planning their time?
   5. **A:** Is the psychologist's answer good?

5

2. **A:** Is ^*it* late?
   B: No, it's early.

3. **A:** ^*Is he* ~~He~~ Korean?
   B: No, he isn't.
4. **A:** Am I in the right room?
   B: ~~You are yes~~. *Yes, you are.*
5. **A:** Is this English 3?
   B: Yes, I think ^*so*.
6. **A:** Are they in room 102?
   B: I ~~no~~ *don't* know.

6

1. b   3. b   5. c
2. b   4. a

8

1. d   3. e   5. c
2. b   4. f   6. a

UNIT 3 **The Past of *Be*** (pages 22–30)

After You Read 1. yes   2. no   3. no   4. yes

1

Dear Emily and Rob,
   I <u>was</u> happy to meet you finally. Jay <u>was</u> right—you are both very special. Thanks for the CD. It <u>was</u> a good idea. The songs <u>were</u> perfect for the party.

                          Sincerely,
                          Gina

2

1. **A:** Was Emily at the party?
   B: Yes, she was. Why?
   A: She's not in the photos.
   B: She was the photographer.
2. **A:** Were Ali and Mo in school on Monday?
   B: Yes, they were. Why?
   A: Their names are not on the attendance sheet.
   B: I think they were late.
3. **A:** How's the weather in Montreal?
   B: It's cold. It was cold yesterday too.
   A: Was it cold the day before?
   B: I think so.

3

A. 1. wasn't   2. wasn't, was   3. were, weren't

B. *Possible answers:*
1. was, wasn't OR wasn't, was
2. was, wasn't OR wasn't, was
3. were, weren't OR weren't, were
4. was, wasn't OR wasn't, was
5. was, wasn't OR wasn't, was

4

2. was	5. were	8. wasn't	11. were
3. Were	6. wasn't	9. was	12. Were
4. was	7. Was	10. were	13. weren't

5

2. it was cold
3. My friend was in Seoul
4. It was sunny
5. She was in class
6. He wasn't at the airport
7. was in Lima
8. was busy

6

2. **A:** Was Dave in Ottawa on business?
   B: Yes, he was at a meeting there.
3. **A:** Was the airport closed?
   B: No, but all the planes were late.
4. **A:** Were Emily and Rob at the party?
   B: Yes, they were there for hours.
5. **A:** Were you at home last night?
   B: No, I was at a party.

7

2. It was cold in Toronto yesterday.
3. It wasn't cold two days ago.
4. Were you in Toronto last month?
5. Were they in Toronto last year?
6. A week ago we weren't there.

8

Hi Victor,
    Right now Bob and I are in a taxi on our
                                    were
way home from the airport. We ~~was~~ in Mexico
                was
all last week. It ~~were~~ great. The weather ~~it~~ was
dry and sunny. The people were warm and
                        were
friendly. Last night we ~~was~~ at the Ballet
                        were
Folklorico. The dancers ~~was~~ terrific. There was
                        was not good
only one problem. My Spanish ~~no was good~~.
See you soon.

                                Rina

9

1. concert was, seats were
2. was, town, last week, back, 917-865-4821
3. sorry, wasn't, meeting, 876-421-0090

11

are, are, is ('s), 's (is)

was, was, I, 'm (am)

was, was, was

's (is), It, 's (is), 's (is)

's (is)

're (are)

PART 1 From Grammar to Writing
(pages 31–32)

2

1. This is Ms. Herrera.
2. Her address is 4 Riverdale Avenue.
3. I'm her good friend.
4. She was in Bangkok and Taiwan last year.

3

(See graphic at the top of page 150.)

UNIT 4 Count Nouns; Proper Nouns
(pages 38–47)

After You Read 1. photographer   2. artist
3. France   4. photos

1

1. accountant
2. *any two:* photo, school, teacher, photographer, library, world, life, show, month
3. *any two:* Jasmine, Brazil, Bob, New York, Amy, India
4. friends, photos

2

A.

1. a	5. a	8. an
2. a	6. a	9. a
3. a	7. an	10. a
4. an		

B. *(See photo on page 151.)*

> Ruth
> Hi ~~ruth~~,
>
> John · I · Acapulco · It's
> ~~john and i are in acapulco~~ this week. ~~it's~~ beautiful
>
> The · It's
> here. ~~the~~ people are friendly and the weather is great. ~~it's~~
>
> sunny and warm.
>
> Last · Mexico City · I
> ~~last~~ week we were in ~~mexico city~~ for two days. ~~i was~~
>
> My
> there on business. ~~my~~ meetings were long and difficult,
>
> Hope
> but our evenings were fun. ~~hope~~ all is well with you.
>
> Regards,
>
> Ellen
> ~~ellen~~

To:
Ms. Ruth Holland
~~ms. ruth holland~~
Oldwick St
~~10 oldwick st~~
Ringwood, New Jersey
~~ringwood, new jersey 07456~~
U.S.A.
~~u.s.a.~~

3			
1. a	**5.** a, a	**8.** Ø, Ø
2. Ø	**6.** Ø	**9.** Ø, Ø
3. an	**7.** a	**10.** Ø
4. Ø		

4		
2. countries	**6.** fish	**9.** husbands
3. museums	**7.** classes	**10.** people
4. watches	**8.** wives	**11.** flowers
5. clothes		

5

Mike Cho, Doug, Mike, Mike, Phoenix, San Francisco, San Francisco, India, Kuwait, Turkey, Jordan, Egypt

6

2. This is ^a^ photo of Henri Matisse.
3. Henri Matisse was ^an^ artist.
4. Matisse's paintings are in ~~museum~~ ^museums^ all over the world.
5. We see four ~~bird~~ ^birds^ in this photo.
6. In this photo Matisse was in the south of ~~france~~ ^France^.

7			
2. classes	/ɪz/	**5.** pants	/s/
3. scissors	/z/	**6.** glasses	/ɪz/
4. boxes	/ɪz/	**7.** books	/s/

9

A.
1. an audio tape
2. a board (chalkboard)
3. a bookbag
4. CDs
5. a clock
6. a desk
7. a dictionary
8. notebooks
9. a wastebasket

UNIT 5 Descriptive Adjectives
(pages 48–52)

After You Read

1. F	3. F	5. F	7. F
2. T	4. T	6. F	

1

fun, old, modern, high, fresh, helpful, friendly, delicious, easy, great

2

1. We are at an old market.
2. Beautiful carpets are for sale everywhere.

3 hat

7 eye

8 ear

4 earring

9 lip

10 woman

flower 5

man 1

suit 6

hand 2

3. The prices are reasonable.
4. It is warm and sunny. OR It is sunny and warm.
5. I'm tired but happy. OR I'm happy but tired.

<table>
<tr><td>3</td></tr>
</table>

beautiful
A: The colors are ~~beautifuls~~.

an
B: I got it at ˄old market in Cappadocia.

interesting things
A: Were there many ~~things interesting~~ to buy?

great colors
A: They're ~~colors great~~.

<table>
<tr><td>4</td></tr>
</table>

1. a   **2.** b   **3.** a   **4.** b   **5.** b

<table>
<tr><td>5</td></tr>
</table>

2. b	**5.** j	**8.** a
3. g	**6.** i	**9.** c
4. h	**7.** f	**10.** e

UNIT 6 Prepositions of Place

(pages 53–58)

After You Read

1. between   **3.** near   **5.** at
2. next to   **4.** on

1

What's the message? I LOVE ENGLISH

2

2. between   **5.** at
3. on the, of   **6.** on the
4. next to   **7.** under

3

1. 3rd   **4.** between, bakery
2. between, Streets   **5.** Moon Palace
3. in front of   Restaurant

4

Answers will vary.
2. in, (305)
3. at, at
4. in (Turkey)
5. in (Istanbul)
6. on the (fourth) floor
7. at (65 Main Street)

5

2. The bookstore is on the corner ^*of* Main Street.

3. He lives on ^*the* first floor.

4. √

5. He's not ^*at* work today. He's home.

6. I'm ^*on* the corner of Main and Second.

7. A man is in front ^*of* the stationery store.

8. √

9. √

10. Her office is ^*at* 78 Elm Street.

11. He's ^*in* Osaka now.

12. We're ^*on the* third floor.

6

1. KOREA   **3.** MADAGASCAR
2. ECUADOR   **4.** SPAIN

UNIT 7 *Wh-* Questions   (pages 59–63)

After You Read   **1.** b   **2.** a   **3.** b   **4.** a

1

1. Georgia O'Keeffe
2. Museum of Fine Arts
3. *White Rose with Larkspur*
4. Boston, Massachusetts

2

1. What's   **3.** Where's   **5.** Why is
2. Where's   **4.** What's

3

1. What is surrealism?
2. Who are René Magritte and Salvador Dali?
3. Where are they from?
4. What is the name of Dali's most famous painting?

4

2. Who ^*is* the teacher ~~is~~?
3. Where ~~he~~ is **he**?
4. Why **are** the students ~~are~~ so quiet?

5

1. a painting.
2. brother.
3. 2nd Avenue.
4. It's always closed on Monday.

6

A.
1. What is the Hermitage?
2. Who is Salvador Dali?
3. Who is René Magritte?
4. What is the Museum of Fine Arts?
5. Who is Auguste Rodin?

PART II From Grammar to Writing   (page 64)

2

1. and   **2.** but   **3.** and   **4.** but

3

and, and, and, but, and, and, and, but

UNIT 8 The Simple Present: Affirmative and Negative Statements (pages 70–77)

After You Read 1. T 2. F 3. T 4. T 5. F 6. F

1

2. like   **4.** carry   **6.** means
3. knows   **5.** shop   **7.** have

2

2. don't buy   **6.** doesn't look
3. don't like   **7.** aren't
4. don't need   **8.** isn't
5. doesn't like

3

2. a. need   **b.** don't need
3. a. wants   **b.** doesn't want
4. a. like   **b.** don't like
5. a. has   **b.** doesn't have
6. a. goes   **b.** doesn't go

4

A.
2. is   **7.** prefers   **11.** doesn't have
3. has   **8.** aren't   **12.** wants
4. have   **9.** think   **13.** don't want
5. loves   **10.** give   **14.** thinks
6. wants

B. want, agree, works, thinks, sounds

5

She ~~work~~ *works* for a big advertising company. She studies teenagers.

She ~~say~~ *says*, "Teenagers change things.

They ~~doesn't~~ *don't* think like the manufacturers.

Manufacturers ~~thinks~~ *think* of one way to use things. Teenagers find another way. For example, pagers are for emergencies. But teenagers ~~are~~ think they are fun and cute.

They don't ~~uses~~ *use* them for emergencies.

They ~~uses~~ *use* them for fun."

6

2. buys /z/   **6.** carries /z/
3. uses /ɪz/   **7.** misses /ɪz/
4. costs /s/   **8.** watches /ɪz/
5. knows /z/   **9.** thinks /s/

8

1. comes, removes, puts
2. wear
3. wear, takes
4. give
5. don't work, have, watch
6. bangs

UNIT 9 The Simple Present: *Yes/No* Questions and Short Answers (pages 78–86)

After You Read 1. F 2. T 3. F 4. F 5. T
6. F 7. T

1

2. d   **3.** c   **4.** e   **5.** a

2

2. Q: Does, have   **6. Q:** Does, have
  A: doesn't   **A:** it does
3. Q: Does, know   **7. Q:** Does, rain
  A: he doesn't   **A:** it doesn't
4. Q: Do, like   **8. Q:** Do, have
  A: they do   **A:** you do
5. Q: Does, wear   **9. Q:** Does, go
  A: she doesn't   **A:** she doesn't

3

2. Q: Does   **8. Q:** Do
  A: he does   **A:** do
3. Q: Are   **9. Q:** Does
  A: are   **A:** doesn't
4. Q: Do   **10. Q:** Are
  A: they don't   **A:** are
5. Q: Are   **11. Q:** Are
  A: they aren't OR   **A:** we are
    they're not   **12. Q:** Do
6. Q: Do   **A:** don't
  A: they do
7. Q: Is
  A: she isn't OR
    she's not

3. Does he come **9.** Does he have
4. No, he doesn't **10.** Yes, he does
5. Does he come **11.** Do you see
6. No, he doesn't **12.** Yes, we do OR Yes, I do
7. Do you like **13.** Do you bring
8. Yes, we do **14.** No, I don't

5

1. **B:** Yes, she ~~goes~~ *does*.
2. **A:** Does he ~~needs~~ *need* help?
3. **A:** Do they ~~are~~ like jazz?
4. **A:** ~~Do~~ *Does* she live near the museum?
   B: Yes, she ~~lives~~ *does*.
5. **A:** Does he ~~has~~ *have* a roommate?
6. **B:** Yes, we ~~do~~ *are*.

6

likes: to see one or two people at a time OR to be alone

listens to: jazz

studies: at night, in her room

Answers to next two questions will vary.

9

1. No. I'm busy all afternoon.
2. Yes. It's 9:45.
3. Yes, thanks. We need a salad.
4. Yes, it's more than two hundred dollars.
5. No, it's broken.

UNIT 10 The Simple Present:
Wh- Questions (pages 87–95)

After You Read **2.** d **3.** e **4.** c **5.** a

1

2. b **3.** e **4.** d **5.** a **6.** c

2

2. Where does the baby sleep?
3. How do they feel at night?

4. Who does she dream about?
5. What does he dream about?
6. Who daydreams?

3

2. When does school begin?
3. Where does Doug have lunch?
4. What does Doug have for lunch on Mondays?
5. Who does Doug meet at the soccer field after school?
6. Who plays soccer in West Park?
7. How does Doug feel after soccer practice?
8. Why does Doug stay up late?

4

 S O
2. My brother sees his friends after school.
   Q: Who sees his friends after school?
   A: My brother does.
   Q: Who does my brother see after school?
   A: His friends.

 S O
3. My mother wakes me on weekdays.
   Q: Who wakes me on weekdays?
   A: My mother does.
   Q: Who does my mother wake on weekdays?
   A: She wakes me.

 S O
4. Maria helps her neighbor.
   Q: Who helps her neighbor?
   A: Maria does.
   Q: Who does Maria help?
   A: Her neighbor.

 S O
5. Shira and Carolina meet friends at a club on weekends.
   Q: Who meets friends at a club on weekends?
   A: Shira and Carolina do.
   Q: Who do Shira and Carolina meet on weekends?
   A: Friends.

5

2. Why ^*do* they need two pillows?
3. Who ~~sleep~~ *sleeps* on the sofa?
4. When does she ~~goes~~ *go* to bed?
5. Who ~~wake~~ *wakes* you?
7. How ^*does* he ~~feels~~ *feel* about that?

6

1. a forest
2. beard
3. catch her
4. he walks fast, he runs, she wakes up
5. too busy, a vacation

PART III From Grammar to Writing
(page 96)

2

Example paragraph:

First, I take a shower. *Next,* I have breakfast. *After that* I drive to the train station. *Then* I take a train to the bus. *Finally* I get to work.

UNIT 11 *When, What* + Noun; Prepositions of Time; Ordinal Numbers
(pages 102–111)

After You Read 1. November 8th

1

Her yoga class is on Tuesdays **at 6:00 in the evening**.

She has a dentist's appointment **on Friday, September 4, at 10:00 in the morning**.

Mary's plane arrives **on Sunday, September 6, at 10:00 at night**.

Labor Day is **on Monday, September 7**.

2

1. In	**4.** first	**7.** 29
2. In	**5.** In	**8.** 30
3. on	**6.** on	**9.** four

3

1. Two	**3.** Fourth	**5.** first
2. thirty-first	**4.** third	**6.** second

4

2. Q: When is Thailand's national holiday?
  A: It's on December 5.
3. Q: What country has a national holiday on July 1?
  A: Canada does.
4. Q: What country has a national holiday in August?
  A: Korea does.

5

2. American Thanksgiving is on the ~~four~~ *fourth* Thursday in November.
3. Many people ~~at~~ *in* Japan visit the Palace on New Year's Day.
4. (no mistakes)
5. Americans celebrate Independence Day ~~in~~ *on* July 4.
6. On Independence Day, many people watch fireworks ~~in~~ *at* night.
7. New Year's Eve is ~~in~~ *on* December 31.

6

1. on Commercial, First and Second
2. on the fifth
3. on 75th Street, Second and Third
4. on the third

UNIT 12 Possessive Nouns and Possessive Adjectives; Questions with *Whose*
(pages 112–121)

Before You Read 1. a   **2.** b

After You Read Left to right: Boris, Kim, Juan

1

1. teacher	**4.** pharmacist
2. pharmacist	**5.** actor
3. teacher	**6.** actor

2

1. a. mother's	**b.** grandmother	
2. a. father's	**b.** grandmother	
3. a. brother's	**b.** son	
4. a. brother's	**b.** nieces	
5. brothers		
6. a. aunt	**b.** mother	
7. a. grandfather's	**b.** uncle	
8. a. daughter	**b.** sister	**c.** me

3

2. her	6. Its
3. Their	7. your
4. his, their	8. her
5. his	

4

2. Where's	6. Whose
3. Whose	7. Who's
4. Where's	8. What's
5. When's	9. Whose

5

1. **a.** your **b.** Leila's
2. Your
3. **a.** Their **b.** Their
4. **a.** her **b.** my
5. Whose
6. Who's
7. women's
8. men's
9. **a.** his **b.** It's
10. father's

6

I, I, my, My, He, his, She, her, They, Their, He, Our OR My, It, My, I

7

1. **A:** ~~Who's~~? *Whose*
   B: ~~Dans~~. *Dan's*
2. **A:** Is ~~Maria~~ sister here? *Maria's*
   B: No, she's not.
   A: Is Maria here?
   B: No, but ~~his~~ brother is. *her*
   A: Where is Maria?
   B: I think she's with ~~his~~ sister. ~~Their~~ at the movies. *her* *They're*

8

1. Maria's	4. partner's
2. Maria	5. partner
3. Marias	6. partners

10

2. Who's	5. Whose	8. Whose
3. Whose	6. Who's	9. Who's
4. Who's	7. Whose	10. Whose

UNIT 13 *This / That / These / Those; Questions with Or* (pages 122–128)

After You Read 1. b 2. a 3. a 4. a

1

1. c 2. b 3. a 4. c

2

1. These	4. this
2. this	5. That
3. that	6. those

3

2. **A:** Is that a snake or a stick?
   B: It's a stick.
3. **A:** Is that campground open all year round or only in the summer?
   B: It's open only in the summer.
4. **A:** Is this trail easy or difficult?
   B: It's difficult.
5. **A:** Do they speak English or French?
   B: They speak French.

4

1. These	5. this
2. This	6. These
3. these	7. These
4. this	

5

2. **A:** Do you have a night flight or a morning flight?
   B: ~~Yes.~~ I leave at 9 A.M. *A morning flight.*
3. **A:** Is ~~these~~ your flashlight? *this*
   B: Yes, it is. Thanks.
4. **A:** Are ~~these~~ men on the mountain OK? *those*
   B: I think so. But it's hard to see them from here.

6

Check (√) 2, 4, 5, 6, 7

UNIT 14 *One/Ones/It*

After You Read

2. The woman wants a gift. It's for her ~~cousin~~. *friend*

3. The woman looks at a sweatshirt with pockets and one with a ~~hole~~. *hood*

4. Gift cards are ~~an unusual~~ gift this year. The woman buys one. *a popular*

1

2. b   **3.** b   **4.** a   **5.** a   **6.** b

2

1. one   **3.** ones, one
2. one   **4.** ones, ones

3

1. one   **4.** it   **7.** one
2. one   **5.** it   **8.** it
3. it   **6.** it   **9.** it

4

2. it   **5.** ones   **7.** ones
3. one   **6.** it   **8.** one
4. it

5

2. These apples are delicious. Try one. But first wash ~~one~~. *it*

3. We have two gift cards. ~~It~~ is in your desk and one is on the counter. *One*

4. These ~~ones~~ are new. Those ~~ones~~ are old.

5. Do you need silver earrings or gold ~~one~~ *ones*

6. I don't want a new leather jacket. I have ~~it~~. *one*

6

2. cute, inexpensive ones
3. a funny one
4. a beautiful, nice one
5. a practical one
6. a big one

PART IV From Grammar to Writing

1

Subject: Juan's Surprise Party

Dear Hector,

Are you free on the 16th? I hope so.

Ray and I want to invite you to a surprise party for Juan on November 16th, at 9:00 P.M.

It's his 21st birthday. The party is at Ali and Ted's apartment.

Hope to see you there.

Ron

2

Dear Uncle John,

Bob and I want to invite you to a party for my parents' 25th wedding anniversary. It's on Sunday Dec. 11th. The party is at our home at 23 Main St. It's at three o'clock. I hope you can make it.

Emily

UNIT 15 Present Progressive: Affirmative and Negative Statements

After You Read **1.** e   **2.** d   **3.** c   **4.** b   **5.** f   **6.** a

1

A: 2. ride
3.   watching
4. visit   visiting
5. fly   flying
6. send   sending
7. get   getting
8. use   using

B: She isn't sending it by mail.
She isn't using coins.

2

2. is flying OR 's flying
3. is getting OR 's getting
4. is playing OR 's playing
5. is not watching OR isn't watching OR 's not watching

6. is riding OR 's riding
7. is using OR 's using
8. is sending OR 's sending, isn't sending OR 's not sending OR is not sending

3

2. She is OR 's getting on the train.
3. Now she is OR 's checking e-mail, eating a roll, and drinking a cup of coffee.
4. **a.** She is OR 's going home.
   b. She is OR 's talking to friends on her cellphone.
5. Maria is OR 's eating dinner and watching a video.
6. **a.** She is OR 's not talking. OR She isn't talking.
   b. She is OR 's not thinking. OR She isn't thinking.
   c. She is OR 's not watching TV or videos. OR She isn't watching TV or videos.
   d. She is OR 's relaxing.
7. She is OR 's sleeping and dreaming.

4

2. is preparing OR 's preparing
3. is changing OR 's changing
4. are marrying OR 're marrying
5. are not staying OR aren't staying
6. are working OR 're working
7. are staying OR 're staying
8. are making OR 're making
9. doing
10. cooking
11. cleaning
12. are growing OR 're growing

5

Dear Eun Yung,
   It was great to hear from you.
        'm
   I sitting on a park bench in Prospect Park
   ^

and waiting for Sung Hyun. It's a beautiful day.
            taking   *are*
An older man is ~~takes~~ pictures. Two boys ~~is~~
                              are
running and ~~is~~ laughing. Some women doing
                                       ^
            talking
tai chi. A young woman is ~~talks~~ on her cell
            pushing
phone. A father is ~~push~~ his baby in a stroller.

            is   *drinking*
The baby holding a bottle. He isn't ~~drinks~~ from
         ^
            is
the bottle. He playing with it.
            ^

   I hope your work is going well. Sung Hyun
   working   *I'm*   *planning*
is ~~works~~ hard and ~~I~~ studying hard. We're ~~plan~~
a vacation in Hawaii next summer. I hope you
can join us.

                        Fondly,
                        Bo Jeong

6

1. T	4. F	7. F
2. F	5. F	8. T
3. T	6. T	9. T

UNIT 16 The Present Progressive: *Yes/No* and *Wh-* Questions (pages 150–158)

After You Read 1. c 2. b 3. g 4. f 5. e
6. d 7. a

1

1. Are you reading?, Are you taping the show for me?
2. What's happening now?
3.

Wh- word	*Be*	Subject	Base Form of verb + *-ing*
What	are	you	watching?
Where	are	they	working?
What	's	Lucy	doing?

2

1. b.
2. a. Is he looking at the TV Guide?
3. e. Are they enjoying the talk show?
4. c. Are we paying a lot for cable TV?
5. d. Is the movie starting now?

3

2. Are you feeling any better
3. Are you taking the medicine
4. Where are you calling from
5. What street are you walking on
6. What is she wearing OR What's she wearing
7. Is she talking to anyone
8. What are you doing
9. Are you watching TV
10. What's happening

4

1. 'm waiting for   **3.** Are, looking for
2. 's, looking at   **4.** are, listening to

5

B: No, ~~I~~ *I'm* not.

A: ~~What~~ *What're* you watching? OR What you *are* ^ watching?

B: I'm ~~watch~~ *watching* a cooking show.

A: Oh. What *'s* ^ happening?

A: What he *'s* ^ making?

A: What's he ~~use~~? *using*

A: ~~He~~ *Is h* ^ e making the tomato sauce?

6

ROBERTO: 're you listening to
ROBERTO: 's playing
ROBERTO: are they playing
CESAR: Fenway Park
ROBERTO: Who's winning
CESAR: tie
ROBERTO: 's happening
CESAR: home
ROBERTO: Red Sox

7

A.
Student A
2. Who isn't breathing?
3. What are the man and housekeeper doing?
4. Who is a family friend calling?
5. What are some big men wearing?
6. What are they doing on a playing field?
7. What is a tall man carrying?

Student B
2. What is she wearing?
3. What is she talking about?
4. Where are a young couple and an older couple having dessert?
5. Who is smiling?
6. Who is throwing a pie in her husband's face?

B. 1. c   **2.** d   **3.** b   **4.** a

UNIT 17
The Imperative   (pages 159–166)

After You Read
2. Include your name, ~~e-mail~~ address, and phone number with your story.

3. Don't write more than ~~10~~ *100* words.

4. Visit our ~~office in Pleasantville~~ *website at PC.com* for current information.

5. E-mail ~~*Teachers*~~ *Parents* and Children at PC.com.

1

Sentences checked (√): 1, 3, 4, 6, 8, 9

2

1. Point   **6.** Don't use
2. Shop   **7.** Enter
3. Make   **8.** Please don't write
4. Don't shop   **9.** Send
5. Wash

3

B.
Walk, 72nd, Turn, two

4

2. don't open   **5.** Don't eat
3. Please don't call   **6.** Please show
4. Please come   **7.** Please don't touch

5

1. Pick up   **3.** Send in
2. Fill in   **4.** Check out

6

1. √
2. Please ~~to~~ include your name and address.

3. For information, ~~visits~~ *visit* our website at www.longtrip.com.
4. √

5. Write ~~not~~ *no* more than 100 words.

6. Don't ~~sends~~ *send* money.

7. ~~Send~~ *Please send* your entry ~~please~~ before the end of this month.

Caller	Message for	Message	Caller's Number
Denise	Penny	Please call me.	224-3479
Gary	Steve	I have tickets to basketball game. Call if interested.	420-9097
Penny	Steve	Don't eat cheesecake— for Aunt Lyn.	
Mom	Steve	Don't call before 8. Love to everyone.	

UNIT 18 *Can/Could* (pages 167–173)

After You Read 1. F 2. F 3. T 4. ? 5. F 6. T

1

A. 1. can talk
2. can't understand
3. can't help
4. can't hear
5. can lift
6. can't smell
7. couldn't reach

B. 1. e 2. b 3. f 4. g 5. a 6. d 7. c

2

2. can't see
3. can sit, can't bring
4. can walk
5. can speak
6. can't drive
7. can't open

3

2. Can he ask questions? Yes, he can.
3. Can he make suggestions? Yes, he can.
4. Can Aimee and N'kisi get a car now? No, they can't.
5. Can you believe this conversation? Yes, I can. OR No, I can't.

4

1. b. Could, catch
2. a. could use   b. could make
3. couldn't do
4. could understand

5. couldn't speak
6. could play
7. could lift

5

         can
B: Yes, thanks. How I get to your home?

A: You can ~~to~~ take the train and a taxi.

               can't
A: I'm sorry I can't. I ~~no can~~ drive. Maybe Bob can meet~~s~~ you. He has a car and he can ~~to~~ drive.

6

2. can sit, can't beg
3. can lift, can't
4. can play, can play
5. can read, can't understand

UNIT 19 Suggestions: *Let's, Why don't we . . . ?, Why don't you . . . ?*; Responses (pages 174–180)

After You Read

               Snuba diving
Five friends decide to go ~~snorkeling~~. They also

       a camera
decide to buy ~~phones~~.

              the fish
They want to take pictures of ~~themselves~~. Arda

             front desk
and Rodica get information at the ~~hotel pool~~.

1

B.

A: Let's get some souvenirs.

B: That's a good idea. Why don't we go to the gift shop? They have some beautiful things.

A: That's true, but the prices are high. Why don't we go to the market?

B: OK. The prices there are better.

2

2. Let's take   5. Let's walk
3. Let's not go   6. Let's do
4. Let's not go   7. Let's not sleep

3

1. c   **3.** b   **5.** f
2. a   **4.** e   **6.** d

4

1. pick up, a.   **4.** turn on, a.
2. sit down, a.   **5.** check out, b.
3. find out, b.

5

2. B: ~~Yes~~. *Possible answers:* OK. OR That's a
good idea. OR That sounds good.

3. A: Why ~~do not~~ _don't_ we help them?

4. A: Let's ~~us~~ go Snuba diving.

5. B: That's a little early. Let's _meet_ at 6:30.

6

Checked sentences (√): 1, 6, 7, 8

PART V From Grammar to Writing
(page 181)

2

I _'m_ in Central Park. It _'s_ a sunny day in September.
~~Is~~ _It's_ crowded. Some children _are playing_ soccer. They're
laughing and *shouting*. Some people *are*
running. Three older women _are_ on a bench. ~~Are~~
watching the runners and soccer players. A
young man and woman *are holding* hands. ~~Are~~ _They're_
smiling. ~~Are~~ _They're_ in love. Central Park _is_ a wonderful
place to be, especially on a beautiful September
day.

UNIT 20 The Simple Past: Regular Verbs—Affirmative and Negative Statements
(pages 188–197)

After You Read
1. Karen and Gene visited Rio de Janeiro.

2. Karen and Gene **watched** foot-volley on Ipanema Beach.
3. Karen and Gene enjoyed a meal at a **barbecued meat** OR a **churrascaria** restaurant.
4. Karen and Gene's plane arrived **at night**.
5. The people at the hotel were **helpful**.
6. Karen and Gene **don't** speak Portuguese well.

1

2. visited, visit
3. walked, walk
4. invited, invite
5. baked, bake
6. carried, carry
7. dropped, drop, cried, cry
8. walked, walk
9. talked, talk
10. called, call, thanked, thank

Time markers: on Thursday, Yesterday afternoon, last night, yesterday morning, After dinner, This morning

2

2. arrived /d/   **7.** borrowed /d/
3. visited /ɪd/   **8.** watched /t/
4. cooked /t/   **9.** joked /t/
5. walked /t/   **10.** hugged /d/
6. wanted /ɪd/

3

2. arrived, didn't arrive
3. wanted, didn't want
4. rained, didn't rain
5. invited, didn't invite
6. helped, didn't help
7. wanted, didn't want

4

1. rented   **8.** visited
2. arrived   **9.** attended
3. shared   **10.** called
4. rained   **11.** invited
5. didn't stop   **12.** didn't want
6. carried   **13.** promised
7. walked

5

1. a. last **b.** ago **c.** Yesterday **d.** last
2. a. last **b.** last **c.** ago

6

1. usually travel, traveled
2. doesn't like, liked
3. usually opens, didn't open
4. rarely travel, traveled
5. usually start, started
6. usually naps, didn't nap, played

7

Dear Ilene,

    Paris is magical at night! It's 10 P.M. and I'm writing to you from a café. We arrived here

two days ~~before~~ *ago*. Paul's friend Pierre ~~picks~~ *picked* us up. We toured the city during the day and at night we ~~did~~ walked along the Seine River.

Today we ~~dining~~ *dined* in Montmartre and we visited

the Louvre Museum. I *did* not like the Mona Lisa,

but maybe I ~~understood~~ *didn't understand* it ~~not~~. Now we're at the Eiffel Tower and it looks just like it does in the photo.

    We hope all is well with you. Don't work too hard.

Love,
Michelle and Paul

8

1. √
2. √
3. She **didn't rent** a car.
4. She **used** public transportation.
5. √
6. √
7. √
8. She **enjoyed** the trip.

UNIT 21 The Simple Past: Irregular Verbs—Affirmative and Negative Statements (pages 198–205)

After You Read 3, 1, 4, 5, 8, 7, 2, 6

1

Past	Base Form
won	win
disliked	dislike
did	do
worried	worry
had	have
became	become
began	begin

2

1. wasn't	11. went
2. was	12. studied
3. moved	13. moved
4. was	14. opened
5. didn't like	15. bought
6. didn't do	16. made
7. felt	17. used
8. didn't fit	18. lost
9. wanted	19. didn't give
10. were	20. rebuilt

3

1. was	11. started
2. named	12. had
3. began	13. ended
4. didn't have	14. moved
5. loved	15. wanted
6. studied	16. didn't have
7. became	17. sold
8. wasn't	18. gave
9. moved	19. became
10. taught	20. wrote

4

1. took	10. said
2. sat	11. understood
3. sat	12. explained
4. looked	13. knew
5. didn't speak	14. came
6. didn't understand	15. didn't say
7. stood	16. smiled
8. happened	17. stood
9. met	

5

My grandfather *was* born in Peru. He had an older brother and sister. Their dad (my great grandfather) ~~were~~ *was* a dreamer. The family *didn't have* ~~have not~~ much money. When he was 13, my grandfather's mother ~~did~~ died and his dad remarried. My grandfather ~~no~~ *didn't* like his stepmother. He ~~move~~ *moved* in with his sister and

her husband. All three ~~leave~~ *left* for America. They
~~did start~~ *started* a small business. They worked hard
and the business ~~growed~~ *grew*. Today my sister and
I are running the business.

6

1. beautiful blue blanket	**6.** lost, case
2. didn't look	**7.** terrible
3. book bag	**8.** Forget about it
4. book bag	**9.** forget, wrote
5. pencil case	**10.** son

UNIT 22 The Simple Past: *Yes/No* and *Wh*- Questions   (pages 206–214)

After You Read **1.** b   **2.** a   **3.** b   **4.** b   **5.** b   **6.** a

1

A. finish
read
buy
see
read
1. *Yes/No* questions: 1, 4, 5, 6
2. Question about the subject: 3

B. 1. f   **2.** a   **3.** b   **4.** e   **5.** d   **6.** c

2

2. Did, enjoy	**5.** Did, like
3. Did, have	**6.** Did, expect
4. Did, understand	**7.** Did, see

3

2. No, they didn't	**5.** Yes, it did
3. No, you didn't	**6.** No, I didn't
4. Yes, we did	**7.** Yes, I did

4

1. When did you write
2. Did you always want
3. Were you
4. Did you like
5. When did you start
6. How long did you work
7. Why did you start
8. Who helped you
9. How did you feel

5

Q: When John Steinbeck ~~was~~ *was* born?
A: He *was* born in 1902.
Q: Where *was* he born?
A: He was born in Salinas, California.
Q: Where did he ~~studied~~ *study* writing?
A: He studied writing at Stanford University.
Q: *Did he* ~~He~~ graduate from Stanford?
A: No, he didn't.
Q: ~~Does~~ *Did* he marry?
A: Yes, he did. He married in 1930.
Q: When he publish~~ed~~ *did* Tortilla Flat?
A: In 1936.
Q: What year did he publish~~ed~~ The Grapes of Wrath?
A: In 1938. It was his best book.
Q: What ~~were~~ *was* it about?
A: It was about a family who lost their farm and became fruit pickers in California.
Q: Did he ~~won~~ *win* many prizes?
A: Yes, he did. He won a Pulitzer Prize, a Nobel Prize in Literature, and the U.S. Medal of Freedom.
Q: When did he ~~died~~ *die*?
A: He died in New York in 1968.

6

1. T	**2.** F	**3.** F	**4.** F	**5.** T	**6.** F

8

B. 2. When was he (she) born?
3. Where did he (she) grow up?
4. What did he (she) do in his (her) free time?
5. Did he (she) have a happy childhood?
6. Did he (she) travel?
7. Did he (she) work hard?
8. Did he (she) make a lot of money?

PART VI From Grammar to Writing

PART VI From Grammar to Writing

(pages 215–216)

1. You're kidding!
2. She's twenty-one years old.
3. He said, "I love you."
4. He worked for many years before he became rich.

Whose Baby Is It?

Solomon was a king. He lived about 3,000 years ago. Everyone came to Solomon because he was very wise.

One day two women approached King Solomon. One carried a baby. The woman said, "We live nearby and had our babies three days apart. Her baby died in the night, and she changed it for mine. This baby is really mine."

The other woman said, "No! That woman is lying. That's my baby."

The two women started arguing. They continued until King Solomon shouted, Stop!

He then turned to his guard and said, "Take your sword and chop the baby in two. Give one part to this woman and the other to that one." The guard pulled out his sword. As he was about to harm the baby, the first woman screamed, "No! Don't do it. Give her the baby. Just don't kill the baby."

King Solomon then said, "Now I know the real mother. Give the baby to the woman who has just spoken."

UNIT 23 *There Is / There Are; Is There . . . ? / Are There . . . ?*

(pages 222–230)

After You Read **1.** T **2.** F **3.** ? **4.** T **5.** ?
6. F **7.** T

1

Checked (√) sentences: 1, 3, 4, 6, 7, 8

2

2. There's a **shoe store** on the **second level**.
3. √
4. √

5. There isn't a **men's clothing store** in the **mall**.
6. There aren't any **desks** in the **furniture stores**.

3

1. There aren't
2. There aren't
3. they aren't
4. they aren't
5. there isn't

4

1. there's
2. There are
3. They're
4. there's
5. there
6. there
7. there

5

2. There's, He's
3. There are, They're
4. There's, It's
5. There are, They're
6. There's, It's
7. There are, They're

6

1. **B:** It's playing at The Woods
2. **A:** Is there a comedy at Main Street Cinema?
   A: Are there any shows after 6:00 P.M.?
3. **A:** Is there an art auction at the Town Plaza Hotel?
   B: It's
4. **A:** Is there a concert at New City Library on May 24?

7

Pizzas come in all shapes and sizes. There are pizzas with mushrooms, pepperoni, broccoli, and tofu. There ~~is~~ *are* also pizzas with curry, red herring, and coconut. In the United States ~~they~~ *there* are over 61,000 pizza places. ~~There~~ *They* represent 17 percent of all restaurants. ~~Are~~ *They are* popular with young and old.

8

1. Y 2. ? 3. ? 4. N 5. Y

Possible Answers: **1.** In Picture A there's a hardware store, but there isn't one in Picture B. **2.** In Picture B there's a flower shop, but there isn't one in Picture A. **3.** In Picture B there are flags on top of the supermarket. **4.** In Picture A there is a man looking in the bakery window. In Picture B there is a woman looking in the bakery window. **5.** In Picture B there are signs on the supermarket window; there aren't signs on the supermarket window in Picture A. **6.** In Picture A there are two people coming out of the pizza place. In Picture B there are two people going into the pizza place. **7.** There are parking meters in Picture A. **8.** There is a parked car in Picture B. **9.** There are 13 people in Picture A. There are five people in Picture B. **10.** There are shopping carts in Picture B.

UNIT 24 Subject and Object Pronouns; Direct and Indirect Objects (pages 231–238)

After You Read **2.** Masako, Maria   **3.** Masako, a phrase   **4.** Maria, the phrase, the phrase **5.** Masako, Maria

1

2. d <u>your work</u>, **i** <u>your partner</u>
3. i <u>me</u>, **d** <u>Spanish greetings</u>
4. d <u>a note</u>, **i** <u>her</u>
5. i <u>me</u>, **d** <u>an answer</u>
6. i <u>you</u>, **d** <u>word</u>
7. d <u>it</u>, **i** <u>them</u>

2

1. them	**5.** them	**8.** him
2. it	**6.** her	**9.** them
3. it	**7.** me	**10.** them
4. them		

3

1. b. them
2. a. me   **b.** We   **c.** you
3. a. me   **b.** me   **c.** it
4. a. I   **b.** me   **c.** I
5. a. us   **b.** he   **c.** us

4

2. He taught me a song.
3. I gave her my dictionary.

4. My friend and I showed him your work.
5. Don't e-mail it to me.
6. Send it to me by regular mail.
7. I wrote him a letter.
8. He gave the book to them.
9. They gave me the money.
10. My husband and I read it yesterday.

5

1. B: <u>your notes</u>
2. A: <u>my composition</u>
  B: <u>the composition</u>
  A: I handed it to my teacher.
3. A: <u>a lot of money</u>
  B: <u>a lot of money</u>
  A: She owes it to her roommate.
4. A: <u>the rolls</u>
  B: <u>the rolls</u>
  A: Please pass them to Ranya.

6

1. A: I hate to lend or borrow money. Last
  month I ~~Sue lent~~ *lent Sue* $10. She still owes ~~I~~ *me* the
  money. I reminded ~~she~~ *her* last week and she
  promised to pay me back. I see her in
  school, but now she doesn't want to look
  at ~~I~~ *me*.
  B: That's too bad.
2. A: Who's teaching ~~boxing you~~ *you boxing*?
  B: Sachiko is.
  A: Really? Who taught ~~her it~~ *it to her*?
  B: Her brother's friend. He's a champion boxer.
3. A: ~~I and my cousin~~ *My cousin and I* are learning Italian.
  B: That's great. Who's your teacher?
  A: Fiore. He's teaching ~~to~~ us useful phrases.

7

1. lemon
2. gave, heart
3. teach, lesson
4. tall
5. lend, hand

UNIT 25 Count and Non-Count Nouns; Articles
(pages 239–249)

After You Read   **1.** GG   **2.** AB   **3.** GG   **4.** AB
5. GG   **6.** AB   **7.** AB

1

A.

2. information,	non-count
3. menu,	singular count
4. customers,	plural count
5. bread,	non-count
6. napkin,	singular count
7. server,	singular count
8. kilometers,	plural count
9. coffee,	non-count
10. rolls,	plural count
11. food,	non-count
12. people,	plural count

B.
1. a   **2.** a   **3.** a   **4.** b

2

1. the	**5.** a	**9.** an
2. the	**6.** a	**10.** a
3. a	**7.** An	**11.** the
4. a	**8.** a	

3

Kel Warner is a college student. He's ^*an*
English major. He has ^*a* great part-time job.
He writes for ^*the* school paper. He's ^*the* OR *a* food
critic. Kel goes to all ^*the* restaurants in town and
writes about them. He can take ^*a* friend to ^*the*
restaurants and ^*the* school newspaper pays ^*the* bill.
Kel really has ^*a* wonderful job.

4

A: some

B: any

B: any, some

B: some, any, some

5

1. any	**3.** Many	**5.** any
2. many	**4.** any	

6

2. many restaurants	**6.** many history books
3. much traffic	**7.** much water
4. much homework	**8.** many pots
5. many people	

7

1. a few	**5.** much
2. a little	**6.** a few
3. much	**7.** a little
4. many	**8.** a few

8

2. He doesn't earn ~~many~~ *much* money.

3. I have ^*a* problem with my car. I think it's ~~a~~ *the* battery.

4. This soup needs a ~~few~~ *little* salt.

5. We bought ~~a~~ *an* apple pie.

6. We don't have ~~some~~ *any* napkins.

7. There weren't ~~much~~ *many* people at the party.

8. There was a lot ^*of* traffic on the highway.

9. We finished the yogurt. There isn't ~~some~~ *any* left.

10. We bought a pie and a cake. ~~A~~ *The* pie was good, but ~~a~~ *the* cake was terrible.

9

1. chips, ice, salsa, soda, tuna

Answers may vary slightly:
2. Boris bought tuna for cats.
3. He usually eats that kind of tuna.

PART VII From Grammar to Writing
(pages 250–251)

1

1. shoe store	**3.** maple tree
2. shoe stores	**4.** maple trees

2. There are three Sunday newspapers on his desk.

3. There are three movie theaters on Main Street.

4. We went to two rock concerts last month.

5. There are two music festivals in the city today.

3 |

My favorite street is Edgehill Street between First and Second Avenue. It's an unusual street. It's long and crooked. There are two <u>shoe stores</u>, a <u>coffee shop</u>, and a <u>fruit</u> and <u>vegetable market</u> on the north side of the street. On the south side there's an Italian bakery, a bookstore, and a Chinese restaurant. There's a <u>traffic light</u> on one corner and a <u>stop sign</u> on the other. There are two <u>apartment buildings</u>. Only one thing is missing from the street—a <u>music store</u>. Then it would have all the things I like. I know the street very well because my grandparents live there. Every time I go to that street these days, it brings back happy <u>childhood memories</u>.

UNIT 26 The Simple Present and Present Progressive; Adverbs and Expressions of Frequency (pages 256–265)

After You Read

Answers may vary slightly.

1. F, It's the **morning**.

2. F, Bob and Nita are talking to Tal on a **radio show**.

3. F, Nita spends a lot of time **cleaning**.

4. F, Bob doesn't spend a lot of time cleaning. OR Nita spends a lot of time cleaning.

5. T

6. T

7. T

8. F, Nita and Bob **never** clean together.

9. F, Bob almost never stays home on weekends.

1 |

2. eats, 's eating

3. appears, is preparing

4. study/listen, 're studying/listening

2 |

2. buy	**5.** says	**8.** says
3. says	**6.** 're wasting	**9.** 'm turning
4. write	**7.** prepare	

3 |

2. never plans	**7.** always wears
3. always helps	**8.** always looks
4. always asks	**9.** always stops
5. is always ('s always)	**10.** never buys
6. never takes	

4 |

Answers will vary. Responses are samples.

2. How often do you e-mail friends? I e-mail them once a day. OR Once a day.

3. How often does your family have dinner together? We have dinner together once a week. OR Once a week.

4. How often does your best friend call you? My best friend calls me once a month. OR Once a month.

5. How often do your relatives get together? My relatives get together once in a while. OR Once in a while.

5 |

2. 'm calling	**7.** talk
3. 're using	**8.** don't
4. always have	**9.** e-mail
5. don't	**10.** need
6. don't understand	**11.** are, doing

6 |

2. A: Can I help you?
              am calling
  B: Yes, thank you. I ~~call~~ about my new air
       does not work OR *isn't working*
  conditioner. It ~~not work~~.

               do
3. A: How often you see them?

  B: About once a month.

4. A: Can I see the doctor on Tuesday?
               work
  B: Sorry. He doesn't ~~works~~ on Tuesdays.

           playing
5. A: Is she ~~play~~ tennis at West Park?

              She never
  B: No, she's not. ~~Never she~~ plays there.

6. A: Where *are* you calling from?

B: Downtown. I ~~walk~~ *'m walking* along Second Street.

7. A: Do you eat there often?

B: I ~~don't~~ rarely eat there. It's too expensive.

7

1. b   **2.** a   **3.** b   **4.** b   **5.** a

UNIT 27
Non-Action Verbs   (pages 266–273)

After You Read

2. Bora Bora looks like **paradise** to Heather.
3. Bora Bora sounds **great**.
4. Rick **wants** to go to Bora Bora.
5. **Heather** doesn't believe in his invention. OR Rick **believes** in his invention.

1

2. love, e   **6.** see, a
3. smell, f   **7.** have, g
4. taste, h   **8.** know, c
5. hear, b

2

1. b. costs
2. a. Does, have   **b.** has
3. a. Are   **b.** are
4. a. like OR prefer **b.** prefer
5. a. belongs

3

2. 'm sitting   **7.** feel
3. eating   **8.** 'm not worrying
4. 's swimming   **9.** love
5. looks   **10.** is
6. isn't worrying OR
   's not worrying

4

2. I'm thinking about our vacation.
3. He doesn't understand French.
4. We have a good guidebook about French Polynesia.
5. They're waiting for us.
6. I want to go to the beach.
7. I'm looking for a swimsuit.

8. I don't remember his name.
9. I'm tasting the soup.
10. It tastes delicious.

5

2. A: How much ~~is~~ *does* it cost to get to the airport?
B: I don't know.

3. A: Do you ~~wants~~ *want* a double bed or two twin beds?
B: A double bed.

4. A: Hurry. The shuttle bus is leaving now.
B: I ~~come~~ *'m coming*.

5. A: ~~Do~~ *Are* you wearing sunscreen? The sun is very strong.
B: Yes, I am.

6. A: ~~Are~~ *Do* you ~~needing~~ need a beach towel?
B: No. I have one.

7. A: How much ~~cost these pearls~~ *do these pearls cost*?
B: They're $200.

6

Checked (√) sentences: 1, 2, 3, 6, 8

UNIT 28 Gerunds
and Infinitives   (pages 274–279)

After You Read **1.** c   **2.** b   **3.** c

1

2. I   **5.** G   **7.** I
3. I   **6.** I   **8.** G
4. G

2

2. to act OR acting   **6.** spending
3. to become   **7.** to give up
4. to have   **8.** trying out
5. to change   **9.** to show

3

2. to get   **4.** telling   **6.** looking
3. to meet   **5.** to find   **7.** to study

To Whom It May Concern:

    I want to apply for a part-time job at Kennedy Library. I am in my senior year of high school. I expect **to** attend State College

next year and I plan to major~~ing~~ in library science.

    I enjoy ~~to read~~ *reading* and ~~to work~~ *working* with the public.

I'm good at computers and I like ~~keep~~ *keeping* OR *to keep* things in order.

    I've enclosed a resume. I hope ~~hearing~~ *to hear* from you soon.

                 Sincerely yours,
                 Joe Reed

5

When false statements are changed to true ones, answers may vary.

1. T
2. T
3. F, Cindy decided to **become a wedding planner**. OR Cindy decided to open her own business.
4. F, Cindy enjoys planning **parties**.
5. F, Cindy likes to work with **people**.
6. F, Ken wants to have **dinner** with Cindy on Saturday.

UNIT 29 Review of the Simple Past
(pages 280–290)

After You Read

A.	B.
2 a	**7** a
1 b	**5** b
3 c	**8** c
4 d	**6** d

1

Answers will vary. Below are samples.

Sentences with *Be* in the Past

He was the first president of the United States.

When was that?

How long was he president?

Was he a good leader?

Yes, he was.

Kemal Ataturk was the father of modern Turkey.

He was also a great soldier and leader.

He was one of Korea's greatest leaders.

Simon Bolivar was the father of half a dozen countries.

Sentences with Other Verbs in the Past

He became the president in 1789.

And before he became president, he led the army during the American Revolution.

He led from 1923 to 1938.

He gave Turkey many things including a modern alphabet.

George Washington didn't do anything about the English alphabet.

King Sejong gave Korea an alphabet.

He led many countries to independence.

He didn't change our alphabet but spelling is not so hard in Spanish.

2

2. married	14. lost
3. had	15. didn't forgive
4. lived	16. started
5. wore	17. was
6. worked	18. used
7. was	19. turned
8. made	20. did
9. didn't like	21. didn't want
10. didn't like	22. didn't want
11. followed	23. died
12. invested	24. left
13. went	

3

A.
2. When was he born?
3. What did he always love?
4. How many degrees did he have?
5. When did he receive a philosophy degree?
6. What (kind of) degree did he receive from Presbyterian College?
7. What kind of degree did he get from the University of Colorado?
8. When did he make his biggest contribution to the world?
9. Why did he want them to play an indoor sport?
10. What game did he invent?
11. What happened in 1936?

B.

2. Was he a good student? Yes, he was.

3. Did he finish college? Yes, he did.

4. Did he become a lawyer? No, he didn't.

5. Did he invent the game of volleyball? No, he didn't.

---

4 |

2. Q: Where ~~she was~~ *was she* born?

　　A: She was born in England.

3. Q: When was she born?

　　A: She *was* born in 1821.

4. Q: When ~~she did~~ *did she* come to the United States?

　　A: She ~~did come~~ *came* to the United States in 1833.

5. Q: Was it hard for her to become a doctor?

　　A: Yes, it ~~were~~ *was*. Most medical schools didn't want women.

6. Q: How ~~was~~ *were* her grades in medical school?

　　A: She was an outstanding student. Her grades were excellent.

7. Q: When *did* she graduate?

　　A: In 1849.

8. Q: What did Dr. Blackwell fight for?

　　A: She ~~did fight~~ *fought* for the admission of women to medical schools.

9. Q: Where did she ~~goes~~ *go* in 1869?

　　A: She returned to London. She worked there for many years.

10. Q: When **did** she die?

　　A: She died in 1910.

---

5 |

1. painted

2. did Rembrandt live, seventeenth century

3. was Rembrandt born, Holland

4. Rembrandt's full name

5. married, John Lennon

6. was the name, group, The Beatles

7. did the Beatles come from, Liverpool, England

8. did the Beatles make, 1966

PART VIII From Grammar to Writing
　　　　　　　　　　　　　　　　　　　(page 291)

1 |

1. in the evening

2. At present

2 |

(See figure below.)

A COUNTRY DOCTOR

Michelle Hirch-Phothong is a country doctor. Her day begins at six-thirty <u>in the morning</u>. <u>At seven o'clock</u> she is at the hospital. She visits her patients and discusses their problems with the nurses and other doctors. Michelle enjoys talking to her patients. She listens to them carefully and never rushes them.

　　<u>In the afternoon</u> Michelle works at a clinic. The clinic is busy, and patients are often worried about their health. Michelle and the other doctors try to help them.

　　<u>At six o'clock in the evening</u> Michelle leaves the clinic. She goes home and relaxes. <u>Every evening at seven o'clock</u> Michelle goes to "Bangkok in the Boondocks." That's my restaurant, and Michelle is my wife. Michelle and I enjoy a delicious Thai dinner alone.

　　Sometimes, however, people come to the restaurant and tell Michelle their medical problems. I say, "Tell them to go to the clinic." But Michelle never sends them home without listening to their problems and offering advice. Michelle is a wonderful doctor.

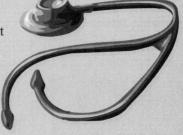

UNIT 30 *Be Going to* for the Future
(pages 300–309)

After You Read
For the Fitness Center: b, c, f
Against the Fitness Center: a, d, e

1

A. 1. 's going to seat
2. 're going to build, 's going to have
3. 's going to talk
4. 're going to build, are going to provide
5. is going to destroy
6. 'm going to write

2. a   **3.** f   **4.** e   **5.** d   **6.** b

B. 3: The mayor **is giving** a speech on Wednesday afternoon here in our school.

2

1. It's not going to rain.
2. We're going to move to a bigger apartment next weekend. Our friends are going to help us move.
3. They're going to build a new high school next year. They're going to raise taxes to pay for the school.
4. I'm not going to write to the school paper. I'm going to talk to the student leaders.
5. Are you going to be home? Are you going to watch the show?
6. Are you going to visit him tonight?

3

2. isn't going to look
3. is going to have
4. are going to be
5. aren't going to be
6. 's going to be
7. is going to tower
8. 's going to look

4

1. **b.** 's going to be
2. **a.** are, going to do   **b.** 're going to visit
3. **a.** did, say   **b.** 's going to make
4. **a.** Did, see   **b.** 'm probably not going to see
5. **a.** Are, going to watch   **b.** 'm going to visit
6. **a.** doesn't work   **b.** are, going to fix
   c. 'm probably going to buy

5

2. Who is she having lunch with on Monday? Community leaders.

3. What's she doing on Monday afternoon? She's giving a speech at State University.
4. Is she flying to Los Angeles on Monday? No, she isn't. She's flying on Tuesday.
5. What's she doing in Los Angeles? She's meeting with (the) mayors at noon. OR She's going to a mayors' meeting at noon.
6. What time is she flying home from Los Angeles? At 2:00 P.M.
7. Is she going to a dinner for the police chief? Yes, she is.

6

Dear Residents:
  Last week the mayor talked about building a sports stadium in our neighborhood. I think it's a terrible idea.
  It's going ^to cost taxpayers millions of dollars.
  ~~It~~ It's going to mean traffic jams. Parking ~~is being~~ is going to be difficult, and it's going to bring~~ing~~ noise and dirt to the area.
  Next Monday at 7:00 P.M. the mayor is ~~goes~~ going to answer questions at the public library. I ask everyone from Peaceful Place Apartments to come and speak out about the new stadium.
  Sincerely,
  Dale Ortiz
  President, Residents' Association

7

Answers will vary.
1. The new building is going to have 200 new apartments. OR It's going to have a pool. OR There are going to be shops.
2. There's going to be more noise and traffic. OR It's going to spoil the view for people in nearby homes.
3. He's for the new building.

UNIT 31 *Will* for the Future; Future Time Markers
(pages 310–318)

After You Read   **1.** a, c   **2.** a, c, d   **3.** a, b, d
4. b, c, d

1

2. d   **3.** c   **4.** e   **5.** a

2

1. b. won't last   **e.** 'll meet
    c. won't finish   **f.** 'll bring
    d. 'll finish   **g.** 'll bring

2. a. will, be   **d.** 'll spoil
    b. won't be   **e.** won't
    c. 'll have

3

2. g. Will you marry me?
3. d. I won't be long.
4. b. I'll never forget them.
5. f. It won't hurt much.
6. a. I'll bring the hamburgers. You bring the rolls.
7. c. Will you please be quiet?

4

2. Will taxes stay the same? No, taxes will decrease.
3. Will the cost of health care stay the same? No, the cost of health care will decrease.
4. Will the percent of people under 25 decrease? No, the percent of people under 25 will increase.
5. Will the percent of people over 65 decrease? No, the percent of people over 65 will stay the same.

5

2. was   **5.** 'll learn   **7.** Did, like
3. will be   **6.** 'll, be   **8.** knows
4. 'll take

6

           move
B: Many young people will ~~moves~~ to the area.
        increase
    Taxes will ~~increases~~. The value of homes will also ~~to~~ increase.
        increase
A: Will it ~~increases~~?
        won't
B: No, it ~~doesn't~~.

7

Answers will vary slightly.
1. She'll probably leave her job. OR She'll travel to Ireland. OR She'll buy a house.
2. He'll give all the money away.

UNIT 32 *May* or *Might* for Possibility   (pages 319–325)

After You Read   **1.** a   **2.** a   **3.** c, d

1

1. d   **2.** b   **3.** e   **4.** a   **5.** c

2

2. might / may not be
3. might / may need
4. might / may not have
5. might / may not see
6. might / may return

3

2. 'll be
3. may be
4. might need
5. won't start, may be cold

4

2. There might (or may) be one in that library.
3. They might (or may) be.
4. It might (or may) take two or three hours.
5. They might (or may) be good friends.

5

        might
2. A: We ~~maybe~~ go to the park.
     Will
3. A: ~~May~~ you take another course next term?
    might not
4. B: I ~~mightn't~~ have enough time.
5. B: It's sunny now, but it may ~~to~~ rain this afternoon.

6

2. It might rain.
3. He might need one for the sun, and one for the rain.
4. He might wake up during the night.
5. They might go to a fancy restaurant.

PART IX From Grammar to Writing (pages 326–327)

1. When I was six years old, I loved to play with dolls. OR I loved to play with dolls when I was six years old.
2. When I graduate next year, I will work for a newspaper. OR I will work for a newspaper when I graduate next year.

Example paragraph

My Dream

When I was a child, I loved to play "make-believe" games. Sometimes I was a cowboy, and sometimes I was a prince. **When** I became a teenager, I got a job at a video store. I saw many movies. I also made a couple of videos and I acted in all the school plays. Now I'm studying film and acting at school. When I finish college next year, I will move to Hollywood. I hope to become a movie star.

UNIT 33 Questions with *Any / Some / How Much / How Many;* Quantity Expressions (pages 334–343)

After You Read Steve scores 14. Jackie scores 8.

1

	Singular Count Noun	Plural Count Noun	Non-count Noun
1. a	pear		
2. an	apple		
3. one	apple		
4. two		pears	
5. some		eggs	water
6. any		vegetables	cheese
7. How much			meat
8. How many		carrots	
9. enough		onions	salt
10. a lot of		potatoes	time
			soup

2

2. **A:** Do we have enough water?
   B: Yes, but we don't have enough ice.
3. **A:** Do you want some more yogurt?
   B: No, thanks. I'm full.
4. **A:** Are there any more glasses?
   B: Yes. They're on the top shelf.
5. **A:** Did you go to the gym this morning?
   B: No. There wasn't enough time.
6. **A:** Are you going to bake a pie?
   B: Yes, but we don't have any flour.
7. **A:** I need to get some napkins.
   B: Is the store open yet?
8. **A:** We need some milk.
   B: How much do we need?

3

1. How many	5. How much
2. How much	6. How many
3. How many	7. How many
4. How many	8. How much

4

1. a few	6. a few
2. a few	7. a few
3. a few	8. a little
4. a little	9. a few
5. a little	10. a few

5

1. teaspoon	4. roll
2. bottles	5. package
3. piece	

6

      much
2. **A:** How ~~many~~ time do you spend at the gym?
        enough water
3. **A:** Do we have ~~water enough~~ for everyone?
      many
4. **A:** How ~~much~~ yoga classes do they offer at the gym?
  Are   *enough treadmills*
5. **A:** ~~Is~~ there ~~treadmills enough~~?
        some OR *a few*
6. **B:** There are ~~any~~ near the swimming pool.
         towels
7. **A:** Do you need any ~~towel~~? OR Do you need
  a
  ~~any~~ towel?

7

1. cans of vegetable soup
2. containers of yogurt
3. lettuce
4. packages of frozen vegetables
5. of nuts
6. of grapes

8

1. How many	5. How much
2. How much	6. How many
3. How many	7. How many
4. How many	8. How many

UNIT 34 *Too Much / Too Many / Too + Adjective* (pages 344–352)

After You Read

Climate: c	Health: f
Employment: b	Environment: e
Culture & Leisure: d	Education: a

1

1. b., <u>cold, windy</u>
2. d., (teachers)
3. a., <u>expensive</u>
4. f., <u>crowded</u>
5. h., (bugs)
6. g., (problems)
7. c., (homework)
8. e., (money)

2

1. too many	5. too much
2. too much	6. too many
3. too much	7. too much
4. too much	

3

2. There was too little rain
3. There are too few jobs
4. There are too few affordable homes
5. There are too few spaces
6. There is too little food

4

2. It was **too** violent.
3. Am I **too** late for the movie?
4. I don't eat there because it's **too** dirty.
5. They're **too** high for me.
6. Is it **too** far to walk to the beach?
7. Homes are **too** expensive in that area.
8. It's **too** heavy.

5

Answers will vary slightly.

4br / 3ba / 2-car garage / nr trans $2,000/mo

2. There are too few bedrooms in this house.
3. There are too few bedrooms and it is too expensive.
4. The garage is too small.
5. (no problem)
6. This house has too few bathrooms and it isn't near public transportation.

6

1. **a.** too	**b.** too little
2. **a.** too	**b.** too many
3. **a.** too much	**b.** too
4. Too few	
5. **a.** too	**b.** too few
6. too	
7. too many	
8. **a.** too	**b.** too much
9. **a.** too	**b.** too many

7

1. **A:** I'd like to change my class. It's too hard.
   And there's too ~~many~~ *much* homework.
2. **B:** There are too many bosses and too ~~little~~ *few* workers.
3. **B:** No. It was too ᵃmoney *much* and too ~~very~~ *much* complicated.
4. **A:** Don't go by bus. It will take too ~~many~~ *much* time. Take the train. It's a lot faster.
   B: Yes, but it's ~~a lot more~~ *too* expensive. The bus is half the price.

8

	What They Liked	**What They Didn't Like**
1st Apt.	on a beautiful street	too small too few closets not big enough
2nd Apt.	the right size had a great view	too noisy too many people
3rd Apt.	big enough not too noisy kitchen big enough to build more cabinets	kitchen had too few cabinets

UNIT 35 Possessives (pages 353–359)

After You Read

left to right—Amy's bike, Johnny's bike, Jasmine's bike, Roger and Ted's bike

1

Subject pronouns: they, We

Object pronouns: us, you, you, us

Possessive adjectives: Our, their

Possessive pronouns: ours

2

1.   **b.** his   **c.** Mine
2. a. Theirs   **b.** ours   **c.** Yours   **d.** ours
3. a. hers   **b.** Mine

3

1. a. my   **b.** Yours   **c.** her
2. a. Her   **b.** Mine
3. a. their   **b.** Their   **c.** yours   **d.** Ours

4

1. a. mine   **b.** me   **c.** I
2. a. he   **b.** his   **c.** him
3. a. Theirs **b.** They   **c.** them

5

1. are   **4.** Is   **7.** has
2. Is   **5.** Do   **8.** live
3. Is   **6.** are

6

1. B: No. Ours is in room 304. Theirs ~~are~~ *is* in 306.
2. A: I like ~~yours~~ *your* watch.
   B: Thanks, but it isn't ~~my~~. *mine* OR *it isn't my watch.* It's my uncle's. He
   lent it to ~~my~~. *me* Mine ~~watch~~ is broken. OR
   ~~Mine~~ *My* watch is broken.
3. A: Where are ~~yours~~ *your* keys?
4. A: ~~Mine~~ *My* phone doesn't work here. OR Mine
   ~~phone~~ doesn't work here.
   A: ~~Your~~ *Yours* doesn't work either.
   B: Try Mary's. ~~Hers~~ *Her* phone works everywhere.
   OR Hers ~~phone~~ works everywhere.

7

him, keys, red, sports, present, him, his
eighteenth

PART X From Grammar to Writing (pages 360–361)

1

1. at the top left of the page
2. below your address
3. below the date; skip two lines
4. *Dear* <u>Name</u>: OR *Dear Sir/Madam:* OR *To Whom It May Concern:*
5. explain what you want
6. thank you
7. *Sincerely yours,* OR *Yours truly,*
8. Your signature, and your name below your signature

UNIT 36 *Can* or *May* for Permission (pages 368–375)

After You Read
1. T   **4.** T
2. F   **5.** F
3. T   **6.** It doesn't say.

2. a. Student A   **b.** Student B
3. a. Salesperson   **b.** Customer
4. a. Police Officer   **b.** Driver
5. a. Student   **b.** Teacher

2

2. a	**5.** b	**8.** d
3. g	**6.** i	**9.** h
4. f	**7.** c	

3

1. Can I drink coffee?
2. Can I eat ice cream?
3. May/Can I call you with questions?

4

1. B: Yes, you can ~~pays~~ ^pay^ half now and half next month.

2. A: May I ~~speaks~~ ^speak^ to the doctor?

3. B: Sorry. You can't ~~to~~ use a dictionary.

4. B: Fifty minutes. You ~~mayn't~~ ^may not^ continue after two o'clock.

5

1. Her ankle is swollen and really hurts.
2. She can put her foot up and take two extra-strength Tylenol every four hours.
3. She can go to work and she can drive.
4. She can't play tennis or any other sport for three weeks.

UNIT 37 Requests, Desires, and Offers: *Would You Please . . . ?, I'd like . . . , Would You Like . . . ?* (pages 376–384)

After You Read   **1.** G   **2.** M   **3.** G   **4.** M
5. G   **6.** M

1

1. R   **2.** D   **3.** O   **4.** R   **5.** D   **6.** R   **7.** O

2

STEVE: Nice to meet you, Mary. I'm Steve Kaufman.

MARY: Steve, I love to listen to your music, but sometimes I can't get to sleep. Could you please stop practicing by 11:00?

MARY: Thanks so much.

STEVE: Listen Mary, I'd like to do something for you. Would you like to have dinner together sometime?

MARY: Dinner? Sure. I'd love to.

3

2. g	**4.** d	**6.** f
3. b	**5.** c	**7.** e

4

1. Sure.   **4.** Sure.
2. Sorry, I can't right now.   **5.** Of course.
3. Thanks.

5

1. I'd like   **4.** I'd like
2. Would you like   **5.** Would you like
3. Would you like   **6.** would you please

6

2. A: He'd ~~likes~~ ^like^ to go to a concert.

3. A: Would you like ^to^ come for dinner?

4. A: May I ~~to~~ help you?

5. B: Yes, ~~you could~~.   ^of course OR Sure OR OK^

7

1. Bill, him (Robert) an appointment for next Tuesday at nine.
2. thank-you notes to everyone at the meeting yesterday
3. at his (Robert's) report and see if he (John) can find any way to shorten it
4. Dr. Rice calls

UNIT 38 Advice: *Should, Shouldn't, Ought to, Had Better,* and *Had Better Not*   (pages 385–394)

After You Read **1.** E   **2.** C   **3.** E   **4.** H
5. E.   **6.** H

1

should, present
should, translate
should, do
'd better not write
ought to handle, treat

2

1. shouldn't blow
2. shouldn't touch
3. shouldn't be
4. shouldn't do, should wait
5. shouldn't say
6. shouldn't do

3

2. ought to send
3. ought to congratulate
4. ought to get
5. ought to become
6. ought to sell
7. ought to buy

4

2. 'd better not   **6.** 'd better not
3. 'd better   **7.** 'd better
4. 'd better not   **8.** 'd better
5. 'd better   **9.** 'd better not

5

A.

2. A: We're almost out of juice. We *should* get some
on the way home.

3. A: Careful. You have a bad back. You *shouldn't* lift that
heavy chair.

4. A: When *should* we leave for the party?

5. B: You're right. Someone *should* tell them.

B.

1. B: You *'d better* leave earlier tomorrow.

2. A: You *'d better not* leave town. We may
want to speak to you again.

3. B: Early. You *'d better not* call her after 10:30 at night.

6

1. along cash or can I use a credit card
everywhere
Answer: You can use credit cards in major
stores, but when you shop in small stores,
cash is better. So, bring some cash.
2. bow when I meet someone
Answer: No, it's not necessary for you to bow.
3. I remove my shoes when I enter a home
Answer: Yes, you should.
4. Should I learn a few phrases in Japanese?
Answer: You should learn some phrases
because people will appreciate the effort.

UNIT 39 Necessity: *Have to, Don't Have to, Must, Mustn't*   (pages 395–402)

After You Read **1.** b, d, f   **2.** a, c, e

1

1. c   **2.** d   **3.** a   **4.** e   **5.** b

2

1. have   **5.** have   **9.** have
2. have to   **6.** have to   **10.** have to
3. have to   **7.** have to   **11.** had to
4. have to   **8.** have to

3

2. have to wear   **5.** has to be
3. don't have to use **6.** doesn't have to buy
4. don't have to do   **7.** have to hand in

4

2. You mustn't (OR must not) smoke on the
train.
3. You mustn't (OR must not) enter this room.
4. You have to (OR must) wear shoes in the
restaurant.
5. You mustn't (OR must not) drink the contents
of this bottle.

5

2. Now that they are managers, they ~~had~~ *have* to work late several times a week.

3. You ~~mustn't~~ *don't have to* sit in the last row. You can sit anywhere you like.

4. To get to the university, you have ⌃*to* turn left at the third traffic light on this road.

5. You mustn't ~~exceeds~~ *exceed* the speed limit. They give out a lot of traffic tickets here.

6. She ~~have~~ *has* to finish her term paper this weekend. It's due on Monday.

6

Possible answers:

1. You have to have a bachelor's degree and take courses in economics.
2. You have to take a test called the GMAT.
3. You have to check the requirements of the schools that you're interested in.

PART XI From Grammar to Writing (pages 403–404)

1

1. F   2. O   3. F   4. F   5. O

UNIT 40 The Comparative (pages 412–421)

After You Read

Portland, Oregon, has a bigger population, more diverse neighborhoods, and warmer winters.

Portland, Maine, is older.

1

A.
1. worse
2. cooler, warmer
3. less expensive, less expensive
4. busier
5. bigger, bigger
6. more interesting, more interesting

B.
2. bad
3. cool
4. warm
5. expensive
6. busy
7. big
8. interesting

2

2. A two-bedroom apartment in Middletown is more expensive than a two-bedroom apartment in Lakeville.
3. A cup of coffee in Middletown is more expensive than a cup of coffee in Lakeville.
4. It's probably harder to find work in Lakeville than it is in Middletown.
5. Health care in Lakeville is probably worse than health care in Middletown.
6. Summers in Middletown are warmer than summers in Lakeville.

3

2. Which river is longer, the Yangtze or the Nile?
3. Is Texas bigger than Alaska?
4. Which country is farther north, Korea or Thailand?
5. Which country is farther west, France or Germany?
6. Which city is older, St. Petersburg, Russia or Brasilia, Brazil?
7. Is the Indian Ocean bigger than the Pacific Ocean?
8. Is Luxembourg much smaller than Argentina?

4

B.
2. lg
3. bldg
4. bdrms
5. bths
6. nr
7. mo
8. loc

C.
2. Which apartment is more expensive? The one on Cedar Lane.
3. Which apartment is quieter? The one on Cedar Lane.
4. Which apartment is more modern? The one on Cedar Lane.
5. Which apartment is closer to schools and parks? The one on Cedar Lane.

D.
Answers will vary.
1. Which apartment is better for a couple with a child? The one on Cedar Lane.

2. Which apartment is better for a single person? The one on Main Street.

5

2. Florida is ~~more~~ hotter than Maine.

farther
3. Oregon is ~~far~~ north than California.

faster
4. A motorcycle is ~~more fast~~ than a bicycle.

than
5. These days I'm busier ~~then~~ I was last year at this time.

milder
6. The climate in Tokyo, Japan, is ~~mild~~ than the climate in Anchorage, Alaska.

bigger
7. Elephants are ~~big~~ than tigers.

8. Jake's apartment is more convenient than his
sister's
~~sister~~.

6

Possible answers:

Advantages
1. an extra bedroom (apartment is larger)
2. a newer building
3. better heating and plumbing
4. a better view
5. quieter neighbors

Disadvantages
1. a lot farther from school
2. not as convenient to shopping
3. neighbors not as friendly

UNIT 41 Adverbs of Manner (pages 422–427)

After You Read Checked (√) advice: 2, 5, 8

1

clearly, long, fast, frequently

2

2. well, good
3. fluently, fluent
4. neatly, neat
5. fast, fast
6. dangerously, dangerous
7. badly, bad
8. slowly, slow

9. hard, hard
10. carefully, careful

3

1. well
2. good
3. beautiful
4. well
5. slowly
6. slow
7. Nervous

4

good
2. B: Everyone loved it. It really tasted ~~well~~.

slowly
3. B: He drives too ~~slow~~.

4. B: They worked hard~~ly~~ and did well.

5. (correct)

softly
6. B: No, I didn't. He spoke too ~~soft~~.

7. (correct)

nervous
8. B: A little ~~nervously~~.

5

1. sarcastically
2. angrily
3. convincingly
4. sadly
5. questioningly

UNIT 42 Enough; Too/Very; As + Adjective + As; Same/Different (pages 428–437)

After You Read Checked (√) sentences: 1, 2, 4, 6

1

2. c. **3.** e. **4.** f. **5.** a. **6.** b.

2

2. It isn't hot enough to go swimming.
3. This steak is much too tough to eat.
4. The doctor is too busy to see you today.
5. They weren't strong enough to move the sofa bed.
6. That restaurant is much too expensive.
7. That meeting was too important to miss.
8. We don't have enough time to eat before the movie.
9. His address wasn't clear enough to read.
10. The movie was way too long.
11. There weren't enough seats.

2. Robert and Jean are the same height.
3. Robert and Russ have the same initials.
4. Robert and Jean come from Arizona.
5. Russ's and Jean's licenses have the same expiration date.

4

2. very	6. too
3. too, very	7. very
4. very	8. very
5. too, very, very	9. too

5

1. as hard as she does
2. as talented as she is
3. as fast and dependable
4. the same university as Mary
5. the same amount of experience as she does

6

2. My new apartment isn't as quiet ~~than~~ *as* my old one.
3. She's very different ~~than~~ *from* her sister.
4. We're ~~very~~ *too* young to vote. You have to be 18 years old. We're 17.
5. She has the same sweater ~~than~~ *as* I do.
6. I'm as tall~~er~~ as my father.
7. Dan~~'s weight is~~ *weighs* the same as his brother. OR

   Dan's weight is the same as his brother*'s*.
8. She wasn't ~~enough old~~ *old enough* to drive.
9. Sally isn't *as* friendly as Penny.
10. He doesn't have ~~money enough~~ *enough money* to pay for all those things.

7

1. M	4. L	6. M
2. M	5. M	7. M
3. L		

9

2. b   3. f   4. d   5. e   6. c

UNIT 43
The Superlative   (pages 438–446)

After You Read 1. emperor penguin   **2.** little blue penguin   **3.** the Antarctic OR Antarctica   **4.** Greenland

1

A.

2. the largest	5. the longest
3. the most venomous	6. the farthest
4. the coldest	7. the highest

B.

2. venomous	5. far
3. cold	6. high
4. long	

C.

of the year, from the sun

2

Guesses will vary.

1. the loudest	5. the fastest
2. the largest	6. the most colorful
3. the tallest	7. the most intelligent
4. the smallest	

3

2. one of the smartest animals
3. one of the best movies
4. one of the biggest problems
5. one of the coldest days
6. one of the most popular sports
7. one of the busiest months

4

1. **b.** shorter   **c.** bigger   **d.** taller
2. the richest
3. The smallest
4. The largest
5. larger
6. **a.** more active   **b.** colder
7. **a.** the most dangerous   **b.** the most aggressive

5

2. **A:** I read that Pluto is *usually* the ~~most~~ farthest from the sun. Why?
3. **A:** What's the ~~most small~~ *smallest* state in the United States?

4. B: I think it's one of the ~~baddest~~ *worst*. My boss can always reach me.

5. A: What's the ~~busier~~ *busiest* day of the week for you?

6. A: What's the ~~most~~ shortest day of the year?

B: December 21st. June 21st is the ~~most long~~ *longest*.

6

1. Saturn	**3.** Jupiter
2. Venus	**4.** Mars

7

2. What's the easiest way to earn a lot of money?

3. What's the most interesting show on TV now?

4. Who is the most powerful person in the world?

5. When is the best time to go to college?

6. What is the best restaurant near your school?

7. What is the most interesting animal to look at?

PART XII From Grammar to Writing

(pages 447–448)

1

1. funny little brown monkey

2. beautiful red silk dress

2

1. big brown Asian

2. new black Italian leather

3. Mexican silver

License Agreement